# NORTH ATLANTIC ARENA

Water Transport in the World Order

1. The North Atlantic Arena, shown by the broken line, is a coined term designating the space-area on the surface of the globe that includes the North Atlantic Ocean with Western Europe on the east and the United States and southern Canada on the west. The North Atlantic Arena ranks first among the world's regions in nearly all components of civilization.

Charles C. Colby

# North Atlantic Arena
## WATER TRANSPORT IN THE WORLD ORDER

Foreword by Delyte W. Morris

Southern Illinois University Press

CARBONDALE AND EDWARDSVILLE

*Copyright* © 1966 by SOUTHERN ILLINOIS UNIVERSITY PRESS
Library of Congress Catalog Card Number 65–13062
Printed in the United States of America
Designed by Andor Braun

THE ORIGINAL IMPETUS for Mississippi Valley Investigations at Southern Illinois University was the realization that the University had on its staff numerous specialists with expert knowledge of one or more aspects of Mid-America, but each somewhat isolated in his own department. To provide a structure which would bring the total knowledge of these experts to bear on the problems of a vast, complex, and important area, the late Charles C. Colby was asked to organize an interdisciplinary seminar, the membership of which included both administrators and faculty members representing a wide range of interests and concerns. This seminar became a forum in which the results of special studies were presented and then discussed by the entire group. Some of the resulting ideas and materials have been brought to the attention of local, state, and federal agencies, where it is hoped that they will stimulate public thought and enlightened action.

In its middle course, the Mississippi River receives water from streams draining more than a fourth of the United States. The Mississippi, Missouri, Illinois, Wabash, Ohio, Cumberland, and Tennessee rivers unite to form the Lower Mississippi, down which flows this great volume of water to the Gulf of Mexico. As this mid-continental area was settled, a pattern of states and counties was spread over the complex drainage of the Mississippi system, thereby creating a threefold political organization of federal, state, and county jurisdictions. Moreover, the way in which and the extent to which these bodies politic expressed residential and economic preferences added complexities to the utilization of the rivers that are a conspicuous feature of the mid-continental landscape.

Although in the current century the population of the United States has increased notably, the consumption of water has increased even more notably; hence, preparation must be made for the development of water facilities for navigation, flood control, and domestic, municipal, recreational, and industrial uses. In addition, the ever-growing problem of pollution abatement needs attention, if fisheries—both game and commercial—are to attain their potential development and if outdoor recreation is to be safe and enjoyable.

Consideration of the unrealized opportunities in Southern Illinois made it evident that a comprehensive program of water utilization is essential in this area, with the Mississippi River on the west, the Ohio on the south, and the Wabash on the east. Dependence on surface water for domestic, industrial, and municipal uses is a basic need because the deep-seated supplies of water are salty, as might be expected in an area underlain with coal and oil. Among other things, Mississippi Valley Investigations should identify further unknowns in the realm of water problems that will call for careful and penetrating investigations by top-flight research talent.

At the outset, it appeared wise for the University also to initiate a program of studies of the utilization of water resources in other parts of the world, especially where the methods, techniques, and technology of water transport witnessed early developments in the Eastern Mediterranean and in the long period of peace in the Roman Empire. Later developments appeared in the North Atlantic Ocean where, after decades of effort, sailing vessels gave way to steam navigation; and finally the Lower Rhine became an arm of the Atlantic and made the Rhine the busiest river in the world. With the Ruhr Industrial District as the most active center, the Rhine, in touch with the most progressive nations of Europe, creates an object lesson for Europe and the world—and especially for the people in the Mississippi and Ohio valleys who occupy a comparable position in the United States.

It is hoped that the present book, by Professor Colby himself, may provide background in depth and continuing incentive to the members of our staff engaged in Mississippi Valley Investigations and to others interested in similar interdisciplinary activities. Already this approach has involved Southern Illinois University in a reconnaissance study of the Mississippi from its source to its mouth. The ultimate result should be better understanding and richer living for all the people whose lives are touched by the great rivers. This result would be a gratifying memorial to a great geographer's scholarly and humane interest in the development of our area.

*Delyte W. Morris*
PRESIDENT

*Southern Illinois University*
*July 27, 1965*

IN TERMS OF SPACE on the earth's surface this study covers a broad expanse, whereas in terms of time it ranges through twenty centuries with a hope for the future. The space is designated here as the North Atlantic Arena, and the time span includes ancient, medieval, and modern times. The motivation represents an attempt to gain a working understanding of the characteristics and functions of water transportation in the development of civilization, especially in the North Atlantic Arena.

Early transport on water and land largely developed in the Mediterranean Sea, the major eastern arm of the North Atlantic, both in size and in the evolution of economy and culture. From Rome, the center of the Mediterranean, Roman rule expanded until all of the known Western world came under its dominion. In time, the Roman legions invaded Gaul and the Danube and Rhine valleys. Hence, Roman roads, Roman law and order, and Roman skills in the construction of vehicles and boats were introduced and became localized in the Rhine and Danube valleys of Europe, and also in the Baltic and North seas.

In the latter part of the fifteenth century water transportation advanced to the high seas where sailing vessels created a new world order with well-marked advances in the distribution of people outside of Europe, especially in North America. In time much of the unknown world was discovered and settled. People in these pioneer areas began the production of commodities needed in Western Europe, where an active market for foods and raw materials came into existence. Hence, world trade was in the making.

Then in the nineteenth century, after much trial and error, the use of steam propulsion on the high seas became a reality. About 1870 the steam-propelled, steel-clad ship made overseas commerce not only a commercial necessity, but also initiated a new world order with a remarkable advance in civilization. This emphasized the values inherent in the seaboard areas. Not, however, in all seaboard areas, but in the few sections suitable for port development and access to interior productive areas. Such access was possible where rivers such as the Rhine were navigable. Even more significant was the invention and use of the steam locomotive and the coming of the railway age in the nineteenth century.

The Rhine River has been a route of transportation from antiquity; but the success of the Ruhr Industrial District after 1870 made the Lower Rhine, in terms of transport, an arm of the sea and a leading factor in world commerce. This development and others in kind made sea trade available for much of Europe; but as the Rhine is now and has been for many centuries an outstanding example of river transportation, in this study it is taken as a continuing center of interest to illustrate how river transport became a component not only of the world order, but also of the progress of civilization. Note, however, that the beginning developments were in the Mediterranean where water transport emerged as a civilizing force and where it functioned along with the remarkable advances in language, philosophy, art, and law—other components of civilization. Hence, this study which emphasizes water transport also moves into a recognition of attributes of such transport in civilization; and finally it considers the prospects for attaining a permanent civilization in the world order.

Three periods of study helped in the preparation of this manuscript. The first and second continued for upwards of three decades, whereas the third covers active effort since 1957. The first period was devoted to research and teaching in the economic geography of North America at the University of Chicago; the second aimed at an understanding of ocean trade and transportation and grew out of service in the Commodity Section of the Division of Planning and Statistics of the United States Shipping Board during World War I, and as consultant to the War Shipping Administration in World War II; the third and current period is associated with my tenure as University Professor at Southern Illinois University in charge of an interdisciplinary research program called the Mississippi Valley Investigations. The preliminary studies under this assignment led us to focus on the Rhine, first as a long term study of continental transportation and second as an arm of the North Atlantic Ocean in modern maritime history.

Field surveys in the Rhine country occupied the summer months of 1960. In this work I was assisted by Mrs. Colby; in fact, without her expert help I could not have undertaken the study. With the cooperation of the Chicago Motor Club an Italian car was purchased for delivery in Napoli. After experience was gained in driving this car, the Alps were crossed via the St. Gotthard Pass. This route was chosen because the headstreams of the Rhine rise in this vicinity. The approach to the pass from the south leads up the valley of the Ticino River, a tributary of the Po. From the south, the pass is reached by numerous switch-backs expertly engineered in the crystal-line south face of the pass. As the time was early June, the air at the pass was bitterly cold and snow still mantled the slopes of the col. The north slope from the pass is longer than the south; but as a bridge had to be built across a deep chasm, it called for more difficult engineering. At the right of the highway a headstream of the Reuss River meanders in an Alpine meadow before plunging into a deep and narrow canyon.

After a brief interval in the Swiss Plateau, we came to the Swiss port of Basel where our survey began. Then, in order down the valley, we studied the French (Alsatian) port of Strasbourg; the German port of Mannheim at the junction of the Neckar and Rhine rivers; the ports of Duisburg-Ruhrort, the most active river ports in Europe; and finally Rotterdam, the Atlantic port only eighteen miles from the North Sea.

The terms Atlantic Europe, Central Europe, and Western Europe are in common use by writers dealing with that continent; but usage varies from one writer to another according to his judgment or inclination. In this study the terms Atlantic Europe, Central Europe, and Western Europe are employed for the needs of the theme under discussion. Atlantic Europe designates the countries of Norway, Denmark, Germany, the Netherlands, Belgium, Great Britain, Ireland, France, Portugal, and Spain facing the Atlantic. Central Europe includes most of Germany and also Switzerland and Austria. Western Europe is a combination of Central and Atlantic Europe, with Sweden and Italy added.

During the field survey we became indebted to many port officials, especially at Basel and Duisburg-Ruhrort. These officials provided recent local publications and a large body of statistical information. We are under deep obligation to Professor Pfeifer, Director of the Geographical Institute, University of Heidelberg, because of his help in studying the port of Mann-heim, and because he loaned us his research assistant, Erdmann Gormen, who spent a week with us as guide and interpreter in the Neckar Valley and in the Duisburg-Ruhrort area.

At Duisburg we were introduced to Dr. Wilhelm Helmrich, who saved us time and effort in our study of the ports of Duisburg-Rohrort and who presented us with an autographed copy of the first edition of his new book, *Wirtschaftskunde des Lande Nordrhein-Westfalen* (Düsseldorf: August Bagel Verlag, 1960.

I am under deep obligation to Mary H. Galneder, Map Librarian in the Morris Library at Southern Illinois University, for translations from German and for help in finding maps and related materials; to Daniel R. Irwin, in charge of the Cartographic Laboratory of the Mississippi Valley Investigations, for designing and drawing the many maps in this volume; to Stephen M. Colby for a critical reading of many sections of the manuscript and for his valuable support throughout the writing of this book; to Curtis C. Roseman, my research and field assistant in the summer of 1964; to John Clifford, Associate Professor of the staff of the Morris Library, in charge of the Division of Social Studies; to Anne S. Sharpe from the editorial staff of the Southern Illinois University Press; and to Marilyn M. Branch, secretary of the Mississippi Valley Investigations.

My greatest obligation is a double one: first, to President Delyte W. Morris for his continuing interest in the project, as well as his financial help in making the study possible; and second, to my wife, Mary McRae Colby, for without her skillful driving, her effectiveness in conducting interviews and in recording the results, and her stimulating interest in the field study the Rhine survey would have been an impossibility; moreover, her invaluable help in editing and processing the manuscript raises my debt to her beyond the realm of obligation.

Finally, I wish to express my debt to the authors of the numerous publications that were consulted as the study advanced from original concept, through field surveys and library compilations, to the completed manuscript; and to Elizabeth A. Stone and other officials of the Morris Library at Southern Illinois University. For the inevitable errors of facts and concept, I assume the responsibility.

*Charles C. Colby*

*January, 1965*

# CONTENTS

# ILLUSTRATIONS

# TABLES

# NORTH ATLANTIC ARENA

Water Transport in the World Order

# 1

# Water Transport in the World Order

## PERSPECTIVE AND DIMENSIONS

IN THE SLOW ADVANCES achieved by mankind in search of civilization, there have been a series of world orders, each occurring during a
recognized period of time and in an inhabited space-area. Probably in each
case hope arose that a world order with a stable civilization might be
established. Such a civilization did not happen. Although, in each case,
some progress was made toward surmounting the inherent difficulties, the
desired progress did not occur because of human frailties such as greed,
ignorance, or misdirected ambition.

## I  World Order of the Twentieth Century

The world order of the twentieth century represents the convergence and interactions of many currents of ideas and technologies, as
well as the full range of human activities. This complex assemblage has
exercised an impact on people in all parts of the world. The extent and
character of the impact on the people in a particular area varies with the
degree of their participation in the currents of transport and trade together

3

1. *The North Atlantic Arena, shown by the broken line, is a coined term designating the space-area on the surface of the globe that includes the North Alantic Ocean with Western Europe on the east and the United States and southern Canada on the West. The North Atlantic Arena ranks first among the world's regions in nearly all components of civilization.*

with the status of the associated triple economy of agriculture, industry, and commerce. Localization of the foregoing giants of productivity, livelihood, and welfare, in large measure, is confined to Western Europe and Anglo-America—the fertile lands that flank the North Atlantic Ocean. Taken together, this great ocean with its bordering lands and tributary seas and rivers makes up the North Atlantic Arena, shown in Figure 1. This convenient term refers to the space-area on the surface of the earth in which transportation—and especially water transport—by means of trial, error, and final achievement has become a vigorous and efficient service in the development of civilization.

As used here, the North Atlantic Arena is meant to convey the concept of leadership in human affairs. It poses the thesis that in the future, as in the present and past, the North Atlantic and the countries and tributary water bodies that border it in Europe and North America constitute the earth space occupied by a large proportion of the people endowed with the inherent capacities and potentialities for progress, not only in the full range of science, philosophy, and the arts, but also in the economic, social, political, and other divisions of human welfare. Under this broad thesis, the present study is limited to the development and utilization of water transport in three segments of the North Atlantic Arena: the Rhine representing river transport in Western Europe, the Mediterranean where the early advances in water and land transport occurred, and the North Atlantic Ocean where the long struggle for improvements in sea transportation finally resulted in the invention and use of the steel-clad steamship, the cheapest long distance carrier in the whole realm of transportation.

*FUNCTIONS AND VALUES OF TRANSPORTATION*

Water transport and, in fact, all forms of transportation demonstrate critical values in both peace and war. As elements of the world order, now and in the past, the transport activities, including the pipelines, have rendered persistent and continuous services to society. Functionally these services resemble the arteries of human anatomy in that they carry the blood of commerce to revitalize the social, economic, and political structures.

In times of war the several forms of transportation help to solve one emergency after another as they move men and materials into strategic positions. In peacetimes, transportation continuously solves the persistent and permanent needs of the body politic. Moreover, in the domain of peace the contributions of transportation, in each of its divisions, may be appraised as to its future requirements in organization, administration, legal clarification, and other characteristics.

Three of the major types of transport are modern attainments. The coming of railways featured in the nineteenth century, whereas the development of highway (automobile), pipeline, and air transport belong to the twentieth century. Water transportation, however, began in antiquity, advanced notably under Roman rule, flowered in medieval times in the rivers and bordering seas of Europe, and came to its full status with the oncoming of well-organized steamship navigation between 1870 and 1914. Transportation by water always has been associated with land transportation. Actually the ancient caravans probably preceded water transport, although the origin of these two types of transport appears to be lost in the shadows of antiquity. Nevertheless, sea ports are mentioned in early records. Hence, there must have been exchange of goods from sea to land or vice versa. Apparently such trade was associated with the beginnings of civilization. Later, during the heyday of Roman dominance of Mediterranean affairs, the vast extent of the Roman road system matched the Roman command of the shipping routes.

Rivalries for the control of trade and the wealth it produces have featured the world order ever since the Phoenicians and ancient Greeks struggled for supremacy in the Eastern Mediterranean. At times since, the leading nations have adjusted their rivalries by dividing the Commercial World into recognized spheres of operation. Under the Papal Bull of 1494, the Pope assigned the Western Atlantic and the New World to Spain, and the Eastern Atlantic and the Oriental lands reached by the Good Hope route to Portugal. At other times, great trading organizations chartered by governments have implemented the rivalries and led the search for commodities. More recently, individuals, corporations, and combines have owned and operated shipping and acted as agents of trade. They have competed openly and actively in the production, transportation, marketing, and processing of raw materials and other commodities. In many cases, governments, by their internal policies and their international agreements, have established the rules but, in large measure, the game has been played by private individuals and organizations. However, as in 1914, commercial rivalries have become so intense that war resulted.

Toward the close of the last century the advantages of widespread trade became so apparent that an ever-growing world trade was taken for granted. In this country many argued that commerce was the best basis for international relations and that world trade had made war a thing of the past. In spite of such theories, tariff barriers were increasing rather than decreasing, and "Trade follows the flag" was a popular adage with many leaders. As we look back at the turn of the century it becomes clear that, insofar as raw materials and trade were concerned, there were two powerful international motivations. One emphasized the acquisition of raw materials by an ever-increasing industry and trade. The other thought of raw materials as one of the prizes to be gained from national expansion, by military might if necessary. Both motivations were observable in the policies and actions of most governments, but in varying degree. Britain's policy of Free Trade was an example of the first, whereas her active participation in the partition of Africa illustrates the second. In theory all nations should have access on equal terms to needed raw materials. This was recognized in the Atlantic Charter, but apparently few, if any, know how the theory can be translated into effective practice.

The modern world order has become increasingly dynamic, increasingly global, and strangely ineffective. New political philosophies and theories, responding to new forces, have appeared in rapid and complex succession. New political divisions, some large—some small, now grace the international scene; even though as national properties they leave much to be desired. Under the scrutiny of a geographical appraisal, some nations of today must be ranked low in human and natural resources, in productive plant, in economy, in governmental organization, and in social structure. As in amateur choral groups where many singers lean on the few members who through long training and experience have mastered the art of reading music, some of the nations bidding for recognition in the international scene lean on other nations rather than systematically demonstrating their disciplined preparation for some part in modern enterprise.

*PATTERNS OF PRODUCTION*

In the constructive decades between 1870 and 1914, four broad patterns of production came into being. They comprised 1] the wide distribution of railway transport on land, and the inauguration of steam-ship services on the major ocean routes; 2] vast increases in agricul-tured lands and in output of agricultural products; 3] development of the European and American manufacturing belts which led to amazing increases in industrial products; 4] the emergence of new political units in the international scene. To a notable degree the advances in transport paced the other developments. Taken together, the output of services and products from these patterns changed the tempo of activities in most of the world and greatly increased the wealth of the nations on the borders of the North Atlantic.

Before 1870 the growth in rail transport had largely been in the physical aspects of engineering. Bridges, tunnels, horseshoe curves, better engines and cars commanded the thought of the time. After that date spectacular advances appeared in the economic and social aspects of tech-nology, that is, in administration and management. Such efforts in West-ern Europe and the United States demonstrated that through the organiza-tion of railway lines into systems, services could be so adjusted to space and time as to produce efficient operation and better financial returns.

In the period from 1870 to 1914 steamship navigation introduced regularity of flow in cargo, passenger, and mail movements between West-ern Europe and the major areas of commerce. This meant that commodi-ties could be purchased for delivery at a specified time. Merchants and manufacturers were relieved of the necessity of buying and holding large stocks of raw materials in advance of use. Hence, savings resulted both in the amount of working capital needed and in insurance and other charges. Furthermore, the spread of railways from the ports to interior points in-creased the area to which imports could go and from which exports could come. Bigger business in larger areas helped to lower the price of com-modities. Lowered prices, in turn, meant more customers, and the total area of the Commercial World increased. Leadership largely came from Western Europe and the United States.

Near the close of the nineteenth century, emigration from Europe to the New World attained a momentum of a million or more a year. Pioneers settled the fertile prairies and plains of the United States and Canada, and also the pampas of Argentina. These areas contained the finest soils in the Americas. Soon huge surpluses of grain, lard, meat, hides, skins, and wool became available. Moreover, from the primeval forests of America, lumbermen produced huge quantities of structural timber both for domestic and overseas markets. Enterprises in tropical lands contributed increasing amounts of coffee, rubber, jute, cabinet woods, and a host of other things. Of minerals, for example, the world produced more in the thirty years from 1880 to 1910 than in all previous time. In much of the world this was a period of increasing production of foods, raw materials, and structural materials. The rapid expansion of industry in Europe furnished an ever-growing market. In this period both the European and the American manufacturing belts took form. The European belt, with its need for imported raw materials and food and its ever-growing surplus of factory products, became the pulse of the Commercial World. The output and the thought of farmers, ranchers, miners, lumbermen, trappers, and fishermen in all productive areas were focused on this belt where the triple giants of modern economy—manufacture, agriculture, and trade—gave increasing employment and prosperity.

Many, if not all, phases of human effort contributed to rapid progress in civilization towards the end of the Victorian era. Peace prevailed except for brief intervals and in highly localized areas. Science flourished in both its pure and applied phases. Literacy and elementary education, or at least a move in that direction, became the rule and the expectation in many countries, especially in those about the borders of the North Atlantic. Cities grew in size and number. The urban influence increased. Engineering in all its spectacular aspects created a new cultural pattern on the face of nature. In this pattern and, in fact, in the gross structure which we call the "World's Economy," transportation probably made the greatest advances and accomplished the most far-reaching results.

*POLITICAL DEVELOPMENTS*

Accompanying the great advances in transportation were political developments of great moment in the working pattern of the world. The Franco-Prussian War of 1870 announced Germany as the major political unit of Central Europe, and modern Italy had come into being by the treaty of Zürich, 1859. The partition of Africa showed that Britain would dominate the political forces which would influence the economic development of the Dark Continent. Japan came out of its long seclusion and in 1869 began its spectacular bid for power in the Orient and the Pacific. Seward's purchase of Alaska in 1867 initiated the extra-territorial expansion of the United States and heralded, although few Americans realized it, the great role which the United States was destined to play in Pacific affairs.

*MAJOR PERIODS AND CURRENT PROBLEMS*

The development of water transportation has been a slow but continuous process. It has been a part of every age and in many areas. In five periods, however, water transport has been of dominate concern; namely, 1] in the period of antiquity, when under the Phoenicians water transport had its first development on a commercial basis; 2] in the period of Roman Rule, when under Pax Romana both water and land transport witnessed a great and somewhat integrated growth; 3] in the penetration of Europe and of European thought after the Fall of Rome; 4] in the Discoveries Period, when shipping and trade moved from the Mediterranean Sea to the Atlantic Ocean; 5] the period of world-wide operation from 1870 to 1914, when sea transport and commerce became a factor in the economy of most nations. Sargent, in his *Seaways of the Empire,* emphasized the dimensions of shipping and trade during this period when he wrote, "The whole is balanced but not the parts." Since the close of World War II, world commerce has not been balanced because it has been impeded by the policies of the Communist Bloc.

The year 1914 not only witnessed the beginning of the First World War but it marked a transition from a time of general peace and prosperity to a period of war-generated turbulence and excessive international tension. In Europe and Anglo-America the turbulence in human affairs included World War I, a postwar boom, a severe and prolonged depression, World War II, and a perplexing period of frustrating economic, social, and political anxiety. In large measure this continuing period was generated by the policies and action of the Union of Soviet Socialist Republics that spread a devastating cloud over Eastern Europe and established the Iron Curtain that divides continental transport, trade, economic, and cultural patterns into two parts, thereby upsetting the civilizing structure of the European continent.

The long period of war, international tension, restrictive Soviet policies, and the continued wave of nationalism disorganized and, in many areas, destroyed ocean transport and trade. Sea transport, as developed before the First World War, attained a world-wide organization and, as will be discussed subsequently, had become a civilizing factor of the first order of importance. Shipping services reached the ports of countries that face the high seas. Fuel stations serving the vessels of all flags were maintained on all the sea lanes, trading and financial agencies featured all port cities, and rapid communication in terms of cablegrams and wireless messages gave unity to the maritime world, thereby keeping the people of all productive areas in touch with world markets. All these and related services fostered industrial and commercial enterprises not only in the North Atlantic Arena but throughout the Commercial World.

PROBLEMS OF THE TWENTIETH CENTURY

The world order of the second half of the twentieth century is confronted by many perplexing problems including  1] the rapid growth of population in most parts of the world;  2] the continued rise of excessive nationalism in many small countries;  3] the development of technology in both its scientific and applied aspects;  4] the development, on the part of many nations, of their economy and financial resources.

Of all the problems that will confront the body politic, none will be more demanding of solution than the ever-present water problems. In addition to the problems of water transportation that are surveyed in this book, there will be the question of water supply for the increasing domestic, municipal, and industrial uses. Moreover, the problem of pollution of rivers, lakes, and underground water resources hovers over the present generation, and if resort is made to use ocean water to augment the waters of the land, the oceans cannot continue to be the dumping place of human and other wastes. Furthermore, the need for bodies of water for recreational purposes will increase as time goes on. Each and every problem of successful living on the space-areas on the surface of the earth will mean investigations to the point of successful utilization. The needs will be great and the rewards to human accomplishment stupendous.

II   Problems of Inevitable Change

Some of the problems now confronting modern society are due to inevitable change, and especially to the rapid pace of change in thought, attitude, techniques, and other motivating aspects of current affairs in the

North Atlantic Arena. Some changes are helping the recovery of sea transport and other forms of transportation, whereas, other changes appear to work in the opposite direction. To the extent that this broad thesis holds true, a great opportunity and responsibility confronts the people of the countries about the North Atlantic Arena. They may follow any one of three directions: 1] recognize that challenge calls for direct, determined, and well-organized attack; 2] sidestep the challenge and hope that everything will come out all right; 3] ignore the challenge completely.

If the people who live and work in the North Atlantic Arena rise to the challenge and obtain workable solutions, the world may anticipate a long period of peace and prosperity. The solution probably will require new dimensions of intellectual effort, new forms of cooperation, and new designs of effectuation beyond any image now visualized. If the challenge to the intellectual and reasoning powers of mankind culminates in success, it should inaugurate a new era in human affairs; in short, a move toward Utopia. If the reaction is to sidestep the challenge in the hope that "everything will come out all right," the situation may mean that the Western world will muddle along much as it is doing at present. If this should be the case, what can be expected of the people in the world's low status areas? Unfortunately, the challenge may be ignored completely. If that is the case, there may follow a period of deterioration, decadence, and retrogression that might lead to a long period of darkness. In this connection it should be remembered that, according to Edward Gibbon in his summary of the principal causes of the Decline and Fall of Rome, the causes continued to operate for more than a thousand years.

If I judge correctly the basic attitudes of the contemporary world order, there is an overwhelming conviction that the first of the stated alternatives constitutes the right road to follow. If this holds true, then we need to return to the opening paragraph of this book in which attention was directed to the complex assemblage of ideas, resources, techniques, and activities which today find their fullest expression in the North Atlantic Arena.

In the search for progress in the world order there will be met a multiplicity of problems so diverse in structure and so widespread in their distribution on the surface of the earth as to defy frontal attack. In all probability, every aspect of human reasoning, every one of the basic disciplines, and in fact, every item of human intelligence will be needed in the exploration of the stratosphere of human intelligence.

# 2

# The Rhine Route

THE RHINE is an international river. It rises in the lofty slopes of the Swiss Alps, and its first port is at the doorway of Switzerland. Then, after forming a boundary for France and Germany, it becomes the commercial, scenic, and industrial waterway of West Germany. Finally it reaches the sea with a glance at Belgium and a commanding position in the economy of the Netherlands. Throughout its course it possesses beauty, but underneath its facade of charm flows the power and the utility that ranks it, in terms of use, among the few really great waterways of the world.

International service of the Rhine fleet may be judged from the composition of the Rhine fleet in 1954.[1] If Table 1 is visualized into action on a summer day, the Rhine becomes a panorama of powerful tugs pulling or pushing convoys of low-riding barges, a multiplicity of motor-powered vessels each bent on its own particular business, tugs rushing to their next assignments, and many excursion and pleasure crafts. The whole moving scene is enlivened with the numerous national flags mingled with the ship-owners' multicolored pennons. On many of the motorvessels lace curtains, aft, show that the owner and his family live aboard, with the crew assigned to quarters in the bow. On these numerous vessels one views international labor at work, all living under and obeying the time-honored regulations under which river traffic operates. Such international work, the common end of commerce, is the major international relation that enriches the life of nations.

1. THE RHINE FLEET CLASSED BY SHIPPING AND NATIONS IN 1954.

| | Tugpower | | Barge Loading Capacity | | Motorvessels | |
|---|---|---|---|---|---|---|
| | Ships | H. P. | Ships | Tons | Ships | Tons |
| Holland | 734 | 207,360 | 2,856 | 2,398,301 | 1,996 | 767,034 |
| Germany | 377 | 181,355 | 1,752 | 1,625,075 | 791 | 486,816 |
| France | 63 | 49,855 | 256 | 274,739 | 299 | 172,965 |
| Switzerland | 19 | 24,800 | 65 | 63,991 | 275 | 201,393 |
| Belgium | 18 | 2,850 | 1,003 | 687,206 | 545 | 226,010 |
| Total | 1,211 | 466,220 | 5,932 | 5,049,312 | 3,906 | 1,854,218 |

Source: *Die Duisburg-Ruhrorter Häfen* (Duisburg, 1956), p. 20.

Edward Gibbon (1737–1794) in summarizing the principal causes of the Decline and Fall of Rome develops the thesis that "The servitude of rivers is the noblest and most important victory that man has obtained over the licentiousness of nature."[2] If this assertion is applied to the Rhine, it is supported by the following excerpts from the writings of nineteenth and twentieth century authorities on the Rhine:

The Rhine is the only Alpine river to reach the North Sea; its valley therefore is the only natural waterway through the central mountains and is of supreme importance to the economic life of Germany. (L. D. Stamp and S. C. Gilmour, *Chisholm's Handbook of Commercial Geography*, p. 408.)

Holland is the gift of the Rhine, just as Egypt is of the Nile. (Sir Halford J. Mackinder, *The Rhine*, p. 360.)

Finally, in the long run, the Romans continued to hold only the rivers Rhine and Danube and also for a considerable period, the angle of country lying between their upper reaches. (Joseph Partsch, *Central Europe*, p. 126.)

The deeply cut valleys, on the contrary, are extremely fertile because of their sheltered position and productive alluvial or loess soils. . . . Plateaus between those valleys of the Rhine system have, for the most part, an inclement climate and infertile soil. (Alfred Kirchoff, "The German Empire," *The International Geography*, p. 287.)

The Rhine has long been the major link in the navigable waterways of northeastern Europe; it is essential to the economic health of the Ruhr Valley of Germany as well as the whole valley from Switzerland to the Netherlands.

(Henry S. Baskin, "Trade and Navigation on the Rhine," *Foreign Commerce Weekly*, Vol. 38, No. 6 (1950), 628.)

Especially important was the valley of the Rhine, and lands along it received a special imprint: a civilization zone was properly generated by the economic and political life of the great river. (Jean Gottman, A *Geography of Europe*, p. 411.)

The foregoing quotations epitomize the opinions and convictions of scholars who have made special studies of the Rhine River and its remarkable valley. Their writings betray a common center of interest; namely, the achievements of the people who have utilized the Rhine and lived and worked in its productive valley. Combined with other sources of information on the Rhine there arises an amazing chronicle of the evolution of society in one of the unique space areas on the face of the earth. In later chapters quantitative evidence is presented which supports the qualitative evaluation represented by the foregoing assertions. It should be understood, however, that the quoted assertions are items in lines of reasoning of the several authors.

I     *The Rhine River in the Continent of Europe*

The high commercial, historical, and political importance of the Rhine River in Western Europe is emphasized by the position of the river and its valley in the complex physical pattern of Europe. As a continent, Europe is almost equally divided into two great physical regions, an eastern and a western. In large measure the eastern region is made up of vast plains with monotonous relief, whereas the western region has a complex assemblage of mountains, valleys, plateaus, hill country, and plains. Shackelton points out that Europe, east of the Carpathian Mountains, "has been a region of great structural stability through vast eras of geological time."[3] In Western Europe, however, the surface has been reshaped and altered by complex diastrophic forces. In this region of physiographic diversity, the structure of mountains, plateaus, and other surface features trends from southwest to northeast. The Rhine River and its well-marked valley, however, trends in general from south to north, thereby presenting a valley route from Switzerland to the North Sea—a route that is a major feature of Western Europe and, in fact, of the Continent (*Fig. 2*).

2. *Western Europe. Countries and major rivers.*

In the drainage pattern of Europe both the Rhine and the Danube are of major importance. The latter, except for the Volga, is the longest river in Europe. Its two headstreams rise in Western Europe not far from the boundary between Switzerland and West Germany. In its upper course the Danube flanks the Alps and the Swiss Plateau for many miles; and, in general, the Danube follows a west-east direction from its source in Western Europe to empty into the Black Sea in Eastern Europe. It resembles the Rhine in that it is a vital traffic waterway; but, unlike the Rhine, it leads to a sea relatively remote from the world's major sea routes.

In Roman times, marked by the long struggle with the tribes of central and eastern Europe, the Roman policy emphasized the desirability of keeping the tribes north of the Danube and east of the Rhine.[4] The policy was implemented by the Roman roads and by the Roman legions maintained north of the Alps. The frontier was a zone rather than a definite line because it separated more civilized or more advanced people from less civilized and less well-organized people. At intervals during the ensuing centuries the zone has marked the distinction between Eastern and Western Europe, much as the Iron Curtain presently signals the conflict between East and West.

## ACCESSIBILITY OF THE RHINE

In the passing of the centuries the Rhine and its valley have been approached from many directions and for many purposes. The terrain and drainage structure of Western Europe provides a multiplicity of routes and passes that give the Rhine a central quality which invites travel and trade. This same quality has made the conquest of the Rhine a necessity for ambitious military leaders with the urge to conquer Europe. The people of the Rhine Valley have witnessed epoch-making events in religious thought and ecclesiastical government. Some of these proved to be constructive in nature whereas others hindered the progress of industry and commerce. However, in the realm of education the Rhine universities again and again have demonstrated achievements in the acquisition and dissemination of knowledge and in the utilization of the scientific method.

Since early times, the Rhine has been a route of travel and trade. At present, practically all forms of modern transport are in use along its valley. In harmony with this form of leadership, the coal, iron ore, and other minerals in the Rhine territory have been and are being utilized in far-reaching industrial and commercial enterprises. Throughout the Rhine's course flow the power and utility that make it one of the really great waterways of the world. It is because of these elements of achievement and leadership in navigation and traffic that this study of the characteristics which make the Rhine one of the major waterways of the world was undertaken. The underlying purpose was to see if any of the patterns, methods, or techniques associated with the Rhine and with the growth of the industries and cities in its valley might be applied to future development in the Mississippi and Lower Ohio valleys.

## II    *The Rhine in Western Europe*

Although the Rhine River has been a route of transportation and travel in Western Europe throughout the course of European history, it has varied in its functions. In antiquity it was a route in the European frontier. It became the eastern border of the Roman exploration and invasion of Gaul. Roman legions traveled along its course and established forts and other posts at strategic points. In the middle ages the Rhine became a continental route in the complex terrain of Western Europe. Some of the forts became trading posts and others became governmental and ecclesiastical centers. In time some of the centers attained importance as members of one or more commercial leagues and prospered accordingly. The route extended to the North and Baltic seas, and much was learned about the organization, financing, methods, and techniques of trade. Finally, after steamship services became common and the Ruhr section developed heavy industry, the Lower Rhine became an arm of the sea; and the busy Rhine attained status as a maritime route with an ever-growing participation in world affairs.

Today eleven countries in the western part of Europe have frontage on the Atlantic and are directly a part of the Atlantic Arena. In addition, Sweden on the Baltic Sea and Italy on the Mediterranean are so closely associated with the Atlantic countries that in this study they are considered as part of this group. Moreover, Switzerland with its connections with the Atlantic via the Rhine, and Luxembourg, closely associated with Belgium, may be included in the group of fifteen nations that are thought of as "Europe of the Sea."

In Rhine transport five countries—Switzerland, France, West Germany, the Netherlands, and Belgium—share the Rhine. As canals connect the Rhine with most of the inland waterways of these countries there results a regional unit of waterways on which the flags of each of the five nations may be seen. Moreover, a system of international regulations has gained acceptance so that the craft of these nations operate together successfully. Hence, in this study the "Rhine Countries" designates the five countries which share the Rhine and constitute the heart of Atlantic Europe.

III    *The Rhine in the North Atlantic Arena*

In the early days of March, 1945, United States troops reached Remagen on the Rhine thirteen miles south of Bonn. An American platoon promptly took over the Remagen bridge just in time to prevent its destruction by the Germans. The possession of this bridgehead across the river opened the way not only to the Ruhr and the interior of Germany, but up valley to the Upper German Rhine. The presence of American troops on the Rhine almost twenty centuries after Roman legions passed this point enroute to the North Sea and Britain emphasizes the high importance of the Rhine not only in the long military history and economy of Western Europe, but also in modern times as an area in direct contact with the multiplicity of shipping services on the North Atlantic Ocean.

How different the outlook of the Rhine country as viewed in periods of peace. Before the First World War, Americans and students from many other countries came to study science, education, and the arts. Moreover, in the final decades of the nineteenth century German scholars were making great strides in geography. Students in this field of learning came to realize that the Rhine is *continental* in its position in Western Europe, and that throughout history it has flowed not only through the diverse terrain it drains but through the culture of the people who have lived and made a living along its remarkable valley. That the Rhine also has vigorous *maritime* qualities is illustrated by recent developments at Rotterdam and its outlying ports along the New Waterway, a channel 18 miles long and 35 feet deep that is the major navigated route from the thriving port of Rotterdam to the North Sea. Along the south side of the channel where it opens to deep water, the new port of Europoort is under construction on piles driven deep into the sand and mudflats of the deltaic border. The new port will accommodate the largest vessels, will have the world's largest dry docks, and will offer sites for warehouses, industrial establishments, and petroleum storage and refineries.

Rotterdam with its numerous ancillary ports comprises the facilities and functions of the most rapidly growing European area of contact with ocean trade and transportation. Rotterdam also is an active river port for it has terminal facilities and services for handling the barge traffic on the Rhine. Daily ferry-like services are maintained with Duisburg-Ruhrort, the major river ports for the Ruhr industrial area, and ocean-going vessels clear from Rotterdam enroute to Duisburg-Ruhrort, Düsseldorf, and Köln.

Rhine navigation, the first focus of interest, begins at Basel in northwest Switzerland at the point of contact of the Swiss, German, and French boundaries. From Basel, the Rhine in its course to the Hoek van Holland has been so engineered as to provide 550 miles of navigable waterway. Enroute the river flows through a series of highly developed urban, industrial, commercial, and cultural areas.

Historically the Rhine Valley has been not only a battleground for the campaigns of ambitious military leaders with an urge to conquer Europe, but also the scene of epoch-making conflicts in religious thought and religious influence. These wars and ecclesiastical conflicts disturbed creative effort; hence, handicapped the livelihood of the people. However, in spite of the exigencies associated with the occupancy of desirable space, the people of the Rhine Valley became distinguished by their contributions to science and by the application of scientific methods and techniques to agriculture, industry, and trade. At the inner margins of the North European Lowland the Rhine flows through a belt rich in coal and other minerals. The utilization of these resources spurred the development of the Ruhr and other industrial districts.

As has been mentioned, the Rhine, with Rotterdam as its major port, has become an arm of the North Atlantic. Its extensive transportational, commercial, and industrial activities make it at present the most rapidly growing port in Europe, ranking with New York and London in world commerce. In the past, similar activities localized at or near the mouth of the Seine, the Thames, the Schelde, the Noordzee Kanaal, the Weser, and the Elbe, with Le Havre, London, Antwerpen, Amsterdam, Bremen, and Hamburg respectively as the great ports. The distance from Le Havre to Hamburg of about 600 miles comprises only a short segment of the long coast of Western Europe, but along with Liverpool on the west coast of England, these cities have been for many years the leading ports of Western Europe.

The Eastern Seaboard of the United States, on the west flank of the North Atlantic, is the other area of great world ports. The Eastern Seaboard, as defined here, extends from Boston on Massachusetts Bay to Norfolk at Hampton Roads and constitutes another segment of about 600 miles where important ports are localized. In addition to Boston and Norfolk, this segment contains New York on the Hudson, Philadelphia on the Delaware, and Baltimore on Chesapeake Bay. New York, in the center, dominates the Eastern Seaboard both in services by sea and by land. Actually more railroads from the interior focus on New York than on Boston at one extremity or on Baltimore or Norfolk at the other. Furthermore, there are more frequent sailings and faster ships from New York to Western Europe and other areas than from any other American port.

In effective penetration into the interior today, the transport services of the two continents facing the North Atlantic stand in sharp contrast with each other. In Europe the Iron Curtain, and the policies that support it, constitute a barrier to transportation, trade, and social contacts from the North Atlantic to Eastern Europe, thereby largely restricting such contacts to the Rhine countries and contiguous areas. In this age where transportation and communication are developing rapidly, the Iron Curtain is an anachronism both in time and space. Politically it savors of defeat and constitutes an unwarranted handicap to the welfare of Eastern Europe. Nature provided two sea routes to Eastern Europe: the long Mediterranean and the Black Sea extension at the south, and the Baltic sea at the north. Both have been utilized since ancient times, but today the prevailing policies restrict rather than promote commercial enterprises along these sea routes. Air services have become a new feature in world transportation and constitute a new phase of North Atlantic transport. They extend into Eastern Europe, but again their full usefulness is denied by governmental edicts and regulations.

In North America the vast mid-continent lowlands are reached by rail, highway, and airway services. Moreover, the St. Lawrence River and the Great Lakes along the northern border of the United States provide a developing water route to Chicago and other mid-continental centers, while from the Gulf of Mexico tow barge services on the Mississippi and Illinois rivers reach the same continental points. Thus, barge services carry such huge quantities of bulky commodities at such low cost that they constitute an entirely new means of commodity transport.

The question of transportation is acute in all parts of the world. Leadership in solving the problems, however, probably lies in the North Atlantic Arena. Here is the world's greatest development of transportation on the sea, on the land, and in the air. Here also is the greatest localization of science, industry, and technology; and, in all likelihood, here is where the problems of transportation will move progressively towards solution.

The high significance of the North Atlantic Arena has been recognized by other writers. For example, Barbara Ward in her outstanding study of *The Rich Nations and the Poor Nations* states that in this revolutionary age four revolutions are underway. These four revolutions are 1] the revolution of equality of men and nations; 2] the idea of progress in the possibility of "material change leading to a better world"; 3] the fact of rising birth rates; 4] the progress of scientific change. She also states that these revolutions "started in the North Atlantic Arena, in those nations which lie around the North Atlantic Ocean."[5] Other writers or speakers, in recognizing the high significance of the area of which the North Atlantic is the center, use such terms as the Atlantic Community, the Atlantic System, or the North Atlantic World.

## IV    *Physical Characteristics of the Rhine*

For upwards of twenty centuries the Rhine River has been of major significance in the continent of Europe. The physical characteristics of its source area, its flow and gradient, and the divisions of its valley become matters of concern in the functional achievements of the people who have lived and worked along the course of the river. Hence, this remarkable valley has become a pilot area in modern economy. To a high degree, the characteristics and culture of the Rhine exemplifies the sum of the attributes essential in the development of a riverine civilization.

### SOURCE AREA

The sources of the Rhine are in the Swiss Alps, the central section of the chain of mountains that border the Mediterranean Sea from Spain to the Balkan Peninsula. This Swiss section extends from southwest to northeast for more than 500 miles, and from north to south varies from 80 to 140 miles in width. In large measure the flow of the Rhine depends on melt water from the snow and glaciers of the Swiss Alps. This means a remarkably regular flow throughout the summer navigation season, as compared with the other rivers of Western Europe.

The pattern of Rhine drainage in Switzerland has three divisions; namely, the Vorderrhein and the Hinterrhein at the east, the Reuss and Linth in the middle, and the Aare in the west and northwest (*Fig. 3*). Each river drains through one or more of Switzerland's large lakes that help to regulate the flow of these mountain streams.

According to an early account by Emile Chaix, the surface configuration and geological structure of Switzerland presents four roughly parallel zones from southwest to northeast.[6] The first zone lies in the northwestern border of the country and is made up of the Jura Mountains, a limestone region folded into a series of parallel ridges and valleys. The Swiss

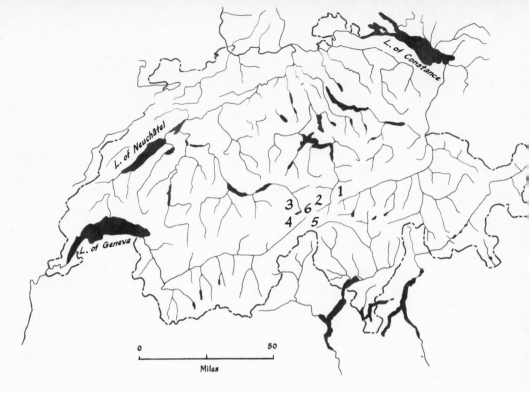

3. *St. Gotthard complex, source area of five major rivers:* 1) *Vorderrhein;* 2) *Reuss;* 3) *Aare;* 4) *Rhone;* 5) *Ticino. Also shown is the St. Gotthard Pass and tunnel, 6.*

section of the Swiss-Bavarian Basin is the second zone. Its irregular but usable surface extends from Lake of Geneva to Lake of Constance. The remainder of Switzerland, about three-fifths of the country, lies in the Alpine zone. This zone divides into two widely different bands. The northern or limestone Alps have been folded and faulted into a high and complicated terrain, whereas the central crystalline Alps (gneiss and granite) occupy the southern and southeastern parts of the country. Both sections of the Alps are broad and in many places rise to over 13,000 feet. At such elevations the Alps contain many glaciers, the total estimated at more than a thousand.

Access to the famous glaciated areas in the western portion of the Alps is obtained by either of two long, narrow and steep-sided longitudinal valleys parallel to the original folds of the structures (*Fig. 4*). These longitudinal valleys separate the northern glaciated section from the southern glaciated section, and thereby facilitate access to each glaciated section. The Rhone River flows down from the western longitudinal valley, whereas the eastern valley is occupied by the Vorderrhein, the head stream

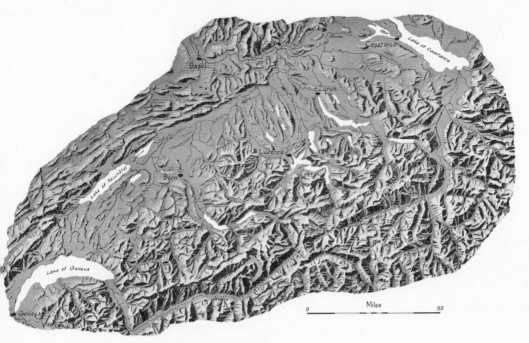

4. *Source area of the Rhine River, showing the deep valley of the Rhone River upstream from Lake of Geneva and the deep valley of the Vorderrhein upstream from Lake of Constance.*

of the Rhine system. Other rivers flow in transverse valleys excavated across the folds.

The two valleys are separated by a high, massive mountainous block between the sources of the Rhone and Vorderrhein which is called the St. Gotthard Block, under which is the tunnel of the same name. Near this high block lie the fountain heads of five great rivers (*Fig. 3*).[7] The Vorderrhein rises at the Oberalp Pass on the east margin of the high block and constitutes the head stream of the Rhine system that drains into the North Sea (*Fig. 4*). At the north end of St. Gotthard Pass is the source of the Reuss River, a principal tributary of the Rhine, whereas at the southern end of the pass, the Ticino River flows into Lago Maggiore and thence to join the Po River in the Po Lowlands. In the northwest flank at Grimsel Pass is the head stream of the Aare River that carries the runoff of northern Switzerland to its junction with the Rhine at Waldshut. Near the foot of Furka Pass on the west flank of the massive block is the source of the Rhone. It then takes its irregular course down the longitudinal valley to Lake of Geneva and the Mediterranean.

*THE VORDERRHEIN AND THE HINTERRHEIN*

The Vorderrhein rises in the vicinity of the St. Gotthard Pass and flows northeastward in its longitudinal valley. Near the city of Chur it is joined by the Hinterrhein. The junction of these two streams marks the beginning of the Rhine proper. From this junction the Rhine flows northeastward to empty into Lake of Constance (Boden See). From the western arm of this lake the water flows over the lip of the basin and follows an irregular course known as the High Rhine to Basel. In this segment the river retains its Alpine characteristics as it drops from 1200 to 800 feet above sea level. Near Schaffhausen a waterfall 100 feet high, inclusive of rapids, and 340 feet wide produces a large amount of hydroelectric power.

*THE REUSS RIVER*

In the middle section of the Swiss drainage pattern, the spectacular valley of the Reuss River forms the northern approach to the highway over St. Gotthard Pass and to the northern end of the St. Gotthard Tunnel, whereas the southern end of the highway and the tunnel opens into the upper Ticino Valley with its southward flowing river.

The Reuss River, a major tributary of the Rhine, rises in the high country in the vicinity of St. Gotthard Pass in the Lepontine Alps in south-central Switzerland. Its upper course is in view from the northern section of the modern highway that is skillfully engineered over the pass from the Ticino Valley at the south. Near its origin, on the north slope of the pass, the Reuss is a small stream flowing in a high, meadowlike valley from which it tumbles into the wild and impressive Schöllenen Gorge that the Reuss has cut through the granites of the massif. This gorge has such precipitous slopes that it defied travel until it was bridged in the thirteenth century. From the gorge the river flows northward into Lake of Lucerne.

Because the St. Gotthard Pass is high (6,929 feet above sea level) it is blocked by snow during the winter and spring. Hence, it was not much used until 1882 when the St. Gotthard Tunnel was opened to railway traffic. The tunnel is nine and a third miles long and extends from Göschenen in the Reuss Valley to Airolo in the Ticino Valley. The tunnel was of great technical significance as it required spiral sections cut in the granitic rock to overcome the differences in the level of the entrances, the southern being at a higher elevation than the northern.

The railway that utilizes the St. Gotthard Tunnel has the shortest route from Zürich and Basel in Switzerland to Milano (Milan) and

Genova (Genoa) in Italy. Hence, commercially the railway makes Genova a Mediterranean port for the Rhine Valley and West Germany. Although all of the Alpine section of the line lies in Swiss territory, its high importance to Germany and Italy led these countries to contribute most of the cost of construction.

*THE AARE RIVER AND THE CONFLUX OF RIVERS*

The Aare River rises near the Grimsel Pass not far from the source of the Rhone. With its tributaries it drains the middle of the Bernese Oberland, a range of the Alps in south-central Switzerland. In its course it traverses the lakes of Brienz and Thun. A tributary, the Thiele, brings in the outflow from the lakes of Neuchâtel and Bienne, and thus the Aare carries the drainage of northern Switzerland to the Rhine.

South of Koblenz where the Aare River empties into the Rhine is the conflux of three rivers—the Aare, the Reuss draining out of Lake of Lucerne, and the Limmat out of Lake of Zürich. The enlarged flow from the union of the three rivers retains the name of the Aare, and within a few miles empties the runoff of central and northern Switzerland into the Rhine that carries the drainage of eastern Switzerland. As only a few small streams join the Rhine between Koblenz and Basel, the Rhine below Koblenz has a flow practically equal to the flow at Basel. This fact helps to explain a plan to canalize the Rhine from Basel to Koblenz, Switzerland. However, a rapids at Rheinfelden will make the effectuation of the plan a costly undertaking. The authors of the plan even contemplate canalization of the river all the way to Lake of Constance in spite of the falls and rapids at Schaffhausen. They argue that the completed canalization would give Germany, Switzerland, and especially Austria an outlet to the Rhine and the North Sea. Each of the three nations would have to contribute to the cost of the work. The cost-benefit ratio would have to be figured in terms of three participants, each of which would view the matter in national terms. The precedents for each joint action are fairly numerous in Western Europe with its many national properties. The arguments, pro and con, would resemble somewhat the interstate compacts in the United States.

v   *Divisions of the Navigable Rhine*

In terms of navigation the commercial Rhine has four distinctive sections. From south to north the sections are:   1] the Upper Rhine Valley that extends for nearly 200 miles from Basel, on the northwestern Swiss border, down a deep flat-floored rift valley to Bingen; 2] the picturesque Rhine Gorge from Bingen 80 miles down river to Bonn, the capital of West Germany, the German Federal Republic; 3] the heavily utilized section from Bonn and Köln across the North German Plain to the border of the Netherlands; 4] the section of deltaic distributaries across the Netherlands to the North Sea. In these navigable sections the level of the river drops from 890 feet above the sea at Basel to sea level at Rotterdam. The steepest gradient is in the 70 miles from Basel to Strasbourg—a drop of nearly 400 feet. As will be shown later, this section and the one downstream to Mannheim has required considerable engineering installations to make navigation feasible above Mannheim, the natural head of navigation.

*UPPER RHINE VALLEY*

Before it reaches Basel, at the southern end of the Upper Rhine Valley, the Rhine has captured the runoff of most of Switzerland. From Lake of Constance to Basel the river flows westward, but at Basel it abruptly turns north and flows into the southern end of the Upper Rhine Valley (*Fig. 5*). This valley is a tectonic depression in the land surface. It commonly is called the Rhine Rift Valley or Graben.[8] It averages about 25 miles in width from east to west and extends northward for 180 miles. Hence, in shape it resembles a long and narrow rectangle with a longitudinal axis from south to north. The Rhine enters at Basel, Switzerland, in the southeast corner of the valley and makes its exit at Bingen, Germany, at the northwest corner.

The valley floor is relatively level, but the entire valley is bordered by mountains, the Schwarzwald (Black Forest) and Odenwald on the east or German side, and the Vosges and Hardt mountains on the west or French side. On the upper end of the east or right-hand side the Rhine is overlooked by the steep, crystalline-faced escarpment of the Black Forest, whereas on the west side a similar steep wall and face marks the upstanding edge of the Vosges.

At Basel, where the Rhine enters the Upper Rhine Valley, its drainage basin narrows to less than a hundred miles in width. To the northeast the Rhine drainage is limited by the head streams of the Danube, whereas at the southwest it is limited by the upper reaches of the Doubs, a tributary of the Rhone. Hence, in the vicinity of Basel the narrow Rhine basin resembles the neck of a bottle with a big glass stopper. In the stopper

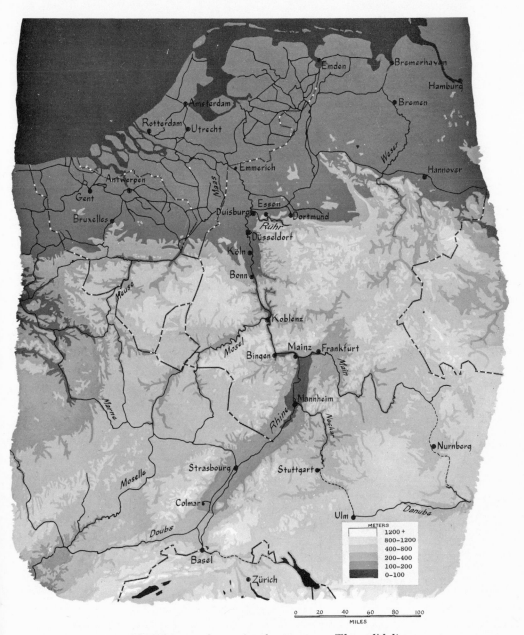

5. Navigable Rhine and associated waterways. The solid lines show navigable waterways. The broken lines indicate proposed waterways. Shown are the Upper Rhine Valley from Basel to Mainz, the historic Rhine Gorge from Bingen to Bonn, the North German Plain from Bonn to Emmerich, and the Rhine Delta from Emmerich to the North Sea.

section, represented by most of Switzerland, the High Rhine and its numerous tributaries coalesce into a single stream to empty through the neck into the elongated bottlelike body of the Rhine Rift Valley (*Fig. 5*).

The southern end of the Upper Rhine Valley is nearly closed by the foothills of the Swiss Jura behind Basel. However, open routes into the valley occur from both the east and the southwest. The narrow trench between the Jura and the steep face of the Schwarzwald (Black Forest) provides a route for the Rhine to reach the rift valley. West of Basel a gap about 20 miles wide and 1200 feet high between the Jura and the Vosges mountains provides a valley route from the Upper Rhine Valley to the valley of the Doubs. This gap in the mountain mass is the Trouée de Belfort, or the Gate of Burgundy, and is followed by the Rhine-Rhone Canal.

The northern or lower end of the Upper Rhine Rift Valley not only is of special interest in Rhine navigation, but also is a focal area in the transportation patterns of Western Europe. This busy area, crossed by the 50th parallel of latitude, is featured by the junction of two rivers and the coalescence of two valleys deeply incised in the surrounding uplands. At its northern end the rift valley, occupied by the Rhine, is blocked by the Taunus Range much as the Swiss Jura blocks the southern end (*Fig. 5*). This norther barrier turns the course of the Rhine westward to Bingen where the river enters its 80-mile gorge by which it crosses the Taunus Range and other sections of the Rhenish Plateau. Although the Rhine turns westward, the floor of the rift valley opens to the east and northeast between the Taunus and the Odenwald to coalesce with the Hessen Lowland. The Main River enters the southern border of the Hessen Lowland at Aschaffenburg and in a great curve via Hanau, Offenbach, and Frankfurt reaches its junction with the Rhine at Mainz.

Transportation routes and services focus on this urbanized lowland that has Frankfurt and Mainz as centers for its diversified economy. As Mackinder pointed out, this sunken lowland is set in a broadly exposed and relatively infertile tableland into which deep valleys have been etched by the Rhine, the Neckar, the Main, and the Lahn.[9] In general, river, canal, railway, and highway routes follow the valleys (*Fig. 5*). However, in modern times some sections of the arterial highways and autobahnen have been engineered across the upland surfaces. From the south, the navigable Rhine with paralleling railways and highways provides a variety of modern transport down the rift valley to Frankfurt and Mainz. From the west, a railway and a highway from the Saarland utilize the lower Nahe Valley to reach the Rhine at Bingen.

*RHINE GORGE*

The upper entrance to the Rhine Gorge is at the river port of Bingen. The port is just upstream from the Binger Loch, a whirlpool at the mouth of the Nahe River (*Fig. 5*). Originally, rapids at Bingen hindered navigation, but long ago channels were blasted through the rapids as another step in making the river a commercial success. From Bingen to Bonn, some 80 miles down river, the Rhine crosses the Rhenish Plateau in a narrow valley deeply incised in the highland. The flow of the river is divided at some points by rocky crags or islands, but in some reaches occupies all of the valley bottom. At the rock of the Lorelei the river narrows to 180 yards and is 90 feet deep. In some places the steep slopes of the valley walls are terraced and covered with vineyards that yield grapes for the famous Rhine wines. Small but picturesque settlements nestle in nooks along the banks or form a narrow fringe along the valley borders. Castles, built to control Rhine traffic in a past era, stand in the midst of the stream or on projecting rocks high above the water. Although they are relics of a past economy, they have income-producing value as tourist attractions. In sharp contrast with these hindrances to the flow of traffic in the past are the railroads and highways which line each side of the river and help to make this deep valley route today one of the great avenues of Western European commerce.

At Coblenz, about halfway between Bingen and Bonn, the valley opens into an attractive basin to receive the junction of the Lahn from the right and the Moselle (Mosel) from the left. Both streams emerge from narrow, winding valleys eroded deeply into the Rhenish uplands. On the point of land between the Moselle (Mosel) and the Rhine stands the massive monument to Kaiser Wilhelm and the period of German history that ended in defeat in the First World War. The Moselle with its major tributary, the Saar River, drains the area between the Vosges on the south and east and the Ardennes on the north and west. The Moselle is highly industrialized and so much utilized for river transport that a plan has been developed to increase the depth of the water so that river craft of deeper draft can bring the Moselle into closer commercial relations with the Rhine. Below Coblenz the valley narrows again, and the river flows with a strong current until the valley walls recede, and at Bonn the Rhine flows out on the broad North German plains. Bonn, an historic center and attractive city, is now the capital of the Federal Republic of Germany.

The narrow Rhine Gorge affords a fine opportunity to view the flow of traffic by rail, highway, and river over this international route from the northern to southern sections of Western Europe. Passenger and freight trains move up and down valleys with amazing frequency. Automobile, bus, and truck traffic along the highways is persistently heavy, while barges and tankers, under their own power, and tows of dumb barges hauled by powerful tugs move up or down river. Because of the narrowness of the gorge, the flow of river traffic can be seen and counted from any vantage point.

*THE PLAIN OF THE NORTH GERMAN RHINE*

At Bonn the Rhine leaves its gorge to enter the North German Plain's baylike extension into the uplands. As the historic city of Köln is near the center of this funnel-like extension, the area has been called the Bay of Köln. Köln lies on the west bank of the river and with its suburbs presents a population of upwards of a million. It marks the beginning of the most notable industrial, transportational, and commercial display in Europe.

The northern border of the hilly upland into which the Rhine has cut its gorge extends in an irregular west to east line from southern Belgium to Poland. The major rivers of Central Europe emerge from this hilly upland and flow across the northern plain to the sea. The Vistula and the Oder empty into the Baltic whereas the Elbe, Weser, and the Rhine reach the North Sea. As the Rhine is the only one that rises in the Alps, it is the only one that in summer is fed by melt water from the Alpine glaciers. Hence, a relatively steady flow is one of its major assets. The border where the upland meets the plain is rich in coal, iron ore, potash, salt, and potter's clay and has become the heart of the principal manufacturing belt in Europe. As much of this part of the northern plain is mantled with loess, it is relatively fertile and responsive to agricultural use.

Although the surface of the plain bisected by the Lower German Rhine is almost featureless, diversity of land rise and drainage introduces some variety into the landscape. The better land for agriculture lies in the reclaimed bogs along the estuaries and in some coastal areas. In other sections the land is so nearly level and the drainage so sluggish that marshes are characteristic. Heath lands, where higher, dryer, and sandy soils prevail, are too poor for cultivation. In some sections skillfully managed forests and parks add variety and color. The most striking landscape features, however, are in the port cities along the Rhine and in the industrial sections such as the Ruhr.

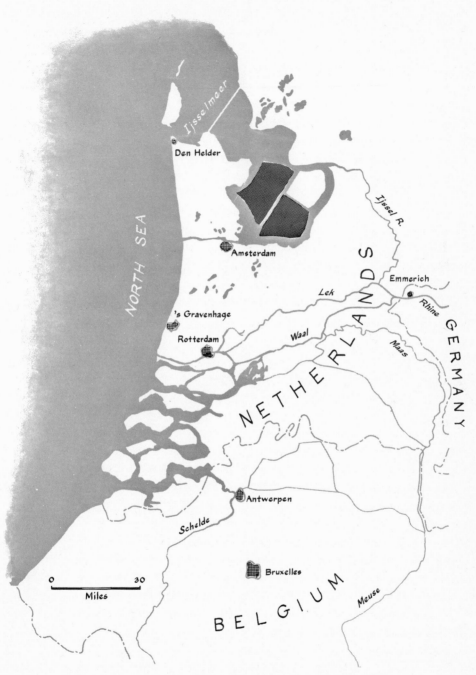

6. Distributaries of the Rhine, and the Maas and Schelde rivers.

DISTRIBUTARIES OF THE RHINE

The Rhine Delta is the major feature of the coastal plain in the Netherlands and the northern part of Belgium. As it leaves Germany and enters the Netherlands the Rhine divides into channels that become the distributaries of the delta, shown in Figure 6. A small distributary, the Ijssel, flows north to the Ijsselmeer (the former Zuider Zee), the broad arm of the North Sea that borders the delta on the northeast.[10]

Two larger distributaries, the Waal and the Lek, flow westward to the estuaries which form the southern flank of the delta. The former carries about two-thirds of the flow, but the latter with only a third of the volume has about two-thirds of the traffic. The Lek is joined by waters from the Maas (Meuse) to reach Rotterdam, the great port of the Netherlands. From Rotterdam a dug channel about 18 miles long leads through the southern part of the province of Holland to enter the North Sea just south of the Hoek van Holland, the point from which service is maintained to the English port of Harwich. Fast railway and highway service are maintained from London to Harwich and comfortable ferry service from Harwich to the Hoek van Holland. From here a major railway crosses the Netherlands enroute to Köln and Switzerland via the west bank of the Rhine. The fast Dutch autostrasse also crosses the country to connect with the German autobahn. Hence, the small area that includes Rotterdam and the Hoek van Holland is a focus of transportation that is so well arranged and the services so efficiently integrated that the visitor scarcely realizes the significance, nationally and internationally, of what he is seeing.

The fairly regular coastline from 's Gravenhage northward to the point Den Helder is bordered by a broad array of sand dunes that protect the low-lying plain to the east where much of the surface is below sea level. North and east of Den Helder, the West Frisian Islands, a chain of offshore islands, characterize the coastal zone. A broad body of water, the Waddenzee, lies between these islands and the mainland. Across the narrow neck of the Ijsselmeer (Zuider Zee) between Noord Holland and Friesland a major dike, 20 miles long and 300 feet wide, was built as part of a great plan to reclaim nearly two-thirds of the Ijsselmeer (Zuider Zee). Inside this enclosure polders were constructed and rimmed with dikes to aid in the reclamation of usable land. Many years will be necessary before the plan is completed for this is one of the great reclamation projects of all time.[11]

# 3

# Mediterranean Beginnings

NAVIGATION AND TRADE have been continuing steps in the pursuit of civilization. Navigation is the forerunner, whereas trade prepares the way for advances in the affairs of mankind. If the advances are of varied character they herald the coming of civilization. In the twentieth century the commercial chain of navigation and trade constitute only a part of the transport complex, and this complex is so interwoven with other factors that affect civilization as to defy systematic analysis. This calls for a recourse from the complexities of the present to the simple beginnings of navigation in the Mediterranean.

I    *The Mediterranean in the North Atlantic Arena*

The Mediterranean, as its name implies, is a sea enclosed by land except at the extreme west where the narrow Strait of Gibraltar makes it a gigantic arm of the North Atlantic Ocean. Until the beginning of the Discoveries Period, the Mediterranean Sea was the active part of the North Atlantic Arena and witnessed the dawn and early development of West-

7. The Mediterranean Sea and Black Sea at the time of the
Phoenicians and ancient Greeks.

ern civilization. The Mediterranean and its bordering lands also comprise
the region in which both water and land transport evolved from primitive
beginnings to well-organized and, in some instances, to integrated undertakings (Fig. 7).[1]

The Mediterranean not only is enclosed by land but, for the most
part, the enclosed quality is emphasized by mountains which rise to spectacular heights above the narrow coastal plains, or by the vast deserts of
North Africa and Arabia. Exceptions to this generalization are the broad
re-entrant valleys of the Nile, Po, Rhone, and Ebro rivers and a multiplicity of smaller valleys. These valleys, endowed with exceptional conditions and resources, have been utilized by generation after generation of
mediterranean people whose skill and enterprise have paced the evolution
of Mediterranean affairs.[2]

The dimensions and the position on the surface of the earth of the
Mediterranean Sea have been of prime importance in its utilization by
mankind. Its longitudinal axis, that is, its over-all length from west to east,
extends through 40 degrees, from 5° 45' west longitude at the Strait of
Gibraltar to Beirut (Beyrouth) at 35° 30' east longitude, or a distance of
approximately 2,300 miles. Its maximum width is 1,200 miles. Including
the Black Sea, with its 750 miles from west to east, there is offered a sailing
length of some 3,150 miles. The immense size of the Mediterranean is

shown by its position between the 30th and 45th parallels of latitude, its over-all dimensions being 965,000 square miles. With the Black Sea included the area is 1,145,000 square miles.

The enormous area of the Mediterranean has continental boundaries on three sides: Europe on the north, southwest Asia on the east, and Africa on the south. On the west the Mediterranean is connected with the North Atlantic Ocean by the narrow Strait of Gibraltar, one of the most important water connections in the world. It not only connects sea and ocean, but also was the doorway through which ancient and medieval civilization passed into the larger world of the North Atlantic. At the east the Mediterranean as a water route is connected with the Black Sea through the Dardanelles, the Sea of Marmara, and the narrow Bosporus. It is separated by the Suez Peninsula from the Red Sea, an arm of the Indian Ocean (*Fig. 7*). In 1869 the 100-mile Suez Canal was completed across the peninsula and thereby opened a sea route from the Atlantic to the Indian Ocean. This route had a great effect on world commerce as it created a navigable waterway for ocean-going vessels between the Occident and the Orient.

In its physical geography the Black Sea almost is a unit by itself. For instance, the *Standard Encyclopedia of the World's Oceans and Islands*, edited by Anthony Huxley, describes it as one of the most unusable bodies of water in the world. Its winter climate with cold and windy "Northers" does not belong in the Mediterranean category. Furthermore, a cross section of its water body shows almost fresh water at the surface because water flowing into the sea from its many tributaries is greater than the loss by evaporation. Under this layer of fresh water is a body of salt water sustained by an inflow from the Mediterranean via the Bosporus. This salt water has no organic life as it has no contact with air that would provide oxygen to support life. It's as dead as the Dead Sea but for a different reason.[3]

In its economic geography, as expressed in shipping and trade, the Black Sea has been associated with the Eastern Mediterranean since the Phoenician and Grecian vessels came in search of cargoes of grain. Furthermore, before World War I British tramps brought coal and took away grain and other farm products. After the war, however, both the imports of coal and exports of grain have given way to the dictates of the post-revolutionary regime in the U.S.S.R.

Taking the Mediterranean as a whole, with its vast size, its position between the Atlantic and Indian oceans, and its numerous extensions into

Europe, there is hardly room for question that it was the best natural setting which the world offered for the early development of commercial shipping. In any case, throughout ancient and medieval times the progress of shipping and trade in large measure was confined to the Mediterranean area and to the Mediterranean peoples.

## II    Civilization in the Border Lands of Eurasia

The early development of water transportation in the Western world rests on the efforts of the people of antiquity who lived and worked before written records. Early civilization largely was confined to the southern and eastern periphery of Eurasia. In broad outline it extended in widely spaced areas from China and India at the east to the Levant at the west. More specifically, it included the four realms of ancient civilization; that is, the Chinese, Indian, and Persian regions in the east to the Egyptians in the west. For the most part, the life of these areas of ancient civilization centered in alluvial plains: the Hwang Ho and Yangtze plains of China, the Ganges and Indus plains of India, the Tigris-Euphrates valleys of the Persian Gulf region, and the Nile valley in Egypt. Outside these alluvial plains much of the land was of poor to medium quality.

The periphery of Eurasia, where the ancient civilizations originated, is characterized by a well-marked series of great peninsulas and archipelagos interrupted by an equally well-defined chain of seas of vast extent and other coastal waters. To the ancient civilizations these water bodies were zones of separation, but they also were lines of primitive trade, as, for example, the spice trade from the Spice Islands to India and Persia. In ancient China, the Chinese junk sailed the East China and the South China seas to carry trade from point to point on the mainland and to reach the long chain of offshore islands. In later times, moreover, they ventured to India and the Persian Gulf. These activities came after, rather than before, those of the Phoenicians and Greeks in the Mediterranean; at least, according to the article on the compass in Encyclopaedia Britannica, no seagoing ships were built in China before 139 B.C.[4] Moreover, from Baghdad and Basra, up river from the head of the Persian Gulf, the Arab dhows sailed to the Malabar Coast, Ceylon, Malaya, and Canton near the north end of the South China Sea.

From the time of antiquity to that of Columbus, the Mediterranean with its associated river routes and land portages served as the means of communication with the Asiatic, African, and European civilizations. The

Mediterranean lanes became the world's major routes, and Mediterranean peoples, one after another, played leading roles in the advance of civilization on this great stage. The cities which became the centers of activity in the trade of the Mediterranean also became the seats of civilization where ideas of liberty were planted in early times and, though constantly plagued by bigotry, ignorance, and other pests of mankind, flowered again as the centuries took their troubled courses. In this slow progress shipping and sea trade were vital instruments (*Fig.* 7).

III     *Commercial Navigation in Phoenician Ships*

The early commercial development of sea trade was in the courageous hands of the Phoenicians who inhabited a narrow coastal strip between the Lebanon Mountains and the eastern margin of the Mediterranean Sea (*Fig.* 7). Their sea trade flourished at least 1500 years before the time of Christ and became a feature of trade of the "fertile crescent" between the Tigris-Euphrates valleys and the Nile.[5]

The Persian Gulf and the plains drained by the Tigris and Euphrates rivers are separated from the Eastern Mediterranean and the Nile Valley by a relatively narrow body of desert and mountainous land that is the lowest and narrowest section of the wide and rugged highland extending from northeast Asia to sourthern Africa, thus separating the Pacific and Indian oceans from the Mediterranean and the Atlantic (*Fig.* 8). Early trade across or around this narrow barrier of difficult terrain commonly followed either an overland route from Nineveh on the Tigris River via Syria and Palestine to Egypt, or via the Persian Gulf and the Gulf of Aden to the Gulf of Suez, the narrow western head of the Red Sea, thence overland to the Nile Valley.

In time the Phoenicians, schooled by their fisheries in navigating the coastal waters, succeeded in diverting some of the caravan trade to their vessels and thereby eliminating the long haul over the land routes which paralleled the eastern coast of the Mediterranean. Sidon and Tyre, Phoenician ports, became the commercial centers not only of this coastal trade but of all the Phoenician enterprises. The Phoenicians first dominated and then controlled the trade between the Nile and the Tigris-Euphrates valleys and also that of the Mediterranean and Black seas.[6]

Early in their adventures the Phoenicians learned to sail westward to Cyprus and along the coast of Asia Minor to Rhodes and the island-studded waters of the Aegean. Subsequently, they expanded their sea trade into the Black Sea to tap the fertile lands about its shores and also to the far reaches of the western Mediterranean. At the time of their greatest power they made the Mediterranean a Phoenician sea. They discovered the Atlantic, sailed up the coast of Europe to Britain, and explored the coast of northwest Africa.[7]

In carrying on trade between southwestern Asia and the Mediterranean lands, the Phoenicians facilitated the exchange of the products of more advanced eastern civilizations for the raw materials of the West. Thus from the East the Arabian merchants brought metal work, fine linen and other fabrics, dyes, drugs, oils, ivory, gold dust and spices, as well as domesticated animals and plants, while the West supplied grains, metals, and other raw materials. The Phoenicians furnished forest products from Lebanon and copper and iron from which the Egyptians made weapons. In time the Phoenicians developed the industrial arts in their own country and thus, even in ancient times, demonstrated the close relation of manufacturing and commerce which prevails today.

Where it became necessary to command strategic points along their sailing routes and to promote local trade, the Phoenicians established a chain of trading posts and colonies along the shores of the Black Sea and especially along the south shore of the western Mediterranean.[8] In this humble commercial fashion, Carthago (later Carthage), Ityke (later Utica), Gades (later Cadiz), and other centers of later civilization had their beginnings. In some places, apparently, these ancient ship operators, as did their modern British and American prototypes, opened mines or encouraged others to do so and took measures to develop trade with agricultural and grazing areas. In these and other ways the Phoenicians demonstrated the character and extent of their leadership.

In order to trade in the Black Sea and the western Mediterranean the Phoenicians built larger and sturdier vessels, learned to direct night sailings by the North Star, and, as has been said, commonly restricted their sailings to the less stormy summer months. Their larger "embarkations" were of two types: round ships, or gauli, and long ships called gallies or triremes. The former were useful in approaching coasts where no harbor existed, whereas the latter were fast ships, highly useful in attacking vessels of their competitors. The Phoenicians were jealous of foreigners and employed every known means to keep the entire trade to themselves.[9]

In all their far-flung enterprises the Phoenicians had just one motive, that of material gain. They were a commercial people and had little or no interest in spreading culture. They were sharp dealers, often

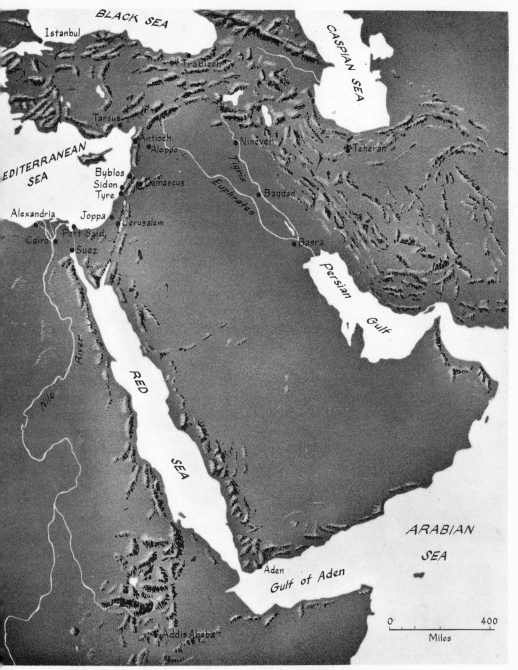

8. The Near East as designated by the Department of State. This small, arid land mass separates the Orient from the Occident.

cruel in their methods, and feared and hated by other people. Their whole effort was to advance their commerce and they affected no empire but the sea. Nevertheless, their trading posts, colonies, and sailing routes became the paths of civilization.[10]

Although the Phoenicians were the earliest people to instigate commercial voyages, they attained their greatest prosperity and became the outstanding traders and colonizers in a period of peace from the twelfth to the ninth centuries B.C. The harbor-ports of Byblos, Arvad, Simyra, and especially Sidon and Tyre grew in wealth and power.[11] The Phoenician influence reached almost every port accessible from the Mediterranean Sea. In all these ports they made settlements and in many established colonies. Information was obtained from correspondents, "from which they drew what was useful to themselves, or might be to others." Thus they demonstrated the three divisions of trade—importation, exportation, and transportation. They also had trade by land or by land and sea with Syria, Mesopotamia, Africa, Babylonia, Persia, and Arabia, and even with India. Phoenice, or Canaan as it was known then, became the "great warehouse of the civilized world where everything that might administer to the necessities or luxuries of mankind was to be found."[12]

In addition to forest products and some minerals, the Phoenicians excelled in the production of dyes and glass. The murex, which yielded the purple and crimson dyes, was a sea product found nowhere more abundantly than in the vicinity of Sidon and Tyre. The expense of extracting and distilling the dye and of dying the purple cloth was so great that only the royalty, aristocracy, and priests could afford to wear it.[13] The Phoenicians derived their skill in glassmaking from Egypt, where the art of glass manufacture had been known and practiced for many years. This phase of their manufacture, therefore, depended on borrowed technology. At the outset the Phoenician glass was crude and clumsy in appearance. Practice, however, developed both skill and design, for in time the Phoenician product, largely made in Sidon, found ready access into many markets.[14]

According to *An Universal History* published in London in 1779, the area commonly called Phoenicia is more accurately termed Phoenice. The Jews named it Canaan and called the people Canaanites. This historical source stated that "The proper Phoenice, as far as we can gather from the ancient geographers, lay between the 34th and 36th degrees of north latitude, bounded by Syria on the north and the east, by Judea with Palestine on the south, and by the Mediterranean on the west."[15] Near the end of the period of peace from the twelfth to the ninth centuries B.C., the three political units together made up an area that not only participated in land and water transport and trade, but advanced in many aspects of civilization, including the use of an alphabet.

Tyre in Phoenice and Jerusalem in Palestine became centers of interest in the area and the time. The Phoenicians under King Hiram of Tyre were the great traders and commanded the forest resources of the Lebanon Mountains, whereas Solomon, king of the Hebrews, was in possession of the grain and oil production of Palestine. When Solomon ascended to the throne after the death of his father, David, King Hiram sent a congratulatory embassy to Jerusalem.[16] Upon the return of the ambassadors, Solomon sent a letter to Hiram requesting cedarwood and cypress from Mount Lebanus to build a temple to the Lord. Hiram replied that he would furnish the desired forest products and that he would have his men bring them to the seaside from whence they could be shipped to Joppa a port only a short distance west of Jerusalem. From Joppa, Solomon had his men move the cedar and cypress woods to Jerusalem. Hiram not only furnished the cedarwood and the cypress, but also sent able architects and workmen to help build the temple. In addition, King Hiram sent purple dyes, rare fabrics, metals, and one hundred and twenty talents of gold. Accompanying these items, King Hiram loaned the services of a man famous in Tyre for working in gold, silver, and other metals. In return, Solomon ordered Hiram a yearly supply of twenty thousand measures of wheat and as many measures of pure oil, commodities much needed in the coastal cities.[17] The temple, known as the Temple of Jahweh, was built, and Jerusalem was started on its career of world influence for later Jews, Christians, and Mohammedans as the Holy City.

Later, when King Hiram learned that Solomon wished to build a fleet of ships at Elath and Ezion-geber, two seaside points near the head of the Red Sea, in order to carry on trade with Ophir, he sent as many builders and shipwrights as were needed to construct the vessels. Afterward, Hiram furnished expert pilots and skillful mariners to conduct the fleet to Ophir. On their return from Ophir, Hiram's crew brought him gold, almug trees, and precious stones. These and other incidents in kind emphasize the flourishing condition which Tyre attained under its great leader.[18]

IV   *Shipping and Trade Under the Ancient Greeks*

The development of sea trade by the Greeks illustrates many of the conditions which influence the growth of seagoing activities. Greece with its array of closely spaced peninsulas, islands, bays, and seas is a natural maritime area about the size of Scotland. Like Scotland, Greece is mountainous in its terrain. The largest three plains taken together form less than a sixth of the surface.[19] In his account of the Athenians Strabo writes: "they lived in a country both thinsoiled and rugged." All points are near the coast and in the clear air of the Mediterranean; every island and headland is in plain view of other islands and headlands.[20] Through the long rainless summer conditions are highly favorable to navigation. The small plains and neighboring hill slopes of many of the islands were fertile enough to support a considerable population and yield a trading surplus of oil and wine.[21] When once population grew beyond the point of local support, other lands, such as the slopes of Asia Minor and the plains of the Black Sea, were within reach.

Sea trade in the hands of the ancient Greeks developed from small beginnings about 1000 B.C. to great dimensions in the fifth century B.C. Their early trade was carried by the Phoenicians, but by copying Phoenician methods of shipbuilding and ship operation they first successfully challenged and then surpassed the Phoenicians in the carrying trades.[22] The seas which surround the coast of Greece are subject to sudden and violent storms. The Greeks depended upon their oars and seldom hoisted the sails, for where the seas were landlocked the stoutest vessels experienced the greatest danger. Although the sea trade of the ancient Greeks was much like that of the Phoenicians, improvements were made. The Greeks, for example, substituted the use of coined money for the simple barter which characterized the Phoenician trade. Athinai (Athens), using silver from local mines, developed a silver currency which was not allowed to depreciate in value and thus found wide use in this early trade. Furthermore, the system of coinage and the code of maritime law developed by Rodhos (Rhodes) in its time became widely accepted in the Mediterranean.[23]

*REGIONALISM APPEARS IN MEDITERRANEAN TRADE*

Although the character of the shipping trade of the Phoenicians and Greeks was much alike, the areas in routes involved were somewhat different. Even in ancient times, the practice of regional differentiation based on position, war, and other circumstances made its appearance. At the time of active competition in the sixth century B.C. the Phoenicians with their settlements and trade dominated the Levantian Mediterranean, especially its east coast, and the south coast of the western Mediterranean. The Greeks, however, controlled practically the whole of the northern Mediterranean and the Black Sea. Such a distribution was not illogical in view of the position of Phoenicia on the one hand and Greece on the other. In this connection, however, historians emphasize the fact that the Phoenicians and ancient Greeks were trading peoples living by and for themselves rather than strong nations controlling territory and routes with the vigor and determination of later times.

## v  *Importance of Cities in Ancient Trade*

Trade, even in ancient times, emphasized the importance of cities at focal points and of trading posts, oases stations, and island bases along the routes. Initiative and leadership, moreover, came from the larger commercial cities like Nineveh, Sidon, Tyre, Korinthos (Corinth), Athinai (Athens), Rodhos (Rhodes), Carthago (Carthage), Siracusa (Syracuse), Gades (Cadiz), and Alexandria. Sidon, for example, was for many centuries skilled in producing all kinds of manufacturing then in demand and was not only the major city of Phoenicia but the dominant influence in developing shipping and trade in the Eastern Mediterranean. As time went on and the quantity of trade increased, the commercial cities became larger and more numerous. Clive Day points out that after the conquests of Alexander of Macedon opened vast areas east of the Mediterranean to trade, the commercial centers grew rapidly. Before Alexander's time only Siracusa, Athinai, and Carthago had a population of 100,000 or more, whereas scarcely more than a century after Alexander's conquests four cities—Alexandria, Seleucia, Antioch, and Carthago—had more than 200,000, and Siracusa, Korinthos, Roma, Rodhos, Ephesus, and possibly others had 100,000 or more. Thus in early times the intimate relation of trade to the growth of ports and other commercial centers became apparent. In fact, P. Vidal De La Blache in his *Principles of Human Geography* points out that "as a result of commerce, safety on the high seas, and colonization there grew up around the Mediterranean a social order which found its highest expression in the city." He continues with the thought that "the city idea was elaborated and amplified by Rome. It became an element of civilization which could be communicated and adopted by an increasing number of groups. Command of Mediterranean sea lanes and the network of Roman roads were its vehicles."[24]

The great cities of antiquity illustrate still another characteristic of the development of commercial centers, namely the close relationship of trade and manufacturing. As previously stated, Sidon and Tyre, copying the skill of the Assyrians, learned the art of making articles which in their earlier history they imported from the East. With imported raw materials they learned to make cloth of fine quality, to work in metals and glass, and to produce perfumes, dyes, drugs, and the like. All these products were useful in trading with other people and were one reason why the Phoenicians not only were the first people to dominate world shipping and trade but maintained dominance longer than any other people.

The Greeks in their bid for shipping supremacy also developed skill in the crafts of manufacture. Athinai and Korinthos, for example, were famous for pottery, and produced bronze, silver, and textile goods in addition to decorative handicraft. The industries of these ancient cities attracted skilled workmen for many lands, and their output helped in developing trade with many areas.[25] Subsequently, the industrial arts and crafts were important in the commercial activities of Carthago and Siracusa, western representatives respectively of Phoenician and Grecian culture.

## VI    Shipping Policies of Antiquity

The shipping policy of the Phoenicians was highly monopolistic. They wanted no competitors, and in critical areas and on major routes they tolerated none. When trade could not be secured by peaceful means, they resorted to force to obtain it. When once the Greeks matched the Phoenicians' skill and organization, many conflicts resulted, and, as has been stated, some segregation of trading routes and areas resulted. Both of these maritime peoples were motivated by desire of profit, and both prosecuted trade with relentless ardor and ambition.

To the ancient Greeks western civilization owes many values, but in no respect is our debt greater than in the realm of trading policies. To be sure, the general scheme was monopolistic in character but, nevertheless, the germ of tolerance made its appearance during the relatively brief periods when Athinai and Rodhos dominated maritime activities.[26]

Both Athinai and Rodhos followed farsighted commercial policies. In the case of the former, the general policy emphasized the interests of the consumer. To this end, restrictions were placed on the exports of grain and shipbuilding materials, some of which were produced locally but not in quantities to supply the local demand. To this end also, duties on imports were low and were for revenue only. Although manufacturers in the limited scale of the time were fostered, they were not protected by tariffs as they are in many countries today. In dealing with other people, commercial advantages were granted or withheld in terms of what appeared to be wise political procedure.[27]

Rodhos (Rhodes), located at the busiest crossroads of the Eastern Mediterranean, commanded the southern coast of Asia Minor on the one hand and the entrance to the Aegean on the other. It became a prosperous commercial city and exercised a policy aimed at securing widespread freedom of trade. Under its farsighted policy its fleet policed the seas and reduced piracy. The Rhodians became skillful navigators and highly efficient traders. As was stated previously, their monetary system and code of maritime law were widely adopted. Moreover, as their commercial reputation and influence grew, trading vessels in large numbers came to their docks, and men from distant points came to learn their methods. The city enjoyed efficient administration and gained what was tantamount to an international reputation for its action against anything which threatened the security of the seas.[28]

### EGYPT AND THE NILE

The Greek republics fostered transport, manufacture, and commerce; but with the decline of Grecian political strength the Greek manufacturers shifted to the cities of Asia Minor and their sea trade was centered in Alexandria, in Egypt on the western flank of the Nile. In time many Greek merchants migrated to Egypt, and Alexandria became the center of commerce of the Mediterranean world. However, the power of Roma was rising, and the commerce of the Mediterranean gradually took on new directions.

The foreign trade of Egypt was carried on by both the Phoenicians and the Greeks, whereas the Egyptians handled the trade on the numerous canals and channels of the Nile Delta. After 650 B.C. when foreign merchants were admitted, even Egypt's interior trade was taken over by the Greeks. When the Mediterranean world came under Roman rule most of the sea trade to and from Egypt remained in the hands of Greek merchants, for the Roman function was to govern and manage the business of the government. The Romans were renowned as capitalists and bankers and apparently exercised their influence as part of the great organization which distinguished Roman rule, much as the holding companies of today function.[29]

As Herodotus in the fifth century before Christ pointed out, the economy of Egypt, with its desert climate, depends on the management of irrigation from the Nile in the production of crops and the welfare of the country. The country then, as now, produced grain and other crops for export. According to Charlesworth, after Augustus, the first Roman Emperor, conquered Egypt, he "realized to the full the position and importance of the country, its wealth, its volume of trade, its immunity from invasion, its contribution to the corn supply."[30] As in the agriculture, Egypt depended on the Nile as its highway of commerce. Roads were not needed for, as Strabo points out, the usual method of transport was by boat and barge on the river and the numerous channels constructed in the Delta area. Even today irrigation from the Nile is the basic factor in the export of agricultural products from Egypt to industrial markets in Western Europe.

VII  *Transportation and Civilization under Roman Rule*

Under Roman rule transportation and civilization made notable progress. Both water and land transport increased in effectiveness as Roman influence advanced from the original pastoral settlements, through the five centuries of the Republic, and the transition period of the triumvirate, to the establishment of the Empire.[31] These advances in the organization and technology of water and land transport helped to widen the dimensions of the space-area under Roman rule, until in A.D. 117 when it attained its greatest extent, the Empire reached from Britain on the Atlantic front to Arabia beyond the eastern border of the Mediterranean.

In the early centuries of the Empire peace was established; and law, transportation, trade, and Christianity became constructive elements in the world order. At this time the bulk of commerce moved to and from Roma (Rome) on the waterways which extended from the Black Sea to most parts of the Mediterranean and even to the Atlantic. Moreover, most of the leading imperial cities had ports on one of these seas.

The evolution of Roman rule constitutes an epic of history and geography. It calls for a knowledge of Roman law and organization, of the fundamentals of military operation, of the structure of the social order, of the high importance of leadership, of the utilization and protection of merchant fleets, of a growing commerce, of a spread of Christianity into the Roman domain, and of the construction of and management of a network of roads that extended into three continents.[32] Roman civilization in its numerous phases has engaged the attention of scholars from many disciplines. The vast amount of published material begets confusion if an attempt is made to deal with the whole complex. As this study is geographic in emphasis, it faces the difficulty of focusing attention on the progress of water and land transport in the space-area on the surface of the globe commanded by the Romans. As much of the aggrandizement of territory occurred under the leadership of the two Caesars, Julius and Augustus, brief consideration of the regime of these historic leaders is introduced at this point.

*JULIUS CAESAR*

Julius Caesar lived from 100 B.C. to 44 B.C. He came from the aristocratic ruling class that dominated Roman affairs in the centuries before Christ. In 60 B.C. he became a member of the triumvirate that marked the transition from the Republic to the Empire. Fired with ambition, he soon dominated the triumvirate and eventually established himself as a dictator over all of Roma. Between 60 and 44 B.C., with the well-trained Roman Legions, he reached the Danube and Rhine valleys and conquered Gaul, the vast territory west and northwest of the Alps. As the Rhine Valley became a major route followed by the Romans in reaching the North and Baltic seas, it was held as the eastern limit of Roman occupation of Gaul.

After the conquest of Gaul, Caesar and his Roman Legions reached the English Channel and the southern end of the North Sea. He crossed into Great Britain and, with London as a base, conquered England and southern Scotland.

Caesar's operations in Gaul and Britain form the theme of his famous *Commentaries* and possess high geographic and historic qualities. In fact, Anthony Trollope in his volume *The Commentaries of Caesar* states that the commentaries mark the beginning of modern history.[33] In view of Caesar's description of the land and water routes he followed in Gaul, of his conquests of people, and the characteristics of the occupied area, it also might be said that Caesar's writings constitute a major link in the long chain of geographic records.

AUGUSTUS CAESAR AND THE ROMAN EMPIRE

A brief interval after Caesar's death was marked by a struggle for power by the strong men of the time. Leadership was established, however, when in 31 B.C. Augustus Caesar's forces under Agrippa defeated Antony and Cleopatra at Actium on the west coast of Greece. Augustus became the first emperor and is recognized as the founder of the Empire. Before his death in A.D. 14 he established a period of peace that continued for two hundred years (the Pax Romana).

According to M. P. Charlesworth in his study of *Trade Routes and Commerce of the Roman Empire*, Augustus Caesar in his early career was ruthless in establishing power over the Roman domain, but in his later years turned his attention "to secure the right ordering of his vast realm." This change in attitude and purpose reflects the fact that Augustus was the son of middle-class parents from whom he gained an interest in trade, rather than the contempt for trade which was held by the aristocratic class of the time. Augustus came to the realization that peace then, as now, was essential to enterprise and trade, and that transport and financial stability were other essentials.

Fired with his new ambition, Augustus visited most of the provinces under Roman rule and endeavored to organize information and intelligence services. He directed Agrippa to draw a great map of the Empire and encouraged the geographer Strabo and other writers to produce information in regard to areas and trade routes. At his death Augustus left the *Breviarium totius Imperii* which contains an exact account of the state of the Empire. In studying this great period of Roman development, it should be remembered that statistical evidence such as is available now was conspicuous by its absence. Hence, as Charlesworth points out, the "authorities fall into main classes: literary and what we may term archaeological." He also writes, "It has been said that the Republic conquered the world without maps; it is certain that the Empire governed the world by using them."[34]

The geography of ancient commerce as developed by the Romans in the Mediterranean Arena portrays adventurous and, in many cases, profitable enterprise on both sea and land. Sailing routes led to strategic points that eventually became ports where contact with land routes was maintained. Vessels, small in size, clumsy in design, and powered with sails and/or oars carried the sea trade. To protect merchant vessels from pirates Roma (Rome) built a navy in which oars manned by slaves enabled quick attack and retreat. Roman roads created a system of land routes over which men on foot, pack animals, and horse-drawn, wheeled vehicles were the land instruments. Protection along these routes was afforded by chains of forts and fast moving cavalry.

## TRANSPORTATION AND TRADE UNDER ROMAN RULE

Under Roman rule many elements of civilization originated or grew to effective stature. None was more fundamental, however, than the advances in the technology and organization of both sea and land transportation. By the skillful utilization of both types of transport, the Roman Empire extended over the known world, thereby creating a pattern of world dominion.

## SEA TRADE UNDER ROMAN RULE

Although shipping and trade connected Phoenicia and Greece with their far-flung trading post and colonies, each part of the ancient world constituted more or less a separate entity. Commerce rather than government was widely spread. Beginning in the fourth century before Christ a great change occurred, for military and political rule was extended over vast domains, first by the Macedonians and later by the Romans. The conquests of Alexander the Great from 336 to 323 B.C. created an empire from Macedonia to India, and the growth of Roman rule after 200 B.C. finally brought the entire Mediterranean and the Black Sea under one government.

When Roma (Rome) came to be the dominant power in the Mediterranean world, political rule maintained by force, rather than commercial enterprise, gained the ascendency. Although sea trade continued and developed rapidly under the Empire, the Romans never became a seafaring people. They conquered the Greeks and the Carthaginians, but trade continued to move on the old routes and to a surprising extent was left in experienced hands. In the Punic wars, however, Roma (Rome) learned the need of a navy, and Roman fleets figured in the conquest of oversea areas and in the maintenance of Roman rule in such areas.

The influence of government on commerce is illustrated by the contrast of conditions at the close of the Roman Republic and with those at the height of the Empire. In early times the landed aristocracy were in control of the government and, content with the income from their estates, had little or no interest in trade. Speculation was rampant, money was loaned at exorbitant rates, and contractors exploited the government in the construction of public works. Taxes were high, especially in the provinces, and the sea was infested with pirates. Conditions went from bad to worse; but, under Augustus, peace was established throughout the Empire. Speculation was curbed and piracy practically eliminated. The sea lanes became safe, lighthouses were erected, and harbors improved. Great systems of roads gave contact with distant land areas, and, according to Hutton Webster, the two centuries following the triumph at Actium—where Roman forces defeated forces of Cleopatra and Marc Antony—became the golden age of Roman industry and commerce.[35]

In the progress of sea trade and shipping in the Mediterranean four geographic areas during four historic periods stand out:   1] the Eastern Mediterranean, or Levant, in which in early antiquity the Egyptians, Phoenicians, and ancient Greeks constituted the prime movers;   2] the central Mediterranean, in which at the time of the Roman Empire the city of Roma (Rome), in the Italian Peninsula, became the center of the Western world;   3] the Byzantium Empire, with its center at Constantinople on the narrow water route between the Aegean and Black seas, which in the early Middle Ages kept commerce alive;   4] the latter centuries of the Middle Ages in which Venezia (Venice), Genova (Genoa), and other city-states dominated the trade of the Mediterranean and much of Europe. In the century between the decline of Greece and the rise of Roma (Rome), Carthago was an important factor; however, it was founded by the Phoenicians and represented a Western and later expression of their efforts. Moreover, the Carthaginians were the first to explore the coast of Europe beyond the Strait of Gibraltar.[36]

## LAND TRANSPORT UNDER ROMAN RULE

Although transportation and trade over land routes featured the economy during the long period in which the Roman Republic held jurisdiction over the lands and seas under Roman rule, Webster contends that the two centuries of peace following the triumph at Actium became the golden age of Roman life.[37] Certainly transportation, industry, and commerce prospered during these centuries of peace.

## ROMAN ROADS AND ROUTES

The invention of the wheel presaged the long series of technological discoveries associated with the development of land transportation. As in many other aspects of civilization, the ancient Mediterranean was the arena or earth space where the principle of rolling rather than walking over the land surface found early expression. In Egypt, for example, there were Egyptian-made chariots in the period of 2000 to 1500 B.C.; the chariot was in use as early as 1360 B.C. The great advance in wheeled vehicles, however, came under Roman rule, especially under the Empire when command of the great system of roads not only gave stability to the Italian Peninsula, the center of the Roman area, but also under Pax Romana brought relative peace to primitive tribes in the Danube and Rhine valleys, and brought a modicum of law and order into Gaul and Britain. In the latter, and probably elsewhere, the Roman roads were preceeded by the trackways developed in the Stone Age.[38]

In the developments of transport technology in Roman times the public roads were outstanding. They were visable and mapable parts of the system organized and maintained by the Roman people. The construction of the roads was delegated to highest rank officials, and the cost of construction as well as the amount of labor and materials needed were immense. Bridges and other special features called for skill in design and in execution. In fact, the ingenuity and audacity of the builders has amazed people in every succeeding period. During the Republic from 509 to 28 B.C., roads were built to consolidate Roman victories over Italy, Carthago in northern Africa, and Asia. These roads were used by powerful legions and messengers of the Roman government. It should be recognized that under the Empire the world enjoyed peace, during which time there was freedom to discover and develop resources. During the crest of the Empire, the road system was composed of main roads or public ways connecting Rome with the larger cities and the provinces. Hence, according to P. Vidal De La Blache, "to the Romans goes the credit of organizing the roads into a system—a network—whose various parts feed into one another."[39] Subsidiary to these main roads were parish roads that led to towns and boroughs off the principal routes. Farm roads reached the farms and hamlets, and many mule paths led to otherwise inaccessible areas.

According to the Itinerary of Antoine there were, during the Empire from 28 B.C. to 476 A.D., 372 main roads with a total length of 53,658 Roman miles. The Roman unit equalled 4,859 English feet or slightly less than a mile. The pattern of main roads as stated by Rose is shown in Table 2. Roman roads were so built as to carry freight and passengers and to provide convenient and durable routes over which Roman troops could move safely in all kinds of weather. Their construction consisted of five distinct layers. At the bottom was a foundation of earth, worked into a compact mass and given a convex surface to aid drainage. On top of this foundation was placed a bed of large stones held together with mortar. The next, or third layer, consisted of small stones or gravel and mortar. Then came a stratum consisting of powdered chalk, brick, or other materials locally available. On top came a paved surface called the dorsam.[40]

The terrain over which the roads were built displayed mountains, hill country, and plains, and such drainage features as rivers, lakes, and marshes. Under the general plan the roads were laid out in straight lines.

2. MILEAGE OF RO-MAN ROADS BY COUNTRIES.

Source: *Annual Report of the Board of Regents of the Smithsonian Institution, 1934* (Washington, D.C.: Government Printing Office, 1935), p. 349.

| Country | Roman Miles |
| --- | --- |
| Italy | 13,024 |
| Gaul | 9,320 |
| Spain | 7,700 |
| Great Britain | 2,579 |
| Sicily | 1,362 |
| Sardinia | 200 |
| Corsica | 125 |
| Africa (less Egypt) | 9,348 |
| Egypt | 1,500 |
| Asia | 8,500 |
| Total | 53,658 |

To accomplish this, mountains were cut through, valleys filled, and water bodies bridged. When the English Channel or the Strait of Dover was reached, for example, roads led to the waterfront in Gaul, the channel was crossed in boats, and from the English coast the road was continued to London—then, as now, the major center of tranport in Britain.[41]

The Roman military roads were constructed by the State and maintained by a tax assessed upon real property. Various means such as donations, statute labor, and requisitions were used to obtain road funds. Parish and secondary roads were built at the expense of the towns and boroughs, with the aid of special donations, and were maintained by statute labor provided by owners of adjoining property. The taxes were based upon the area of land affected or upon the number of interested inhabitants. The statute labor of the Romans established the precedent for the system of road upkeep which is found incorporated in English laws from the time of the Middle Ages.[42]

Among the vehicles in use on the roads in Italy, and probably in Gaul and the Rhine Valley, was the vehicle commonly used by the ancient Romans. The chariot, called the *biga* or *currus*, was employed in war, in hunting, and in racing. For passenger travel a two-wheeled covered carriage known as the *carpentum* was in use by the Romans for upwards of a thousand years. For transporting freight and passengers there was in wide use a heavy four-wheeled wagon called the *clabulare* as well as a large four-wheeled coach called a *rheda* for long journeys. Other types of vehicles were in use in local areas, as might be expected in a region as large as the

Roman Empire and in which the system of roads was essential to Roman rule and to the trade and economies of their domain.[43]

The routes selected for Roman roads emphasized the valleys and passes of the numerous sections. They are described, but not mapped, in M. P. Charlesworth's *Trade Routes and Commerce of the Roman Empire*. As interest in this study largely centers in the relation of the Mediterranean to the Rhine in Roman times, attention is focused on the major routes followed during the expansion of the Romans into the Rhine.[44] In general, communication from the Mediterranean to the Rhine and the northern seas depended on a combination of land and water transport; however, most Romans preferred the roads. Roman engineers not only built roads over which horse-drawn vehicles were essential and which represented notable advances in highway technology, they also built and utilized river craft in which goods, passengers, and soldiers could be transported. Of no less importance was the organization under which routes were selected and the construction of roads so planned as to divide the units into convenient lengths. Along the routes, in fact, the advances both in physical and social technology bore the earmark of progressive civilization.

The Roman roads were so useful that in many areas commerce was carried on chiefly by land. Distances carefully marked out along the major roads made it possible to prepare time tables that proved to be useful to travelers as well as to the military forces. Villas or other resting houses maintained at regular intervals increased the usefulness of the roads. At the larger centers fresh horses were available in time of need.[45] In some cases the *carpentum* was made into a covered wagon for transporting distinguished citizens. One cannot insist too forcibly upon the immense influence these roads exerted, not only upon commerce but upon civilization in general. They were part of the great system of transportation which distinguished Roman times.

*THE MEDITERRANEAN WORLD AND THE RHINE*

From the ancient Mediterranean world, civilization, as developed under Roman rule, expanded into many areas including Gaul and the Danube and Rhine valleys (*Fig. 2*). Under the Roman Empire this expansion took the form of conquest followed by the construction of military roads and Roman rule. Settlement and trade followed, and Roman law and organization were transplanted.

In Roman times the Rhine Valley was a major link in an overland route connecting the Mediterranean Sea with the North and Baltic seas.

Access to the Rhine was possible from the head of the Aegean Sea via a pass leading to the Middle Danube, and from the head of the Adriatic Sea over the Brenner Pass to the Inn Valley, a tributary of the Danube. When once the Danube was reached, travel up valley led to points from which passage over relatively low divides led to the upper reaches of the Main, a major tributary of the Rhine.[46]

The western route by which the Romans reached Gaul and the Rhine began at the ancient seacoast port of Massilia (Marseilles) on the eastern flank of the Rhone Delta. From Roma (Rome), Massilia was reached by sea or by the Via Domitia along the narrow foreshore between the Maritime Alps and the sea. As the sea voyage along the coast was considered dangerous, especially in the Gulf of Lyons, the preferred route was by the coast road through Liguria and along the Riviera, the main road to Narbonensis (Narbonne), the well-settled southern province of Gaul, and to Spain.[47]

Because the Lower Rhone presented conditions that made navigation difficult from Massilia, a much traveled Roman road followed the left or east bank of the Rhone to Lugdunum (Lyons) at the junction of the Saône and the Rhone. Lugdunum, according to Charlesworth, became the center of the five roads as planned by Agrippa, the map maker under Augustus Caesar.[48] The road south to Massilia and the Via Domitia was the first of the five. The second ran almost due west to the port of Burdigala (Bordeaux). The third led northwest to the coast from which a passage was maintained to Britain. The fourth, and the one of special interest in this study, extended in a northeasterly direction to reach the Rhine and the Roman camps along it. The fifth branched from the fourth, then climbed the Jura and the Alps to reach northern Italy and eventually Roma. These major roads formed the beginning of the road system of Gaul. Later additions were developed upon lines devised by Agrippa.

From Lugdunum north, the Saône, a Rhone tributary, furnished a navigable waterway that led to a broad divide from which the Loire River could be reached to serve as a route westward to the Atlantic. Similarly, an open passage to the Seine furnished a northwesterly route to the English Channel. To the northeast the Doubs Valley, a tributary of the Saône, was followed in later decades to the Gate of Burgundy between the Vosges and Jura mountains and thence to the Upper Rhine Valley at Basel and Strasbourg. From Basel roads led down valley on each side of the Rhine to Strasbourg from whence the Rhine was navigable.[49]

At Köln the Rhine traffic of the Roman Empire divided into three units, each with a different destination. Traffic for Britain left the river at Köln and followed trails or roads along the edge of the upland to the Strait of Dover or the southern coast of the North Sea. Traffic for the Baltic Sea also left the river at Köln and followed the irregular edge of the upland east of the river to Hannover and thence overland to Lübeck. Some traffic continued down the Rhine to its mouth and then continued down the coast of Gaul to Itius before crossing to Britain. Moreover, the map on page 38 in Shepherd's *Historical Atlas* shows a road leading down the left bank of the Rhine to a point just south of the mouth. No mention of this road or its use was found in the literature consulted during this study. Since the time of Caesar, the mouth of the Rhine has shifted southward in harmony with the outlet or outlets of a river on its delta.

According to Charlesworth, some merchants from the Rhone had reached the Rhine Valley before Caesar. They found that the Menapii, a local tribe, had trade connections in the valley and that small craft were much used to navigate the river. By Caesar's time vessels reached the mouth of the Rhine and then worked southward along the Gallic coast to Itius, from which point they crossed the water to reach Britain. In fact, Caesar followed this route to reach England. Moreover, Drusus, stepson of Augustus, as a Roman general constructed dikes along the Rhine at the head of the delta and also, by using the legions under his command, dug a canal from the Rhine to the Zuider Zee. From the latter, vessels could reach the North Sea.

# 4

# Penetration

AMONG THE MEANINGS of the verb "penetrate," two epitomize the scope and purpose of this study. Geographically, "penetrate" means to reach the interior of a space-area, whether land or water, on the surface of the earth; but philosophically it means to reach the mind or to affect deeply the progress of the intellectual process. When and if the two meanings are contemporary, that is, if they occur at the same time in the same space-area, the result is an advance in culture or civilization. In the long story of water transportation their coexistence has appeared in six periods of time and by six peoples in five space-areas.

When the Phoenicians took to the sea from their narrow coastal plain fronting the Eastern Mediterranean some 1500 years before Christ, they set in motion both types of penetration. Their resources were few, but did include the forest-clad Lebanon mountains—the source of the timber of which boats were built—an abundant curiosity, and an ambitious urge that led them successfully through the necessary stages of technology in boat construction and operation. Bit by bit they advanced from fishing grounds to offshore islands that acted as stepping stones to the future. They discovered, bartered, settled, and colonized the vast Mediterranean, and thereby mastered the techniques of shipping and trade and learned the arts of contact with more primitive people. Their enterprise also looked eastward to tap the caravan trade from the older civilizations of southern Asia. In their centers such as Sidon and Tyre they established and developed the warehouse function and the beginnings of the manufacture of dyes, cloth, and metal products. Their rewards were great, as their private enterprises yielded amazing profits. They introduced not only water transport and trade into the Mediterranean world but also the benefits of colonization, the values of information, the importance of profits, and the use of the alphabet which had been discovered in Egypt. Along with Egypt, ancient Greece, and the lands watered by the Jordan River, they advanced civilization in the ancient Mediterranean.

In the fourth and fifth centuries the Roman Empire lost its command of the Mediterranean world. The decline of Roman power led to strikingly different results in the two major divisions of the Empire. In the west there came a period of depression and chaos caused by a deterioration of governmental authority, accompanied by a marked decline in tranport, trade, and the productive pursuits. This period witnessed the infiltration and conquest of Roma (Rome) by the Teutonic tribes. The Germans, in their turn, were harassed by the Huns and other hordes from the grasslands of eastern Europe and northern Asia. Invasions and counter movements resulted in such a decline of commerce and the associated decay of civilization that this period in the west has been called the Dark Ages.[1]

In the Eastern Mediterranean commerce flourished with its center at Constantinople, the splendid capital of the Byzantine Empire (395–1453 A.D.). In fact, from the decline of Roma (Rome) in the fifth century to the Crusades, Constantinople commanded the long-distance trade between Europe and Asia.[2] In true commercial style the city became famous for its manufacture of textiles, metal work, leather goods, and porcelains. Its money was widely used in trading operations, its principles of banking and credit became the standards of the day, and loans were made at reasonable rates of interest. The practice of insuring vessels was inaugurated.[3] All these and other developments kept Mediterranean commerce alive through the difficult early centuries of the Middle Ages.

During the Dark Ages some of the most productive sections of Western Europe so declined as to become unfruitful. Conditions went from bad to worse, but under Charlemagne in the eighth century civilization and trade again came to life. His empire covered much of Europe, and education, agriculture, and industry were encouraged. Gibbins, writing about this period, notes that the great works included the construction of roads, bridges, and canals.[4] However, Charlemagne was followed by weak administrations, and much of the progress was lost.

For a thousand years after the Fall of the Roman Empire most of Europe knew little or nothing of long distance commerce. Instead, each local area lived within itself, producing for local needs. If craftsmen made products for local use, the products were marketed by the same craftsmen. Such exchange as occurred was for short distances, and they represented trade rather than commerce. Centuries went by with little or no penetration. However, both in the Mediterranean city-states of southern Europe and in the merchant leagues of the North Sea and Baltic Sea in northern Europe notable contributions to long-distance commerce were made.

I    *Mediterranean City-states Attain Commercial Leadership*

Venezia (Venice), on the islands at the head of the Adriatic Sea, together with Genova (Genoa), and Firenze (Florence), facing the Ligurian Sea, were the major centers that contributed to Mediterranean commerce, especially from the eleventh to the fifteenth centuries. These Italian city-states occupied a middle position between the eastern and western divisions of the Roman Empire; hence, between the eastern and western Mediterranean.

Long before Constantinople lost its leadership, Venezia and the other city-states began their progress towards commercial importance. Venezia, on the islands at the head of the Adriatic, had both the best site and situation for commercial success. The islands gave the Venetians a high degree of security, whereas their situation furnished an opportunity to evolve a commercial domain over the sea routes of the Eastern Mediterranean and Black seas. Opportunity was their greatest asset, and they capitalized it to the full, thereby escaping the bondage of inherited restrictions and unsound commercial ideas of the past.

The case of Venezia illustrates the commercial leadership of the greatest of the city-states in the Middle Ages. The city, founded in the fifth century, had tangible assets of fish and salt, and commanded the trade of the rich Po Valley and the Adriatic Sea. In time the Venetians developed trade in the eastern Mediterranean Sea, with Alexandria as the major center. They also established chains of trading stations along the coasts of the Euxine, the ancient name of the Black Sea, and up the Danube River to Augusta Vindelicorum (Augsburg) and other cities. Other entrances to the Danube country were via the land route over the Brenner Pass or the sea route via Gibraltar. In addition, the Venetians sent fleets of vessels through Gibraltar to trade in London, Brugge, and other North Sea outposts. From the Danube, country commodities were hauled overland to tributaries of the Rhine.

Both Venezia and Genova prospered in transporting Crusaders and their supplies to the Holy Land. The Genoese were friendly to the Pope, and in 1097 at the suggestion of Pope Urban II dispatched a fleet to Syria and thereby initiated trade with the Eastern Mediterranean—trade that brought them into competition with the Venetians. Genoese merchants became a leading factor in the western Mediterranean and rivaled Venezia in the sea commerce with the Low Countries and England. This double effort in penetration in new areas demonstrated that transport by sea was cheaper and more profitable than that via the difficult land routes. In time the rivalry between the two merchant fleets generated such severe competition that war between Venezia and Genova resulted. When the merchants of Venezia and Genova became wealthy they created a merchant aristocracy, thereby demonstrating that successful merchants could penetrate upper social circles.

In his notable book *Merchants Make History*, Samhaber points out that the major profits in the industrial and financial efforts that are ancillary to commerce in this period were realized by Firenze (Florence). This city-state was situated away from the sea at the point where the Arno River escapes from its mountain valley. The local monks learned the art of weaving from their contacts with Orientals. They evolved a method of dying wool and learned a method of finishing cloth by giving it a sheen-like finish. As no other merchants could match this process, a steady demand resulted. In transporting these and other products they obtained a low rate of maritime insurance. Moreover, they increased their capital from their highly profitable financial transactions. The success of Firenze is said to have been due to the shrewdness of the merchants, supported by the skillful work of the artisans. The city also emphasized the quality of its merchandise and the value of its coinage.[5]

The Italian city-states contributed much to the technology of shipping and even more to merchandising methods. They promoted the commercial business of south and north Europe, of the Mediterranean lands, of the Middle East, of parts of the Far East and Africa, and the connecting land and sea routes. Banking was made a respectable business. Most of all, their profits enabled them to grant credit and take great risks. They demonstrated that commerce brought both profits and power.[6]

II    *Merchant Leagues of the North and Baltic Seas*

The merchant leagues that developed in northern Europe in the closing centuries of the Middle Ages represented substantial efforts in the association of merchants and the development of trade, in the welfare of cities engaged in trade, and in penetrating into new areas with new methods. The operative idea was that peace might be established and trade encouraged by a united effort of some or all the cities along a trade route. An early example was the Rhenish League which was established under the leadership of the merchant traders in the city of Mainz at the junction of the Rhine and Main rivers. At its peak, this league had ninety cities along the Rhine as members.

A somewhat similar effort, called the Swabian League, was organized a century later and included the cities along and near the Danube River. This was the era of the Fuggers, a family of merchants with headquarters at Augsburg on a tributary of the Danube River. They brought goods in covered wagons over the Alps, across the Black Sea, and up the Danube or Rhone valleys to Alsace. Prosperous cities furnished markets along these routes. This civilization, although continental in position, nevertheless depended largely on water transport.[7] Both the Rhine and Danube rivers were routes of transport and trade in Roman times. In the devastating period of the Dark Ages their trade had sunk to low proportions, and the Swabian League represented a first step in recovery and demonstrated the power of organized effort.

During the early Middle Ages when shipping, trade, and other instruments and arts of civilization withered in Western Europe, the Norsemen of Scandinavia became a truly seafaring people. They fished in the teeming waters of the Baltic and North seas and on the fishing grounds off the coast of Norway. They raided and, in some places, settled the coasts of England and Germany. They ventured out on the open sea to discover Iceland, Greenland, and the northeast coast of America. The Scandinavians also followed river routes and portages from the Baltic to the Black Sea and brought back Oriental goods. They were not, however, a truly commercial people and contributed to navigation, exploration, and settlement rather than to the growth of trade and to the establishment of commercial centers.

The latter centuries of the Middle Ages witnessed a great development of trade in the Baltic countries, both on land and sea. The trading activities were under the competent direction and protection of the Hansa, a medieval guild of merchants that managed and protected the trade of the Hanseatic League. This league was an association of merchants of a great group of towns and cities, including Lübeck and Riga on the Baltic, Hamburg, Bremen, and London on the North Sea; Köln and Düsseldorf on the Rhine. At the time of its greatest influence, it had seventy-two members, and it almost monopolized the trade of northern and Western Europe. Unity on a common front, according to Samhaber, was the whole meaning and purpose of the Hanseatic League.[8]

In the twelfth century an alliance existed between Hamburg on the Elbe River and Lübeck on the Baltic Sea. The objective was to maintain safe and regular exchange of goods between the towns by land and to protect navigation by sea. This involved the organization of Hansa towns into a league. Bremen was another coast town in the league, as were the inland centers: Dortmund, Münster, Brunswick, and the ancient city of Köln. The union of Köln with the northern cities had important results as it connected the seaboard areas with the waterways of the Rhine and the Alpine routes to the Mediterranean. In the twelfth century, also, German rule was obtained over the tribes of the forests and marshes south of the Baltic. This gave the Germans control of most of the southern frontage of the sea. The Germans multiplied rapidly, and in the thirteenth century, under the direction of the German Hanseatic League, colonized in Slavonia territory. In many cases, according to Partsch, they turned nearly worthless areas into productive lands, thereby gaining favor with their Slavonic rulers. This did much to remove the sharp divide which previously had separated the German race from their neighbors on the east.[9]

The Hanseatic League demonstrated the necessity of peace and order, if commerce was to be a positive factor in civilization. The League survived for upwards of four centuries, but at the end western Europeans looked to the Atlantic and America; gradually they lost interest in their eastern outlook. The work of the Hansa merchants showed the benefits of skillful organization and leadership in the realm of transport and commerce. They did not gain fabulous wealth as their commerce was based on small, sound, and secure gains.[10]

The foreign commerce of England in the Middle Ages largely depended on the initiative of foreign merchants who came to find supplies of wool and hides. The efforts of Venetians and other Italian traders have been mentioned previously. Moreover, near the close of the thirteenth century, merchants from the Hanseatic League gained special privileges in London, then a crude frontier town. They were allowed to build and maintain headquarters and warehouses known as the Steelyard, and at one time the Hansa were hired to operate a police force for London. Hence, German merchants had a foothold in London until 1598 when Queen Elizabeth withdrew their charter. During the period of the Steelyard, the commerce of England largely consisted of exports of wool and imports of "artificiality," as manufactures were called. Duties on the exports represented a considerable part of the king's income. For convenience in collecting the duties, the export movement was restricted to certain designated ports where the duties were collected. Later, the entire export of wool, hides, leather, tin, lead, and such foods as cheese and butter were consigned to Calais, which the English held until 1558.

As trade developed, an organized company of English merchants, known as the Merchant Adventurers, endeavored to participate in the business. Henry IV granted this company a charter in 1404, after which headquarters were first established in Antwerpen and later in Hamburg. The special point here is that this company served as an example for the great trading companies to be constituted in later times.[11] This illustrates the slow evolution of English participation in overseas trade and in penetrating the mysteries of distant lands and seas.

Many of the business, financial, and legal practices of today are founded on methods developed by the Hanseatic League. Thus, the League in northern Europe laid the basis for modern commerce in much the same way that the shipping and trade of the Italian cities prepared southern Europe for the great exploits of the Discoveries Period.

# 5

# Beyond Gibraltar – the Atlantic

SHIPPING TOOK to the high seas beyond Gibraltar, and civilization escaped from its time-honored bounds in the Mediterranean in a single momentus decade at the close of the fifteenth century. In that decade Columbus crossed the Atlantic to discover the New World, and Vasco da Gama reached India by the long sea route around Africa. These great mariners, braving the unknown, demonstrated that overseas voyages were practical and added two vast and highly productive realms to world trade and geography.

The explorations and trade which followed the original discoveries enlarged enormously the dimensions of the Commercial World and moved its center to the Iberian Peninsula. There it divided into two spheres of political operations, one dominated by the Portuguese and the other by the Spaniards. The Peninsula also demonstrated that it is both intercontinental, as it links Europe and Africa, and interoceanic, as it connects the Mediterranean and the Atlantic (*Fig.* 2).[1] Hence, in the span of a few decades the ports of Portugal and Spain changed from frontier ports on the peripheral sea routes of Europe to become the most active ports on the Continent. The scene of activity in the world's shipping and trade had moved to the Atlantic.

The discoveries of the Spanish and Portuguese not only introduced overseas navigation but brought Europe into direct contact with the humid tropics. Except for the Nile Valley and the Canary Islands, in 1490 Europeans had only remote and indirect knowledge of the tropics; for northern Africa, the section of the tropics nearest to Europe, is made up largely of the arid reaches of the Sahara. Within the half century following 1492, however, the exploits of the Spanish and Portuguese gave Europeans commercial acquaintance with most tropical lands.

## I    Portuguese in World Shipping and Trade

The exploits of the Portuguese in bringing the lands bordering the Indian Ocean into world trade exemplify many of the motives, opportunities, and hazards of sea trade. The Portuguese were a courageous, adventuresome people living in a land of restricted area and limited resources. Much of the terrain is too steep for agriculture, and other resources are not abundant. However, from their fisheries in the shallow coastal waters the Portuguese had learned the art of navigation and gained experience in alongshore trade.

For the great adventure down the coast of Africa the way had been prepared by the able leadership of Henry the Navigator. His brilliant mind, great wealth, and well-laid plans enabled him to face both the scientific and the practical problems connected with his consuming ambition; namely, to find an all-sea route to India. Apparently he also was not unmindful of the profits which might accrue from such a route.[2]

To further his purposes, Prince Henry encouraged mathematicians, astronomers, and geographers from other parts of Europe to come to study and work in the observatory and school of navigation which he founded. Among other activities, these men of science compiled maps and charts for use by his navigators. At about this time the mariners compass was greatly improved so that it became an effective instrument for showing direction by sea. Also, the instrument which was used to measure the altitude of a star, the astrolabe, underwent major improvements.[3]

Prince Henry induced experienced and able mariners to sail under the command of the most daring captains of the time. He outfitted voyage after voyage, each of which pushed the front of known territory southwards and added to the knowledge of navigation. Under stern necessity the flimsy half-decked vessels with which Henry began were replaced with vessels of improved design, larger size, and more substantial construction. Slowly the sea lost its imaginary terrors, and navigation under strange skies and new conditions of winds and currents became accepted practice. After the sterile coast of the Sahara was passed, the negro settlements in the rainy coastal areas provided opportunity for the slave trade which, with its profits, helped sustain Portuguese interest in Henry's undertakings.[4]

The combination of sympathetic government, able leadership, improved techniques, better facilities, gratifying profits, and active public interest brought results. Shortly after Prince Henry's death the intrepid da Gama turned the Cape of Good Hope, pushed up the east coast of Africa, and, with the summer monsoon at his back, sailed across the Indian Ocean to Calicut on the Malabar Coast of southwest India.[5]

When da Gama returned to Lisbon in 1499 his tiny vessels brought cargo which repaid sixty times the cost of his voyage. The successful monetary outcome of this first voyage led to a long series of voyages and an equally long period of profit. Spices and other goods were bought so cheaply in India that the Portuguese merchants could sell them in Europe for much lower prices than had held previously and still make immense profits. To Lisbon eventually came pepper from the Malabar Coast, calicos from Calicut, brocades from Gujarat, muslins from Bengal, spices from the Molucca Islands, tea and silks from China, and the special products of many other areas.[6] To Lisbon also came ships from other European countries in order to secure the products brought in Portuguese bottoms from the tropical lands.

As a result of trade with the Indies, Brazil, and its other Atlantic possessions, Portugal, a small country with only about a million inhabitants, became in the sixteenth century a great commercial and political power. Its trading posts and colonies, supported by naval and military might, commanded Brazil, the west, south, and east coasts of Africa, India and Ceylon, and the Spice Islands in the East Indies. Outposts were established in south China and Japan, but the power of the empire largely ended at the Spice Islands.

In view of the non-liberal ideas which long had characterized European thought, it is not surprising that the Portuguese were at great pains to monopolize the trade of their new empire. Such a monopoly was sanctioned by the Church in the Papal Bull of 1493 which designated a north-south line in the mid-Atlantic as the demarkation between the territories of Spain and those claimed by Portugal. In fact, trade between parts of the empire, and all trade between Portugal and its possessions was limited strictly to Portuguese vessels.

Because of their relatively few merchants and traders the Portuguese, in most cases, did not attempt to penetrate into the interior sections of their new possessions but left this trade in the hands of the Arabs, Hindus, or other native people. However, they strictly regulated the trade to the end that most of the profits went into Portuguese pockets. Restrictions, special privileges, and other forms of monopoly were the order of the day. Such a policy, accompanied by governmental inefficiency and corruption, led to a rapid decline of sea trade so that in less than a century Portugal had become a nation of low rather than high rank in the commercial world.[7]

## II    Spain as a Sea Power

In the century following the discovery of America, Spain became a great commercial nation and the leading power in Europe. The way for her rapid advance after 1492 had been prepared by the marriage of Ferdinand and Isabella, which united the crowns of Aragon and Castile and brought most of the Iberian Peninsula under one rule, and by the conquest of Granada, which ended the long exhausting war with the Moors.[8]

In her rise to wealth and power Spain faced three great problems, each worthy of a nation's entire energies. The first was the development of an overseas empire in the New World—an undertaking in which both the route and the territory were previously unknown. The second called for the replacement of the primitive existing economy, which emphasized subsistence living with the export of a few raw materials, by an economy better suited to the needs of a great international power. The third problem confronting Spain was its relation to the rest of Europe, more especially with Napoli (Naples), Spanish Navarre, Austria, and the Netherlands which had been brought more or less under Spanish rule by a series of intermarriages and conquests.[9] On account of the high importance of the first in our narrative, these problems confronting Spain are presented in reverse order.

Under the existing circumstances Spain's relations with Europe were bound to be difficult, but they were brought into the center of European affairs when the death of the only son of Ferdinand and Isabella opened the Spanish succession to numerous claimants and eventually dissipated the wealth and power of Spain in fruitless intervention in the affairs of Europe. In time such intervention brought a swift decline in Spain's power for it diverted the minds and energies of the Spanish government and the Spanish leaders from active development of Spain's overseas trade and possessions. It is scarcely an exaggeration to say that the potentialities in the Spanish overseas possessions were the greatest ever presented to a nation. In large measure they were thrown away by the preoccupation of the Spanish monarchs with the affairs of the Austrian House, and, as will be developed subsequently, by a monopolistic commercial and industrial policy inherited from the Middle Ages.[10] The tragedy of European intervention is emphasized by the fact that the peninsular character of Spain and the high Pyrenees isolate Spain from Europe almost as efficiently as the English Channel and North Sea isolate Britain from the Continent.

For a time Spain made substantial progress in her domestic affairs. As compared with the previous seats of sea power in Phoenicia, Greece, and the Po Valley, Spain was large in size and possessed a variety of producing areas. Her geographic position, moreover, favored trade with the Mediterranean countries, with western Europe, and with the New World. Barcelonia (Barcelona), Seville, Bilbao, and other ports developed rapidly.[11] To long term exports of wool, wine, and iron were added woolen, silk and velvet goods, soap, armor, leather, and other manufactured articles. Webster states that "under Philip II, Seville employed 16,000 looms and 130,000 hands in her textile industries," and according to Day "the laborers employed in the textile industries of Toledo rose from 10,000 to 50,000 in about twenty-five years, and still merchants could not supply the demand."[12] Some progress was made in agriculture, but unrestricted sheep pasturing in many areas ruined both the agriculture and the soil. Under an enlightened point of view and a wise government industry and agriculture should have been greatly benefited by Spain's overseas trade. The resources and opportunities were in hand, but men's minds were not equal to the task. In general, Spain's internal affairs profited but little from the wealth which was taken from her colonies.

The most striking aspects of Spain's development were the growth of her overseas trade and shipping and the development of a colonial empire. Shipping developed rapidly, not only in the number but in the size of vessels. Each year more than one hundred ships left Spanish ports for the colonies, and as many or more were engaged in trade with European ports.[13] Because of the hazards and perils of navigating vessels on the new routes, Spain led in the compilation and use of charts and in examining and licensing pilots. In fact in 1519 Sebastian Cabot was made Pilot-Major in charge of licensing and other services.[14]

The steps in the development of Spain's overseas empire are familiar to most readers. Its real growth began when the rich native empires of the Aztecs in Mexico and the Incas in Peru were subjugated. From them, between 1519 and 1609, almost $5,000,000,000 of gold and silver were taken.[15] This wealth gave Spain a great influence in Europe and was the envy of other nations, especially the Netherlands, France, and England. Gold was considered to be wealth in itself rather than a mere medium of exchange. This error inflated the prices of commodities and led Spain on a ruinous course in Europe.[16] In time sugar, rice, tobacco and other plantations were developed in the West Indies and elsewhere in Spain's possessions. These commodities represented the real potentialities of the New World, and to a degree Spain profited from them. In general, however, the big development in these and other plantation products in America came after, rather than during, Spain's dominance of New World trade.

Spain's policy towards her overseas trade and possessions was founded on monopoly and was implemented by all the known devices of restriction and special preference. Ideas of the freedom of the seas and of equal treatment of all flags in all trades were still to come. Spanish ideas of trade, like those of Portugal, were under the influence of the thought of the Middle Ages. Keller describes the situation in the following passage:

> In the Middle Ages trade was cramped and restricted by regulations that had their origin in applications of scriptural texts wrought out by men ostensibly removed from the world and its doings (ecclesiastics) and thoroughly permeated by the unreal scholastic atmosphere. They were recluses, yet they lucubrated over trade . . . where reasoning of this type ran out at all into practical policy, as in Spain, the result was grave injury to industry and trade.[17]

The commercial policy of Spain during this formative period of overseas trade was restrictive both in pattern and in administration. In the case of the latter, the New World possessions in the sixteenth century were divided into two vast viceroyalties. That of New Spain included the West Indies, Mexico, Central America, Venezuela, and the Philippines; whereas that of Peru was made up of Panama, New Granada, and the occupied regions of South America except Venezuela, Guiana, and Brazil.[18]

In terms of pattern, Spain held the overseas trade to a few channels and to stipulated times. In the mother country the trade was limited to

Seville so that it could be taxed and regulated at will. In the colonies, Vera Cruz in Mexico and Puerto Bello at the Isthmus were the prescribed centers through which the trade was required to flow. The famous "House of Trade" in Seville controlled the "routes, destinations, manner of sailing, passengers, freight, and correspondence" of the overseas traffic. For the sake of the necessary protection, all sailings were confined to fleets and to stipulated times. All fleets, moreover, were convoyed by war vessels. At Puerto Bello trade was limited to a few weeks, and the trade of Buenos Aires was forced to move via Panama, the west coast to Lima, Peru, and then eastward across the Andes.[19] The whole idea was to derive a big profit from handling a small amount of goods in the easiest possible way. Under such restrictions, accompanied by corruption in government, disorganization and failure was inevitable. Spain missed its chance at continued greatness.

## III     *European Seaboard as a Focus of Transport*

As the maritime and commercial status of Spain and Portugal declined, that of the Atlantic Seaboard of Europe increased. Slowly but surely the coastal arc between the peninsulas of Brittany and Jutland became the major commercial coast of Europe. Frontage on this coast was divided between France, Belgium, and the Netherlands on the continental side, and England on the great offshore island. The English Channel, the Strait of Dover, and the narrow southern section of the North Sea form a chain of waterways that provides entrances to the two land bodies. For the sake of convenience these waterways have been called the Narrow Seas (*Fig. 9*) and that designation is used in this study.[20]

9. *The Narrow Seas and major ports of Western Europe. The Narrow Seas is a convenient term designating the narrow waterway that is made up of the English Channel, the Strait of Dover, and the southern part of the North Sea.*

In terms of sea transport today the active section of the seaboard arc extends from Le Havre at the mouth of the Seine River to Hamburg on the Elbe. Spaced between are Antwerpen on the Schelde, London on the Thames, Rotterdam on the Rhine, Emden on the Ems, and Bremen on the Weser. These ports of today had emerged as trading points under the Hansa and before the Discoveries Period were visited by the Venetian traders. In fact, according to Gibbins, "by 1300 A.D. there were seventy cities in the League of Rhenish cities, including every center of importance from Levonia to Holland."[21]

As modern transport developed, ocean highways focused on the seaboard ports; and railroads, highways, and airways now radiate from the ports into the Continent, or from London into other parts of Britain. The meeting of sea and land traffic long ago led to the growth of the ports as commercial and manufacturing centers. In fact, Bruges in Flanders, the center of the famous Flemish textile district that paced Western Europe into the industrial age, lies within the seaboard area.[22]

The trade and associated manufacture of the seaboard are most intensely developed in the area served by the Narrow Seas, especially in the section centering about the lower Rhine (Fig. 9). Here were the early settlements that became the continental ports of Rotterdam and Antwerpen and the island port of London that during the long period of English dominance became the world's greatest port and city.

No one can deny the high importance of the struggles of the Dutch, French, and British to gain control of sea trade. In global terms, however, these conflicts obscure the great power which the Narrow Seas as a region has exercised. For nearly four centuries the world has profited by the extent to which this part of the European Seaboard has acted in its true geographic role; namely, as a leading region in world transport and trade. Conversely, as will be discussed later, the world has suffered by the repeated inability of the nations of this seaboard region to work together. This inability has been, and still is, a tragedy of our civilization.

Until about 1600 this seaboard of Western Europe was a frontier area on the periphery of the Continent. Politically it included three relatively unimportant governments—the Netherlands, France, and England. Even in 1600, England, for example remained a sheep raising and wool exporting country and, up to the time of Elizabeth, imported nearly all "artificiality" as manufactured goods were called.[23] The Netherlands developed rapidly and in both trade and manufactures was ahead of England and France. The latter had the largest mentioned area under its political control and was increasing its strength in overseas trade. In all three countries, agriculture supported most of the people. Manufacture was still in the hands of guilds and represented handwork using simple tools rather than machines. Fish supplemented the food produced on the farms, and the fisheries trained men in seafaring activities. Trade in wool, woolen goods, wine, boots, shoes, metals, and other articles in kind was carried on within the area. Sea trade was in the making but employed few men, and as yet had not begun to overshadow other activities in the policies of these budding maritime countries.

Of the countries facing the Narrow Seas, the Netherlands and Belgium, in the middle of the seaboard arc, made rapid progress, and during the early part of the seventeenth century the Netherlands was the leading maritime nation.[24] Her fishing activities were the most extensive, her manufactures the largest and most varied, her shipyards built more vessels than were built in all the rest of Europe, her skillful sailors dominated many of the coastal and overseas trades, and her commerce extended into most known parts of the world. These activities, together with religious tolerance, attracted skilled artisans from neighboring countries and money from all Europe. As a result, the Dutch made rapid progress in education and in their general welfare.

The rise of the Dutch in shipping and trade gives another illustration of the stages in the rise of a seafaring people. The Dutch first gained shipping and trading experience from their herring fisheries. The fishing fleets gave training in seamanship, and the organization of the fishing trade furnished equally valuable commercial experience. Building the fishing vessels, moreover, gave experience in another essential phase of the shipping industry. At an early stage, there also developed alongshore trade in the North Sea and subsequently more distant voyages to the Baltic. In discussing this matter, Clive Day states that in the seventeenth century more than half the Dutch ships cleared for ports on the North or Baltic seas. Dutch ships sailed each year to the White Sea to bring back furs and forest products from northern Russia. Other vessels plied regularly to the ports of Spain and Portugal seeking goods from the distant possessions of those powerful countries. The Dutch, moreover, persistently sought the North East passage to India and dispatched exploring vessels to the South Seas. Finally, the famous West and East India trading companies carried the Dutch into world trade.

All in all, the Dutch gained a degree of leadership in world shipping and trade not attained by any other nation. Then followed a long series of European wars in which the Netherlands was involved in one capacity or another. After 1750, Dutch shipping and trade gradually lost ground. According to Clive Day, ineffective government, absence of a well-defined commercial policy, inadequate domestic resources, rule by family rings, inordinately high taxes, decline of manufactures, and loss of colonies combined to bring about the decline of the Dutch as the British rose to first rank among the commercial nations.

The advances in the Netherlands were first followed, then matched, and finally surpassed in France and England. France began as a separate dominion in 870 when the great Empire of Charlemagne was divided between France and Germany.[25] France had emerged from the Middle Ages with a strong government spread over an area approximately that of the modern nation. The first half of the sixteenth century witnessed strong advances in French agriculture, manufactures, and trade. Many vessels were added to the merchant marine and the navy. Explorers carried the French flag into many areas. The "capitulations of 1536" signed with Turkey permitted the French to trade with the Ottoman Empire and thus stimulated shipping to and from the Eastern Mediterranean. This progress was slowed towards the end of the sixteenth century, due, in part at least, to the severity of English and Dutch competition; but, nevertheless, France continued its advance and in the seventeenth century became an increasing factor in the trade of Europe.[26]

After the Romans abandoned the British Isles in the fifth century, Great Britain was invaded by the Angles and Saxons who were the real founders of the kingdoms of England and Scotland.[27] These kingdoms were small countries on the western frontier of Europe until England began its career as a commercial nation early in the sixteenth century. By that time, English vessels were carrying English traders and English wool to most of the seaboard countries of Europe. In addition, within fifteen years after the discovery of America fishermen from western England had appeared on the banks of Newfoundland. Also about this time, English merchants were taking advantage of the decline of the Hansa to form the successful Merchants Adventurers Company which set the pattern for the formation of other trading companies inseparably connected with England's rise to commercial power.[28] The Russian Company, for example, tapped rich fur, tar, pitch, and other trade from Russia. Other companies traded to the Levant, the Orient, and the New World (Table 3). Explorers and privateers had also brought wealth and territory to England by this time. Beginning with the Cabots, and followed by such men as Drake,

Hawkins, and Raleigh, explorations were made and trade was initiated. All of these factors set the stage for Elizabeth's reign (1538–1602), during which time peace prevailed and commerce flourished.[29]

3. ENGLISH COMMERCE, 1500–1776.

| Areas of Trade | | | Major Items of Trade | |
| --- | --- | --- | --- | --- |
| European | Mediterranean | Overseas | Imports | Exports |
| Netherlands | Spain | India | Silk | Woolen Manufactures |
| France | Italy | Persia | Cotton | Broad Cloth |
| Spain | Naples | Arabia | Mohair | Watches |
| Baltic Lands | Sicily | North America | Drugs | Tin |
| Russia | Leghorn | South America | Currants | |
| | Venice | | Jewels | |
| | Turkey | | | |
| | Syria | | | |
| | Asia Minor | | | |

Source: H. De B. Gibbins, *The History of Commerce in Europe* (London: Macmillan & Co., 1923), pp. 138–39.

These and other developments on the seaboard of Western Europe were in sharp contrast to conditions prevailing in Central Europe. Much of the German Empire formed, together with the remaining states of Central Europe, the East Frankish Empire, as constituted in 843 at the close of the Empire of Charlemagne. Germany, however, was marked with political disunion and witnessed the continuation of the conflicts between numerous petty princes and nobles. Germany has been called the cradle of the Reformation, where strife between Protestants and Catholics first broke out. The Reformation, moreover, divided Germany into hostile camps; roughly speaking, the southern and eastern provinces remained Catholic, whereas the northern and western provinces embraced Protestantism.[30] In these and other ways, Central Europe remained disorganized politically and commercially in sharp contrast with the seaboard nations.

In the seventeenth century the struggle for commercial supremacy on the part of the Netherlands, France, and England emphasized again the importance of the seaboard section of Western Europe. In the first half of the century the Netherlands still maintained supremacy, but in the latter half England and France forged ahead. Periods of progress alternated with periods of stagnation, explained in part by the quality of government. There can be no doubt that the character and quality of government has a great bearing on the economy and welfare of a people. France, in this as in many other things, went from good to bad with related periods of progress and nonprogress in shipping and trade.[31] Colbert, for example, attempted to make France industrially self-sufficient (1664–1667).[32] He spared no expense or effort to improve the internal economy of the country. During this century five great trading companies were founded, and settlements were made in New France.

In England the seventeenth century brought an upswing in manufactures, trade, shipping, and colonization, encouraged by a long period of peace. Because of religious troubles and other conditions in the Netherlands and France, thousands of skilled workmen and quantities of capital migrated to England.[33] Wars prevailed on the Continent, as already noted, whereas in England prolonged peace was the rule. During the wars England became the foremost commercial and shipping nation in Europe. Great trading companies opened up commerce with the East and West Indies, the Levant, Russia, the Baltic countries, and the Mediterranean. Colonization began in the New World, especially on the seaboard of what is now the United States. The colonies in the West Indies were more important than those on the mainland because their production of sugar, indigo, spice, cocoa, rice, and tobacco led to lucrative trade. For example, England at this time controlled the sugar market of the world, and thus began the type of trading control and influence which has been of great importance in maintaining Britain's position as the leading commercial nation. The lure of profits from the fur trade in North America, for example, led the Hudson Bay Company to obtain exclusive control of this trade, and incidentally, to the eventual control of much of Canada.[34]

One factor in England's development which should not be overlooked is the importance of demonstrations of profit to be made out of overseas trade. Experiences in the seventeenth century included the tobacco trade of Maryland and Virginia in which England took a large share of the exports. In fact in 1700, Virginia shipped about 18,000,000 pounds of tobacco, and fifty years later the export amounted to 40,000,000 pounds.[35] The rice trade of Carolina was another example. The lumber trade and the trade in furs, skins, and fish also proved to be profitable. North Atlantic trade developed during this period by which the American colonies sent "fish, lumber, staves, masts, horses, cattle, beef and pork" to the West Indies, and in return imported molasses, sugar, rum, and honey. To England the colonies sent fish, salt beef, pork, and staves; and from England manufactured goods were shipped to the colonies and the West Indies. Hence, England began to mold her economy around a central core of trade and thus laid the basis for its mercantile policies which carried into the nineteenth century and affected the areas now designated as the North Atlantic Arena.[36]

The seventeenth century also witnessed the entrance of the English into the Indian Ocean, where until the twentieth century they remained supreme.[37] For a long time after the discovery of the Good Hope route to India, the nations facing the Narrow Seas did not attempt to compete with the strongly entrenched Portuguese. The Dutch, however, began to sail the route and soon learned that the East Indies trade earned substantial profits. With the decline of the Portuguese on the sea, with the Pope's authority challenged by the Netherlands and England at the time of the Reformation, and with the rising tide of interest in overseas matters, English participation in the Indian Ocean trade increased after 1582. To this end, Queen Elizabeth chartered the East India Company in 1600. Beginning with posts or factories at Calicut, Masulipatam, and Delhi, by 1689 strong posts were in operation at Bombay and Calcutta.[38] Thus by 1700 the pattern of European influence in the Indian Ocean trades had taken shape; namely, with the British in India, the Dutch in the East Indies, and the French in Madagascar, Réunion, and other small islands. Nearly a century later, Britain added Cape Colony and Australia and thus ringed the Indian Ocean with British commercial and political influence. In this connection, it should be emphasized and re-emphasized that all these commercial and political developments grew out of sea transportation, increasingly developed and powered by the nations facing the Narrow Seas of the Atlantic seaboard of Europe.

Although all of the western seaboard countries had become influential in sea trade by the early decades of the eighteenth century, England's advance was greater and more rapid than that of either the Netherlands or France. Of the two, the Netherlands' greatest period of influence had passed, and the economy of both countries suffered greatly during the War of the Spanish Succession (1701–1714). In England, however, safely out of the war zone, farming, manufacturing, and trade were stimulated rather than retarded.

The Union with Scotland in 1707 brought the resourceful Scotch into the commercial picture.[39] The British trading companies and the British colonies prospered, and, following the Treaty of Utrecht in 1713, Britain showed clearly that the offshore island rather than the low countries was to lead in maritime affairs. Again, however, it should be emphasized that, in world terms, the rise of the great area about the Narrow Seas as the pulsing commercial heart of the world order constitutes the outstanding concept of the geography of the eighteenh century (*Fig. 9*).

Both England and France gained commercial momentum and

power during the eighteenth century. English merchants entered the Baltic and Mediterranean trades and were increasingly influencial in the Americas, Africa, and India. Trade stimulated inventions of importance to manufacture and eventually led Britain into the industrial revolution.

On the Continent, France, in spite of interruptions occasioned by war (Polish Succession 1733–1735, Austrian Succession 1744–1748), advanced in trade and manufactures. The middle of the century saw France improving its agriculture, its manufacture, and its trade. Both private enterprise and government promoted commerce. Roads were improved, bridges built, and the Rhine diked. Progress in scientific and artistic lines helped to make France the leading industrial area of the Continent. This progress was notable if viewed in terms of either France or England, but the perspective is better if the lens is wide enough to take in the whole maritime seaboard along the Narrow Seas.

The profits from commerce, the exploits of the mariners, growing wealth in these maritime countries, the development of banking and credit institutions, and a growing list of new commodities from the ends of the earth created a rising tide of popular interest in overseas investments. Company after company was organized, many without merit or prospects. As is customary in boom periods, some of the organizations were legitimate enterprises managed by able and honest men; others were wildcat schemes under fraudulent management. In England the climax came in the South Sea Company, whereas in France the center of interest was the Mississippi Bubble.[40] In both countries the result was ruin and disaster for some and bitter disappointment for others. The period, however, showed that this maritime area possessed wealth, and also demonstrated the influence of credit on shipping and trade. The interest in overseas ventures was renewed, but this time led to the migration of men and capital to overseas areas, more especially, to eastern North America and the West Indies.

Speculation has been a fairly constant factor in the settlement of new lands and the growth of overseas shipping and trade. Some men ventured capital in the hope of profits, others wagered their personal welfare and even their lives by settling in the newly discovered lands. If the ventured capital and the new settlements produced goods acceptable to European markets, the speculations commonly were successful if no loss of capital and lives resulted. In all these ventures, ocean shipping was the instrument which made them profitable. The arrival of a vessel from the mother country became the outstanding event in colonial life. Likewise, the return to England or France of a vessel laden with tobacco, sugar, or other goods meant profits and welfare for many in the home country.

As the decades ran into the centuries of the Discoveries Period, demonstrations of the significance of overseas trade in the economy of Western Europe began to shape the policies of the seaboard countries. England, for example, developed the mercantile system, or policy, which gave right-of-way to the trading and shipping interests of the country. On the sea-side this policy found expression in the Navigation Acts, which proved highly obnoxious to the British colonies in North America.

As France and England became powerful in shipping and trade, they became increasingly jealous of each other. By 1756 this jealousy led to the outbreak of the Seven Years War, the American part of which was called the French and Indian War. As far as England was concerned, this war was managed in the interest of English merchants. The supremacy in shipping, commerce, and colonial affairs was at stake. England won the war and gained most of the eastern part of North America, most of the French and Spanish West Indies, and most of India. France was seriously crippled on the sea and lost Canada and her claims in southern Asia.

Events of far-reaching importance, however, were in the making. Flushed with success, England pressed her policy of restricting the colonial carrying trade to British bottoms and tried to make England the sole market for colonial goods. Out of this effort came the American Revolution and an opportunity for revenge on the part of France.[41] The colonies with help from France won the war, whereas Britain lost trade, some of her colonial possessions, and much prestige in Europe.

# 6

# North Atlantic Developments

THE SPANIARDS AND PORTUGUESE, during the century in which they led in overseas activities, demonstrated that both adventure and profit could be taken from the development of ocean transport and trade. Their success encouraged other Atlantic nations to attempt to share this promising activity. The Dutch made the first move. They began by handling trade between the Iberian ports and their own ports at the mouth of the Rhine. Subsequently they ventured around Good Hope to the East Indies and across the North Atlantic to the West Indies and the Caribbean coast of South America. Later came both the French and the English. At first they preyed on the Portuguese and Spanish shipping and then launched into the risk and adventure to be had from overseas enterprise. Under Queen Elizabeth I, Drake and other seamen were granted license to engage in plundering Spanish shipping. The profits were great and encouraged the construction of fast sailing vessels that could attack and retreat in quick fashion. In time England opened trade to many areas under the famous trading companies.

1    *Trading Companies and Their Influence*

In considerable measure, the transfer of control of overseas trade and shipping from the Iberian Peninsula to the lands about the Narrow Seas resulted from the activities of trading companies organized by private enterprise but chartered by one of the three governments which bordered the Narrow Seas; namely, the Netherlands, France, and England.

The Netherlands held sway on the high seas in the seventeenth century almost to the extent that Spain and Portugal had dominated the sixteenth. Dominance of shipping and trade in the eighteenth century was shared by England and France, more especially the former.

In all the countries of the Narrow Seas the trading companies were given exclusive right to trade in prescribed areas, and in most cases, the name of the company disclosed the area in which it held sway. The Dutch East India Company and the Dutch West India Company were the leading companies chartered by the Netherlands. The French organized five great trading companies; namely, the West India Company, the Senegal Company, the East India Company, the Company of the North, and the Levant Company. "A few settlements were made by the French in the West and East Indies, Guiana, and western Africa. Moreover, in North America the Great Lakes Region and the Mississippi Valley were explored and the Newfoundland fisheries and the fur trade were stimulated. Colbert, the French leader of the time, failed to awaken any great enthusiasm for colonizing enterprises, and after his death the colonial ambition of France was for a time stifled by the love of military glory."[1] England, however, like the Dutch, poured much effort into its trading organizations, including the East India Company, the Levant Company, and the Muscovy Company, in Asia, the Mediterranean, and Russia respectively; whereas the Eastland Company traded with the Baltic and French areas. Furthermore, the Merchants Adventurers' Company traded with Germany and the Netherlands.[2] Other companies and individual merchants traded with Spain, Portugal, Italy, and other Mediterranean countries. Many things in Britain helped the growth of trade. For example, the establishment of a government postal system (1656), the creation of the Bank of England (1694), and the reform of the currency (1698) during the seventeenth century proved very beneficial both to English industry and commerce.[3]

From the historical facts, the commercial geography of the seventeenth and eighteenth centuries becomes apparent. The center of trade and of political power was about the Narrow Seas, control changing from time to time, but the area retaining its overwhelming leadership. From this central area sea trade was carried on with northern, central, and eastern Europe via the White and Baltic seas, with Spain and Portugal, and with the Levantian section of the Mediterranean Sea.

The overseas areas of supreme importance to the people of middle Latitude Europe were the tropical regions, more especially the East and West Indies. Strategic settlements rather than colonies were the rule in these tropical areas. Trade and colonies also were underway in other parts of North America. For example, the fishing grounds off Nova Scotia and Newfoundland attracted large European fleets every year, the fur trade led the French into the St. Lawrence, and the Dutch and British to the Hudson. Later, tobacco, indigo, lumber, and other specialized middle latitude products brought the North American colonies into the Commercial World. The accumulation and maintenance of wealth and power which came from this trade and these settlements were clearly dependent on shipping activities.

The great trading companies represented controlled trade and were so organized and managed as to keep all other traders out of the business. Some of them exercised far-reaching political, naval, and military power. The Dutch East India Company, for example, represented great financial resources, and was invested with power to declare war, make peace, and appoint judges and administrative officers in the islands where it operated.[4] Because of dangers from pirates and the privateers of other governments, this Dutch Company dispatched convoyed fleets three times a year. These fleets carried out Dutch manufactured goods and bullion, but returned with spices, cloth, and other products greatly in demand in Europe. The trade of this company, and of the English East India Company which eventually took over much of the trade, was slow-moving, closely organized, and highly profitable. When once the English gained control of the India trade they conducted it in lordly fashion. Towards the end of their power they used large comfortable sailing vessels on which the passengers lived in comfort and even in luxury. Passage ranged from $475 to $1170, and the company paid high salaries to its agents in India and high dividends to its stockholders.[5] The British navy protected the fleets and kept anyone else from cutting in on the trade. The idea was not to have reasonably priced commodities for the many but profitable trade for the few. As a result, there was little or no incentive to try for better methods or better vessels. Out of this controlled and static situation came the opportunity for the success of the American efforts in shipping after the Revolution freed Yankee enterprise from the restrictions and inhibitions imposed by the Navigation Acts.

As has been mentioned, interest in the Navigation Acts had lessened in England as manufacturing came into the nation's economy in the latter half of the eighteenth century. King George III and his advisors, however, continued to enforce the laws against colonial commerce. These restrictions prohibited trading in or carrying articles England wanted, or thought her traders might resell. Moreover, the money the colonial merchants made by trading in the West Indies and other areas was drained off to the mother country. The whole matter was aggravated by the growing skill of the colonials in shipbuilding, an activity for which they had superb local timber and other materials. War resulted, and under the new government skill in handling vessels and shrewdness in bargaining for cargoes was added to the colonial assets in shipbuilding. After the close of the Napoleonic Wars in 1815, Britain became increasingly concerned with manufacture and trade, whereas the Americans specialized in shipbuilding and in the carrying trades. Shipping leadership crossed the Atlantic, but leadership in trade did not.

## II  *British Mercantile and Maritime Policies*

The high geographic significance of the seaboard area served by the Narrow Seas and the Lower Rhine stems from the early and persistent localization of initiative in the area in regard to policies affecting transport and trade. Until the nineteenth century the initiative largely represented the mercantile policies of the Netherlands, France, and Britain. Because of the far-flung transport activities of these nations, their policies were almost world-wide in application. Of the three flags, that of Britain was the most influential. Hence its mercantile and maritime policies deserve especial attention.

In view of the monopolistic policies of Spain and Portugal, it is not surprising that the idea of monopoly carried into Dutch, French, and English policies. The idea of the nationalistic state, whose essence was wealth and power, flourished in all the developing countries of Western Europe. The governments of those countries emphasized the power of the nation as a whole rather than the good of the individual. To this end, these governments regulated trade and controlled shipping so that the wealth and the power of the nation should be increased. If the policies adopted injured the individual, that was not a matter of major concern.[6]

*The first stage* of the Mercantile System, which obtained from about 1600 to the time of the Industrial Revolution, was underlain with the idea of the power of the state which permeated the sixteenth and seventeenth centuries. This system developed slowly during the decades when the policy was taking shape and coincided with a long series of exhausting wars on the Continent during which Britain became the foremost power in Europe.[7]

On the maritime side the Mercantile System took the form of the Navigation Acts, of which the complex provisions and principles lent themselves to evasion. On the land the mercantile system aimed to protect and encourage agriculture, especially the grain grower, to the end that England should be self-sufficient as to food. It also encouraged home industries in order to give employment to native artisans, and aimed to amass wealth and keep it within the country.[8] Wealth meant power, and national power was the sought end.

The first of the many Navigation Acts was passed in 1381 under Edward III, and stipulated that English merchandise must be imported or exported solely in English vessels. Subsequently, many other acts were passed but their main principles and provisions were essentially as follows:

1 ] Foreign vessels were excluded from the inter-imperial and coasting trades.

2 ] Foreign vessels were prohibited from importing into the United Kingdom or any British possession in Asia, Africa, or America, any goods unless such goods were *a*) the produce of the country to which the importing vessel belonged; and *b*) imported in such vessel direct from the country of origin.

3 ] The indirect importation into the United Kingdom via European countries of the produce of Asia, Africa, or America was prohibited.

Like all drastic rules, the Navigation Acts promoted evasion as well as compliance. The rigor with which they were enforced, morevover, varied with the rulers in power and with other circumstances from time to time. Henry VIII, for example, on the one hand enforced them vigorously, but on the other gained a profitable revenue by selling exemptions to them.[9]

As the Navigation Laws affected sea trade and shipping, their enforcement led to disputes with other nations and with the colonies. They represented national legislation in regard to international affairs. Such action can be effective only if the nation in question controls the international situation. For two centuries after the passing of the first Navigation Act, Spain first, and then the Netherlands rather than England, dominated the Atlantic trades. During these centuries, however, England slowly developed her policy of national power, her skill with shipping, and her navy to support the merchant marine. As early as the time of Henry IV (1367–1413) steps were taken to maintain a navy.

Under Henry V both the government and private owners built larger and better ships. Later, both laws and rulers encouraged the growth of shipping. An act in 1548 enforced the eating of fish on fast-days to encourage the fishing industries, rightfully regarded as the nursery of the Navy. These and many other measures promoted the growth of both merchant shipping and the Navy. Thus, during the latter part of the seventeenth and the first half of the eighteenth centuries when the development of shipping coincided with the gradual evolution of the mercantilist policy of promoting national power, with a long series of wars on the Continent which exhausted the efforts of France and the Netherlands, with the beginning of English manufacturing, and with other favoring conditions, England became the foremost power in Europe, and thus was able to enforce her maritime program on most of the world.

To a large extent, the Navigation Laws, in their specific application, were aimed at the carrying and entrepot trades of the Netherlands. In this they were successful. Dutch vessels were no longer able to carry the goods of third countries to the Netherlands for subsequent transshipment to England. Even the produce of the Dutch possessions in the East was excluded from British markets if it previously had been brought to Dutch ports. As a result the Dutch overseas trade was crippled, but Dutch competition in the trade of the North and Baltic seas increased. British participation in these trades declined correspondingly, and thus the British interests that were affected opposed the Navigation Acts. To the extent, however, that these Acts diverted British shipping into the overseas trade, they laid the basis for the great expansion of British shipping in the nineteenth century after the Napoleonic Wars.

As has been stated, the mercantilist policy affected agriculture, industry, and finance, as well as shipping and trade. In this connection it should be remembered that the aim of the government was to develop and maintain the strength and power of the country, rather than the welfare of individuals in the population. Moreover, the period in which trade and other elements in the nation's economy were to be dedicated to making commodities abundant and cheap still lay ahead.[10]

The interrelationships of transport, trade, agriculture, manufacturing, and finance in the economy of a nation were slow in developing and even slower in being understood. For centuries agriculture had been the basic element in English economy. Tillage was encouraged because it provided food for the people and offered more employment than its competitor, pasturage. It also supplied men for the army. However, as has been stated earlier, wool was the principal staple for export as late as the reign of Elizabeth. During this long period, land was the chief evidence and measure of wealth, and the mercantilist policy protected the grain and other products of the land in the home markets. Except for occasional years of poor crops from drought or other causes, English farmers were able to feed the population. Under a policy of power this was highly desirable, and thus Corn Laws were designed to promote the growth of grain by protecting the farmer's products in the nation's markets. With the development of manufacturing, the population increased rapidly, and the prices of food rose gradually but definitely.

The ideas of the Mercantile System were applied to manufacturing as well as to agriculture and trade. In the Middle Ages, manufactured goods, spices, and other products were brought to England by the Hansa and the Venetians. In the fifteenth century, however, the idea developed that it would be a good idea for goods to be made in England, thus giving employment to English artisans. Hence, in time, new industries were introduced and old ones protected. If foreign trade led to the export of English manufactured goods or if it brought raw materials to be made up in England, it was looked upon with favor. If English raw material was exported or if manufactured goods which might have been made in England were imported, the trade was thought to be injurious. Such ideas fostered governmental regulation. As early as 1463, for example, an act excluded woolens, silks, iron and steel, leather goods, playing cards, and many other items under the idea that if imports of such goods were excluded, they would be made at home. By means of such regulations, the government attempted to foster practices which it thought would build up a powerful country and to eliminate those regarded as injurious to this "power" policy.

The second stage in the development of British shipping and trade policy covered the time from 1750 to 1850. During this period of 100 years, major industrial discoveries and inventions, and especially the use of steam power, gradually revolutionalized the economy of the United Kingdom and modified its mercantile policy. After the American and French revolutions the population of Britain grew rapidly in numbers, and the country became wealthy. As a result Britain became increasingly dependent on the outside world for food and raw materials and for markets for its coal and manufactured products. Hence, the Navigation Acts were first relaxed and finally repealed (1849).

As attempts to enforce these laws in the American Colonies were substantial reasons for the Revolutionary War, it is worthy of note that the first relaxations were in favor of the United States, then Britain's chief competitor in shipping. This fact is an early illustration of the emergence of the coming importance of shipping and trade in the North Atlantic Arena.

*The third stage* in British mercantile policy was that of the coming of Free Trade from 1850 to 1914. This period witnessed the rise of the British Merchant Marine from 4,000,000 tons net in 1850 to 11,500,000 tons net in 1914. It also marked, particularly after 1870, the development of steam-driven, steel ships that became the world's most economical carriers. During the third period, Britain developed a policy of equal treatment of all flags in all areas. Foreign flags were given equality in British ports, and Britain aimed at securing similar treatment in foreign ports. This created a sea pattern of operation that had slowly emerged out of the multiplicity of events that had a bearing on the development of shipping and trade through the centuries since the Phoenicians first plied the waters of the Mediterranean.

Britain's policy of Free Trade stimulated ocean commerce, helped to introduce new products into many areas, and worked toward rather than against peace and a rising level of living in most sections of the world. Sea trade during this period of peace became a highly constructive instrument in international welfare. Sargent, in his remarkable study of *Sea Trade of the Empire*, concludes that in view of its world coverage the shipping and trade of the world in this period was balanced, but not the parts.

As has been stated, the Mercantile System governed the thought and policy of Britain from the close of the sixteenth century until the time of the Industrial Revolution. Its object was the development of industry and trade and the creation of a strong, self-sufficing state. To this end, the government attempted to eliminate all rivals and subordinated individual English interests and the interests of the colonies. Apparently the influence of the mercantilist policy declined before its theories and its legislation were abandoned. The policy, however, was still strong enough to be a factor in the American Revolution and in the establishment of the United States. The ideas and forces which led to the abandonment of the Mercantile System, however, were visible before the Revolution, and the change to a new policy came early in the nineteenth century. Interestingly enough, shipping played as prominent a part in the new era as it had in the centuries when the mercantilist policy prevailed.

## III    Industry and Free Trade

Towards the close of the eighteenth century, industrial discoveries by British inventors, new methods of production, increasing use of power, and ever-growing markets for British goods gradually revolutionized the economy of Great Britain. The revolution began with progress in the iron and hardware industries and with inventions and new methods in textile manufacture. It was implemented by the invention of the steam engine and the use of power to run the new machines in the shops and factories. Even in 1800, however, Britain still had a predominantly agricultural and commercial economy. By 1850 the great change had come. Manufactures employed more people than any other occupation, and Britain had become the leading, if not the only, industrial country of the world.

The introduction of machines and the use of power called for large amounts of capital and labor. The former had been accumulating in Britain as a part of the rise in trade and shipping. The latter came from all parts of the British Isles and from the seaboard countries of Europe. As the factory towns grew in number and size; as mining community after mining community developed; as canals, roads, and railroads were built; as the port cities grew and flourished; and as these urban communities furnished ever-growing markets for agricultural products the "whole face of the country" was changed, and the British landscape of today was in the making.[11] An even more profound change occurred in the minds of men—a change which found expression in the coming of the policy of Free Trade.

### MANUFACTURE INTRODUCED INTO BRITAIN'S ECONOMY

The development of manufacturing on a machine and power basis not only increased British trade with other countries but greatly increased internal trade. It did more. It affected practically every aspect of British life and every phase of British policy. It redistributed population, increased the number and size of towns and cities, led to rapid development of internal transportation, and, in fact, created a new economy and a new geography. The developments both affected and were affected by sea transportation and overseas trade. The full story lies beyond the scope of our theme, but certain elements of great significance in the growth of cheap and regular sea transport require emphasis.

The roots of the Industrial Revolution lie deep in British history and deep in Britain's bedrock. They were nurtured in the long series of events, circumstances, and inventions which led to the use of British iron and coal. The manufacturing of iron from British ores is largely a story of fire—first wood and then coal. The use of wood and charcoal in smelting had deforested parts of Britain and Ireland. The decline of the timber resources led to the importation of pig iron from Sweden and the American colonies. Like most other aspects of the growth of manufacture in Britain, this last practice led to sea trade.

*IRON AND COAL*

Since the sixteenth century the possibility of substituting coal or coke for wood and charcoal in the smelting of iron ore had been entertained. Actually, however, not much progress ensued until the latter part of the eighteenth century when the production of machinery called for increasing quantities of iron. In 1760 a blast furnace was built for the use of coal, the blast being supplied by water power. Thirty years later steam engines powered the furnace for the first time and saved a third of the coal in the process. Within eight years the output of pig iron doubled. Moreover, in 1783 pig iron was converted to malleable iron with the aid of coal, and malleable iron was made into bars by passing it through rollers instead of using the slower process of forge hammers.[12]

The use of coal in smelting ores gave momentum to the trade in both iron and coal. Coal mining increased from 4,773,828 tons in 1750 to 7,618,728 tons in 1790 and more than 10,000,000 tons in 1795.[13] Previous to this time the Newcastle pits at seaboard had supplied most of the coal, and sea transport had been used in getting it to London and to the Continent where it was in demand. The increased use of coal, however, led to the opening of new pits in other parts of the country and to serious efforts to improve internal transport by water. Thus an eleven-mile canal was built to carry coal from pits at Worsley, in the Manchester coal field, to the rapidly growing city of Manchester. Savings resulted in spite of the cost of tunnels and an aqueduct over the River Irwell. As a result a network of canals soon was built in central England. These were of direct importance to manufacturing and agriculture as well as to mining. With the success of these enterprises the new physical structure of Britain was well underway, to be improved still further by a system of roads, and even more by the coming of railroads. By 1850 both the economy and the geography of Britain had witnessed great changes. New resources, new industries, new means of transport, new enterprise, new uses for capital, new demands for labor, new social problems, and new policies made a new Britain to which, as we shall see, overseas trade and transportation became all-important matters.

## OVERSEAS EMPHASIS IN THE COTTON TRADE

Although Britain's monopolistic trading policies helped to bring on the American Revolution and thereby led to great losses of territory and prestige, sea trade soon brought England and the United States into close commercial relations. The power of transport on the North Atlantic, as we shall see, is a persistent force on both its borders. It is an international tie of the first order of importance. The sea trade in question was the trade in cotton; raw cotton from our South helped to fill the holds of many vessels, and cotton goods gave valuable, though not as bulky, return cargoes.

The cotton manufacturing industry was the first field of endeavor which showed what the Industrial Revolution was to mean to Britain. The iron and hardware industries were based on local materials and local demand. The industry was written for a long time in strictly insular dimensions. Cotton manufacturing, however, went forward in international terms almost from its beginning. From the outset it depended on overseas trade for raw materials and for the disposal of some part of its product. Britain's position in the Atlantic world, its supremacy in sea trade and power, and its early momentum in textiles were important factors in the rapid rise of this industry in the Lancashire area of western England.

Textile production on a cottage basis apparently was introduced to Lancashire about 1685 by immigrants from Antwerpen. After 1740 a series of inventions paced by Arkwright's efforts introduced a long period of rapid growth. The growth was as much a matter of available capital and enterprising administration as invention, for until the latter half of the eighteenth century conditions did not favor the use of machines. The well-ordered and closely-regulated trade of the seventeenth and early eighteenth centuries left little or no opportunity for the individual initiative which inventions represent. Arkwright and others did interest capital, and a growing belief in the rights and powers of the individual led to the favorable modifications in the legal structure of the country.

The early inventions in both the spinning and weaving industries came out of Lancashire and were put to work there. Streams from the Pennines furnished clean and pure water for finishing and dyeing and some water for power. Nearby Mersey River gave the necessary facilities for import and export, and when steam engines were introduced local coal supplied the power. Conditions in England furnished cheap labor, tragically cheap, for a long time, and skilled labor also came from the Netherlands and France, where for a time social conditions led to considerable emigration. This was a geographic coincidence of the first order, and when the invention of the cotton gin and the use of slave labor made cotton fiber abundant, the industry gained momentum at a rapid rate.[14] It also should be recognized that sea transportation not only brought the raw material at low cost but also distributed the finished goods economically. England's ability to export large quantities of useful fabrics at low cost in the coastal areas of the world is the supreme point of consideration. Manufacture always had been a part of shipping supremacy, but cheap manufacture had now made its appearance in Britain, and a new powerful and stimulating force had appeared in the world order. It remains to see how this force affected British ideas and policies.

## THE COMING OF FREE TRADE

The change of trading policy from the Mercantile System to Free Trade was a gradual process and, directly or indirectly, practically every phase of British life was involved. Throughout the period of change, and in fact, from 1500 to the present, the purpose or objective of Britain in regard to trade has remained the same. The importance of trade—of necessity, sea trade—to this island people has scarcely been questioned. Sea trade long since caught the imagination of all classes of British people, and the desire to increase their trade has motivated British legislation to a remarkable degree. Long since, also, the English gave up their earlier ambition to occupy a part of the Continent. They accepted the sea not only as an all-important part of the defense of their political freedom but as equally important in their livelihood.

The importance of sea power was learned early. The first great lesson was the defeat of the Spanish Armada. Phillip II of Spain, angered by the raids of Hawkins, Drake, and others poachers on Spain's commerce with her trans-Atlantic colonies, declared war in 1585. Phillip prepared a great fleet which was in reality an "army of boats" commanded by a soldier rather than a sailor. Elizabeth rallied Drake, Hawkins, Frobisher, Davis, and her other sea dogs and, taking advantage of all they had learned about quick attack, by expert sailing avoided the hand to hand fight which the Spaniards wanted. Up to this time a ship's guns had been used to damage the enemies' rigging so that a vessel could be boarded for a man to man fight. In their raids the English had learned to damage the vessels themselves with the fire from their cannon, and thus were able to make the fight with the Armada a naval engagement rather than an army maneuver.[15]

The lessons learned in Elizabeth's time never were forgotten, and in the last war Hitler's great army quickly reached the channel but, even with command of the air, the army could not be moved across the channel because the British fleet was poised for attack from both north and south.

Sea power, as we have seen, was developed to assure British freedom, but it also has been used to aid the growth of British commerce. The privateer and buccaneer of Elizabeth's time was an outgrowth of the piracy which had flourished most of the time since the days of the Phoenicians. Gradually, public sentiment changed, England looked with declining favor on the pirates, and in time the sailing skill learned in the buccaneering days along the Spanish coast in America was the factor which eventually did away with piracy.

As time went on, sea power came to mean the service of the merchant marine as well as the strength of the navy. An active merchant marine gave employment and brought the raw materials and food of ever-increasing necessity to the British economy. Merchant vessels also served as auxiliary craft in time of war. As factory towns grew in number, manufacturing became more and more significant in British economy. Enterprise flourished, and government regulations of shipping and trade became unpopular. In the decades of peace following the Napoleonic Wars, employment increased, and the population grew rapidly in number. The national wealth and strength increased enormously. Gradually there emerged the modern position of Britain, with its dependence upon all the world for food and raw materials, with its great use of coal for power and for export, and with its great export trade in factory products.

The growth of manufacture and the associated overseas trade naturally affected British thought. Gradually there developed the idea that restrictions on shipping and trade paralyzed the industrial growth of the country. As time went on, the Navigation Acts came into disfavor. Concessions were made to individual countries. As stated earlier, the first breach was made in favor of the United States, then the principal competitor of Britain in sea trade. Reciprocity with other governments followed, and gradually the Acts were relaxed or rescinded until finally they were completely repealed in 1849.

As previously stated, the coming of Free Trade meant that the vessels of foreign flags were given equal treatment with British vessels in the ports of the United Kingdom, and the British aimed at securing similar treatment for their ships in foreign ports. Foreign vessels could, and did, work the alongshore trade of Britain. Britain no longer levied protective duties on its imports. They relied on their momentum and skill in manufacture, on their strategic position in Europe and the Atlantic, on their all-important resources of coal and iron, on their free access to the markets of the world for food and raw materials, and on the willingness of the nations to accept their goods and services.

By 1850, therefore, the Mercantile System had been replaced by Free Trade, and the Atlantic had become the leading realm in world affairs. Maritime Europe, with London as the dominant port, continued as the center of world trade but, as we shall see, leadership in shipping had crossed the Atlantic. Manufacturing had become the leading element in British employment and was developing on the continental side of maritime Europe and the Atlantic seaboard of the United States. Of these developments the rise of American shipping to challenge British supremacy calls for special treatment.

IV    *America Enters the North Atlantic Arena*

The lands about the Narrow Seas were the scene of momentous changes as the eighteenth century turned into the nineteenth. Napoleon's attempts to create a continental system led all Europe into war. The Industrial Revolution and the move toward Free Trade were under way. In shipping terms, however, the great developments were in the western Atlantic where the American Revolution initiated a new nation and where shipbuilding and ship management, freed from the rules and regulations which had strangled them under British rule, began a growth which soon made the United States merchant fleet the standard of comparison in the maritime world.

## SCANT IMPROVEMENTS IN SHIP DESIGN

The two centuries before 1800 saw but scant improvement in ship design and construction. Vessels remained small in size, clumsy in design, and slow in speed. Shipping in all the major, and most of the minor, trades was a monopoly in the hands of a trading company. In the highly profitable trade, as that allocated to the British East India Company, new ships were ordered from the same builders decade after decade. Such a monopolistic circle provided small incentive for the costs and risks inherent in new designs and methods.[16] In terms of competition, of which there was none, the East India vessels were not commercial craft. Much space was occupied by the guns and the fighting men necessary to man them against the pirates and privateersmen of other flags. The East India men traveled in convoys and, as Thornton points out, carried "on commerce with noncommercial instruments."

In addition to the enterprise and drive befitting the men of a new country in a new world, the United States had the advantage of abundant supplies of shipbuilding materials. The northern pine, the hardwoods of the Middle States, and the naval stores of the South surpassed anything in Europe. From the time of the early settlements, vessels had been built in colonial yards, and skill and experience, added to the materials conveniently available at seaboard, produced fine ships at low cost.

## AMERICAN SKILL IN SHIP DESIGN

The naval blockades and the edicts of Napoleon and the British against neutral shipping during the Napoleonic Wars demonstrated to the Americans the need and value of speed. In this respect the American designers made great strides by studying the principles involved in propelling a vessel by sails. It is said that in fifty years the American shipbuilders accomplished as much in the art of building sailing vessels as the whole world had done in the previous three centuries.[17] Probably this is an overstatement, because the French naval designers in developing the frigate, a fast warship, had substituted mathematical computation for the time-honored rule of thumb method of square and compass still employed by the British. According to Stevens and Pendelburg, "When colonial shipbuilding started, Europe was just beginning to learn how to 'reckon' with the easily used Arabic symbols we have today. The American designers adapted the French methods to their use and the long, narrow, fast and low riding New England schooner and the famous Baltimore clippers were the result. These speedy vessels not only were the reliance of the Americans in the Revolution and the Napoleonic Wars but later were the fleets with which American traders won an enviable place in the world's commerce.[18]

The American designers gave much thought to the size and proportion of their vessels. They increased the length in proportion to the beam, and gained riding qualities as well as speed. They discovered that in a well-proportioned ship greater size meant more economical carrying power. By 1840 the average size of the American Atlantic fleet had increased to 1200 tons from the 500 tons or less which prevailed at the close of the Napoleonic Wars.[19] The American designers also improved the rigging, replacing "the elaborate 'top hamper' of yards and cordage carried by a square-rigger" with fore-and-aft sails. The masts, moreover, "were raked—that is, slanted—sharply back from deck to topmost truck" and thereby gained speed.[20]

*SKILL IN SAILING*

Not only were the American vessels expertly built, but they were skillfully sailed. The officers commonly had a better knowledge of mathematics and navigation than British officers, and both they and their crews were paid much better. In many cases, an American captain had a financial stake in his vessel and was a man of high character and reputation. They developed exceptional ability in negotiating cargoes and thereby making their vessels earn money.[21]

Another far-reaching innovation introduced by the American shipping industry was that of scheduled sailings. Previously, vessels sailed loaded, and no one could tell exactly when that would occur. About 1816 an American company announced sailings for a specified time and place in the trade between New York and Liverpool. Their contracts were carried out scrupulously, and they gained a fine reputation on both sides of the Atlantic.[22]

*EMIGRANT TRAFFIC*

In addition to their speed and regular sailings, the American vessels of the time gained a well-deserved reputation for cleanliness and food. This was of much importance in the emigrant traffic from Europe. Before

1840, some 50,000 emigrants annually left Europe for America, mostly in Yankee vessels.[23] Regular services were maintained from Bremen, Le Havre, London, and Liverpool. Hence, the hopeful emigrant got his first impressions of his new home as he sailed from Europe under the stars and stripes.

## LAST OF THE DOMINANCE OF THE SAILING VESSELS

Between the early decades of the nineteenth century when the sailing vessel dominated transportation on the sea and the latter decades when the steamship came into its own, there was a middle-century period in which both were developing significantly, but in different services and on different routes. The initiative also was different. The Americans dominated the sailing trades, whereas, in large measure, the British led the way in the steam packet business. Furthermore, the sailing vessel's bid for supremacy marked its last stand, as against the experimental stages of steam propulsion.

In large measure, early honors went to the sailing vessels and to the Americans because the steam packets burned so much coal that for an ocean voyage it filled most of a vessel's hold. Steam-driven vessels simply could not pay in competition with the sailing vessels as the Americans had developed them.[24] For river navigation where fuel could be loaded at convenient intervals; in ferry service where regularity is an all-important matter; and for passenger, express, and high class freight between closely spaced ports in the North and Baltic seas and other regional maritime areas, steam-propelled craft could pay their way. On the high seas they could not. This fact, obvious now, was not understood or accepted in 1840. Thus a good deal of effort and money was wasted in attempts to use steam on the high seas. So much space was needed to house the fuel and the awkward engines of the time that there was but little space left for cargo. In the "Britannia," built for the Atlantic service about 1840, for example, the engine department occupied nearly half the total underdeck space. Moreover, the necessary coal for the voyage occupied three-fourths of the space which could be used for fuel and cargo. As these early steam packets cost three times as much per ton to build as did the American sailing vessels, it is clear that the advantage in earning power was altogether with the latter.

After 1837, in the North Atlantic and some other trade routes this disadvantage was offset by the subsidies paid by the British government in the form of mail contracts. The justification for these subsidies grew out of the fact that before 1840 the mails between England and America were carried by more or less obsolete government sailing vessels. Hence, the mails were irregular and uncertain. These mail contracts enabled the British to continue the use of steam on the sea until the inventive techniques of the Industrial Revolution could be applied to steam navigation. British preoccupation with other types of manufacture retarded such application in spite of the high importance of sea transport in the British way of life.

It should be remembered that at this time, although British tonnage exceeded the American, the general run of American vessels and of American seamanship was much higher than that of the British or any other flag. The American merchant marine dominated the Atlantic and was respected on every important sea lane. Hence, the momentum of America in the sailing vessel traffic tended to make them less interested in steam navigation on the ocean routes than were the British who had nothing to lose and much to gain if steam triumphed over wind.

The Americans first met the challenge of the subsidized steam packet by bringing the sailing vessel to its highest level of achievement. With their acknowledged advantages in building and operating sailing vessels, it is not surprising that the Americans built an ever-growing tonnage of larger, faster, and more efficient schooners and clippers.[25] They introduced mechanical devices to reduce the number of seamen required to man their vessels, and in many other ways reduced their costs of operation by improving their service. The Americans also met the British challenge by an energetic move into the steam packet business. In 1850 the American Collins Line put into service large and fast steam-driven vessels which had been built especially for the North Atlantic route. Contracts granted by the federal government matched and surpassed the British subsidies. The Collins fleet outsailed the British vessels but, unfortunately, did not become sufficiently successful financially to hold American interest.[26]

The sailing vessels continued to turn in profits and continued as the center of American competition until the decade from 1855 to 1865 brought two new factors into the situation. On the American side of the water the Civil War took the United States fleet out of competition in many trades, and in Britain the invention and use of the compound engine and the screw propellers more than doubled the power obtained from a pound of steam and eventually turned the steamship into an economically operated vehicle in the ocean trades.

## WAR IN AMERICA—STEAMSHIPS IN BRITAIN

As in other great wars, the Civil War between the states exercised a profound influence on overseas trade and shipping. The approach of the war led to the withdrawal of government subsidies to steam shipping. To the opposition of certain merchants and shipowners was added the South's fear that the subsidies were building up the sea power of the North.[27] Depredation by armed vessels on the part of both the North and South destroyed much sailing tonnage. The war also emphasized the construction of ironclad vessels and the use of steam engines to drive them. In fact, the North alone built a fleet of some six hundred war steamers, which at that time comprised the most modern and formidable navy in the world. The blockade of southern ports by northern vessels during the war destroyed the cotton trade and caused loss of business and suffering in the British textile industry. The war also lessened American competition on many sea routes and thereby increased British business. In short, the Civil War and the western movement localized American interest within the confines of the American continent and conversely heightened and widened British interest on the sea lanes.

During the period before and during the war in America, several matters developed abroad which increased British interest in merchant shipping, both steam and sailing. The improvement in the cargo carrying capacity of the steamboat through the invention of the compound engine already has been mentioned. Thus, for the first time the steamship became effective on the all-important North Atlantic Route. Another was the large emigration to Australia following the first shipments of Australian gold to England in 1852.[28] It will be remembered that the earlier emigration and other passenger traffic to America had been handled largely by the clippers and packets of the United States fleet. The only other large overseas passenger traffic of the time was to India, where the carriage of merchant traders, civil servants, and troups called for considerable tonnage. This traffic to India was still in the hands of the East India Company where monopoly and conservatism held back rather than stimulated changes in ships or services. "The East India men remained a 'slow coach' giving well-ordered service on a familiar basis rather than to become a forward-looking agency encouraging innovation in design and organization."[29]

The new Australian trade, however, was open to all comers, and British shipowners rose to the opportunity. Liverpool interests wanted to get into the Australian business but had no suitable ships. However, they purchased "second-hand a whole fleet of American packets—well-suited to the large emigrant traffic to Australia." The Liverpool merchants also placed orders with Boston and New Brunswick yards for new vessels. In 1854, Donald Mackay, the "genius of American ship building," delivered four great clippers, and thereafter Liverpool dominated the Australian emigrant trade.

The rich profits from the Australian trade demonstrated the benefits of competition as against the cherished monopoly of London in the East India trade. It also demonstrated the value of the sailing vessel on the long route to Australia. At this time, therefore, two sea routes—the North Atlantic Route and the Good Hope-Magellan route—were dominated by the clipper ships, the former in the hands of the Americans and the latter under the direction of Liverpool. The sailing vessel also held the tea trade of China for many years and, until the early seventies, the trade with India.

In summary, a concept of high geographic quality may be stated. Into the middle-century period of the nineteenth century two significant trends differentiated the American and British segments of the North Atlantic Arena. In the United States the Civil War between the states, followed by the opening and settlement of the West, deflected American interest from the world scene and engendered a continental attitude and emphasis on the part of the body politic. The nation was engrossed with its continental resources of land, water, and minerals.

In Great Britain, in the same period, the national emphasis was maritime in scope. The increased carrying capacity of steam-propelled vessels generated an ever-growing interest in ocean pursuits. The steamship as a commercial carrier soon demonstrated that it was to be the lowest cost transport yet designed. Moreover, Britain possessed marked advantages in the widespread use of the new forms of transport.

Britain's interest in ocean shipping was increased greatly by the opening of the Suez Canal in 1869. The Canal cut the narrow land block between the Mediterranean and Red seas and opened the Mediterranean-Asiatic trade route. In the Mediterranean, and especially in the Red Sea, sailing vessels commonly were handicapped by calms and contrary winds. But by that time the compound engine and screw propeller were available, and fuel stations were established at many points along the route. In fact, the Suez route is the only long sea route along which fuel stations could be developed for shipping, as this route almost continuously is in touch with land. It also has along its course a marked variety of productive areas with a high density of population. Moreover, it led to the Indian Ocean almost circumscribed by British colonies. Hence, by the last quarter of the nineteenth century Britain had made ocean-going shipping almost a British institution. It should be understood that Britain's world trade based on its island position, its command of power (coal) at seaboard, its far-flung colonies, and its policy of equal treatment of all flags in all parts of the world represent both the cause and the objective of the British mercantile marine.

## v    Steamships in the New World Order

The steamship with its regularity of service introduced a new factor in the world order. The regularity of performance of the steamship meant that time between regions, especially remote regions, became a measurable matter. Space relations could be expressed in time as well as in miles or degrees of latitude or longitude. Effective distance, as we shall see, became not only a matter of the speed of ships but of organized shipping services. Moreover, as shipping services grow out of the nature and quantity of traffic on particular routes, they reflect the producing and consuming capacities of the areas served. Thus, as shipping services developed in the period from 1870 to 1914 they increasingly modified the inter-relationship of regions and gave the world a new geographic pattern. It should be understood, of course, that railway transportation in areas where it was introduced worked in the same direction. The ocean cables and the telegraph and telephone systems were other features of a new pattern of space relationships.

In the days of sailing ships, the date of sailing in most cases was uncertain. Commonly a vessel received its cargo at one port and did not sail until it was full, or until its master realized that more cargo was not forthcoming. The date of its arrival at the port of destination was even more uncertain. No one could predict with any degree of accuracy when a cargo would be delivered. In order to anticipate the future requirements of a market, shippers habitually consigned large quantities at a time. This meant large, long-term commitments of capital, likelihood of depreciation in quality, and increased insurance. These and other risks inherent in overseas transportation meant high rather than low priced commodities in the world's markets. The world's wealth of resources had not yet been made available for the common man.

In 1816 the American Black Ball line began regular schedules sailing on the first of every month from New York to Liverpool.[30] Although it was followed in this practice by some other American lines, general regularity of arrival did not come until the development of the steamship with its compound engines and screw propellers. Wh^n once the length of time between ports could be estimated accurately, goods could be shipped so as to arrive at the season of the year when a market was favorable. Thus manufacturers could be assured of a supply of raw materials in such quantities and at such times as best suited their business. Obviously, regular sailings and arrivals were a boon to passenger and mail traffic and to the shipment of general merchandise where the variety of goods is great, the orders are small and fluctuating, and consignments are made to many firms and individuals. As a result, both the tempo and efficiency of the world's business were increased.

The differentiation of liner and tramp services was accelerated by the coming of the steamship. Experience soon deinonstrated that steam-ships could be adapted more readily than the sailing vessels to the varying needs of commodities and trades. Most bulky commodities, especially if they are not perishable, do not call for rapid transport or regular sailings. Lost cost is the one essential. Thus, when once slow but capacious steel steamships demonstrated that they could carry bulky goods at lower cost than the sailing clippers, the cargo vessels, called tramp steamers, became familiar sights in many ports and trades.[31] When once the steamship had demonstrated its worth, the organization of ocean transport changed rapidly. Quarters and food for the crews improved in response to public interest. Safety regulations and devices were introduced. Passenger services provided clean staterooms and better food. Steamship lines like Cunard and Hamburg-American became household words in Europe and America. Moreover, in much the same way and for mučh the same reasons as indi-vidual railway lines were consolidated into great railway systems like Pennsylvania or Southern Pacific, so steamship lines were amalgamated into great combines, as for example, the Peninsula and Oriental and the Royal Mail. In this same period, international banking and credit systems spread into most parts of the world. In short, the world order of 1914 came into existence.

## GROWTH OF THE WORLD'S STEAM MERCHANT FLEET

By 1913, the last year preceding the outbreak of World War I, the world acquired a good fleet of steam-driven merchant vessels (*Table 4*). The period from 1850 to 1870 marked beginnings with only four countries —United Kingdom, France, the Netherlands, and United States—covered by the statistics. By 1880, all the present maritime countries are in the record, but the United Kingdom already had outdistanced the field. In the twenty years up to the end of 1913, the world added 25,000,000 tons of steam shipping to its sea lanes. Of this, about two-thirds were built in British yards, with half the total for British order. The 700,000 tons net built in 1894 look small in comparison with the average of 1,500,000 tons a year in the decade from 1904 to 1913, or with the 2,000,000 tons net which came off the ways in 1913.[32]

| Country | Tons Net | Per Cent |
|---|---|---|
| British Empire | | |
| United Kingdom | 11,538,000 | 44.4 |
| Dominions and Colonies | 902,000 | 3.5 |
| Sub Total | 12,440,000 | 47.9 |
| Germany | 3,096,000 | 11.9 |
| *United States | 1,195,000 | 4.6 |
| Norway | 1,153,000 | 4.4 |
| France | 1,098,000 | 4.2 |
| Japan | 1,048,000 | 4.0 |
| Netherlands | 910,000 | 3.5 |
| Italy | 871,000 | 3.4 |
| Other Countries | 4,179,000 | 16.1 |
| Total | 25,990,000 | 100.0 |

4. TONNAGE OF STEAM VESSELS OWNED BY PRINCIPAL MARITIME COUNTRIES ON JUNE 30, 1914.

Source: R. H. Thornton, *British Shipping* (Cambridge, 1939).
* U.S. figures do not include vessels engaged in trade on the northern lakes (1,693,000 T.). The steam tonnage of Norway, Sweden, and Denmark totaled 2,185,000 tons net or 8.4 per cent of the world's steam tonnage.

The figures of growth are impressive in themselves, but become much more so when it is remembered that the world shipping was undergoing a continuing process of improvements. Speeds increased, and more voyages could be made in a given interval of time than before. The carrying capacity of vessels increased in geometric rather than arithmetic ratio to increases in length, beam, and draft. Shipping became more efficient as engineering skill developed and thus in many countries kept apace of the demands associated with economic expansion.

The familiar rapid expansion in Germany after 1870 is shown by the growth of tonnage under the German Flag. The German merchant marine attained second place by 1890 and from then on showed an even greater relative increase than the United Kingdom. This growth was in harmony with the rapid addition of manufacture to Germany's economy, to her increasing efforts in promoting overseas trade, and to her access to frontage on the Narrow Seas.

In the case of the United States, Table 4 does not show the full story of steam merchant tonnage but it does suggest certain geographic qualities of this country. The overseas steam tonnage of the United States grew slowly in the decades under survey. The coastwise shipping, however, grew rapidly as did the shipping on the Great Lakes. For its overseas trade the United States leaned on foreign shipping, but under our law only vessels built in the United States yards and flying the stars and stripes can engage in our coastwise shipping. Moreover, because of the huge size of this country and our enormous ocean frontage, our coastwise business should be compared to that of Western Europe rather than to that of any individual country. The point involved is not the length of coastline but rather the huge productive area tributary to the coasts. When once the Panama Canal was opened, the significance of this matter was increased enormously.

WORLD SHIPPING IN 1914

At the end of the century of general peace from 1815 to 1914, and after less than a half century of steamship service, the world's overseas tonnage, by flags, was distributed as shown in Table 4.

The dominance of European flags in 1914 just before World War I is apparent, for of the countries listed, only two—the United States and Japan—lie outside Europe. Within Europe the dominance of the countries facing the Narrow Seas is spectacular. Sixty-four per cent of the world's seagoing tonnage was directed from a maritime area including the United Kingdom, the Netherlands, France, and Germany. In view of the high importance of shipping to all nations, this was one of the most amazing localizations which have appeared in the world's economy. The present area is even smaller because the Iron Curtain shuts out East Germany. Furthermore, the leadership of Atlantic Europe is shown by the fact that the nearby Scandinavian countries—Norway, Sweden, and Denmark—together had 2,180,000 tons net or 8.4 per cent of the world's steam tonnage.

The dominance of Europe's maritime countries in overseas shipping was paralleled by leadership in world trade and manufacture. The maritime area is the western or seaboard section of the European Manufacturing Belt. This belt is the most densely peopled large area in Europe and has a corresponding position in agriculture. From the eyes of the world in 1914, this densely peopled belt of Europe, with its triple economy of trade, manufacture, and agriculture, was a great market for surplus products from many countries and was a source of manufactured goods for the same countries. Viewed thus, it was a leading space-area among the world's regions. Politically, linguistically, and culturally, however, Western Europe was a much-divided house with Britain on the front porch, Germany in the ultra-modern kitchen, and France in the parlor.

From its front porch position, Britain traded with all the nations. Its merchant fleet represented 44.4 per cent of the world's steam tonnage and 93 per cent of the Empire's shipping. In terms of ships, this great tonnage was made up of 8,855 small craft plying the coasting trades, and 3,747 ocean-going vessels representing 10,170,000 tons of the total 11,273,000 tons under the flag of the United Kingdom. These 3,747 relatively big vessels represented Britain's success in time of peace, for, in general, big vessels are economical vessels. They also, as World War I proved, constituted Britain's danger in time of war. In the early months of Germany's submarine warfare, her submarines sunk mainly little vessels in the North Sea. Such losses had but little bearing on Britain's supply line. But when, after February of 1917, Germany's submarines ventured into deep water and sank big vessels in alarming numbers, the submarine campaign became the most vital aspect of the war.[33]


vi   *World Pattern of 1914*

In the constructive decades between 1870 and 1914 the world pattern of 1914 was established. Emigration from Europe to the New World attained a momentum of a million or more a year. Huge surpluses of grain, lard, meat, hides and skins, and wool became available. United States forests produced huge quantities of white and yellow pine that were used as structural timber in both domestic and overseas markets. Tropical lands contributed increasing amounts of coffee, rubber, jute, cabinet woods, and a host of other things. Of minerals, the world produced more in the thirty years from 1880 to 1910, than in all previous time. Large-scale manufacture penetrated deeply into Europe and our own Middle West.

In four realms of activity the world's pattern changed significantly between 1870 and 1914. The steamship introduced regularity of flow in cargo movements between Europe and the major areas of commerce. This meant that commodities could be purchased for delivery at a specified time. Merchants and manufacturers were relieved of the necessity of buying and holding large stocks of raw materials long in advance of use. Hence, savings resulted both in the amount of working capital needed and in insurance charges. Furthermore, the penetration of railways into the interior from the ports increased the area to which imports could go and from which exports could come. Bigger business in bigger areas helped to lower the price of commodities. Lowered prices meant more customers, and the total area of the Commercial World increased, but largely with motivation from the North Atlantic Arena.

All this expansion of trade meant new railways and new demands for rails and rolling stocks. In the process of railway construction many mineral deposits were discovered and, in many cases, new mines opened. Settlement bred construction as well as production and manufacturing, and commerce profited thereby. Profits created great wealth and international credits, and, for the first time, financial structures became worldwide in scope and function.

Emigration from Europe during this period relieved pressure on employment there, and employment also was to be had in ever-growing quantity in Europe's industrial and commercial centers. The world's outlook became increasingly commercial and increasingly optimistic. The economic and social values of commerce became so clear that by the turn of the century many leaders of thought argued war on a large scale to be unlikely if not impossible. Such ideas probably were more common in the United States and other parts of the world than in Europe where the heritage of language barrier (Phelps' legend for his map of linquistic divisions carries forty-nine language divisions), religious prejudices, nationalistic ideals, and other social conflicts generated trends toward war rather than peace.

By 1870, railway transportation had become sufficiently developed and widespread to demonstrate its significance. The big developments had come in Europe and the United States. In the former, railways had reached the capitals and leading cities, and some of the international services had been inaugurated. In the latter a network of lines had been built in the eastern half of the country, and in 1869 the first transcontinental line to the Pacific had been completed. In both Europe and the United States, well-integrated through services had yet to come. However, in the following decades the numerous individual lines were organized into great systems, and through services and schedules became possible. Before 1870 the developments in rail transport had been in the physical aspects of engineering. Bridges, tunnels, horseshoe curves, and multiplicity of adjustments to terrain and drainage commanded the thought of the time. After that date spectacular advances appeared in the economic aspects of engineering, that is, in administration and management. Such efforts in Western Europe and the United States demonstrated that the organization of railway lines into great systems could be so adjusted in time and space as to produce efficient operation and financial benefits in the national economy.

As compared with the map of 1878, the political map of 1914 shows some political changes with commercial implications. Of the four huge national units of 1878, the partition of Africa by European powers added enough territory to the French Empire to make the color for French possessions conspicuous on the political map. To a less extent, Germany, Italy, Belgium, and Portugal had acquired large holdings in Africa. All this expansion represented the conviction that colonies were desirable in terms of political power and commercial gain.

The success of the British free trade policy in the middle of the nineteenth century almost had brought the world to a free trade basis. After 1870, however, industry developed rapidly in Germany and the United States, and these countries, especially the former, competed with Britain in the world's trade. Some writers, therefore, recognize the decades from 1870 to 1914 as a period of competition, with increasing use of tariffs, instead of a period of free trade. British political and especially commercial influence was so widespread, however, that British policy either predominated, or definitely influenced, trade activities in all parts of the world. Nevertheless, belief in the values of colonial expansion was strong enough to create a great interest in colonies on the part of European nations.

Before 1914 the United States acquired additional territory. The Hawaiian Islands had been annexed in 1898. In 1898 American occupation replaced Spanish rule in the Philippines and Puerto Rico, and Cuba was freed from Spain by American arms. The Panama Canal project brought the Canal Zone under the American flag and greatly enhanced the interest and influence of the United States in the Gulf and Caribbean areas. Our Caribbean relations were growing steadily, for example, in the banana industry and the services of the "Great White Fleet" which were essential to the trade in this fruit and other tropical products.

The rise of American influence was accompanied by a decline in the British position and by a growing understanding of Anglo-American relations in the Atlantic. This understanding, climaxed in 1901 when Britain abandoned its naval bases in the Lesser Antilles, has been called the Atlantic System.[34] It represents a rational working agreement by the two English speaking powers.

The dominance of the United States in the "American Mediterranean" is in harmony with the juxtaposition of middle latitude and humid tropical lands. In this respect, as has been stated previously, the United

States is unlike Europe. The latter lies far from productive tropical lands, whereas the fertile islands and peninsulas about the Gulf of Mexico and the Caribbean lie close to the southern border of the United States. The development of manufacturing in the United States, with the need of raw materials and its output of finished products, is another reason for the great influence of the United States in the Caribbean. In 1914, the Chinese Republic still held sway over much of the vast territory held by the Chinese Empire of 1878. Japan, however, had taken Korea in the war with China in 1895, and part of Sakhalin and Manchuria in the Russo-Japan War of 1904–1905. By this time, as we shall see subsequently, Japan possessed an active merchant marine and navy, a growing foreign trade, and a welling ambition to become a world power.

In southeastern Asia, France had increased the area included in French Indochina; Burma and the Malay States under Britain had grown in area; the Dutch, British, and Germans had divided New Guinea; and as has been said, the United States was established in the Philippines. Rubber culture had been grafted onto the plantation industry of the Dutch East Indies and British Malaya. Tin mining was a major activity in both these areas. Subsequently, rubber and tin in the Dutch possessions gave the Netherlands bargaining power with the Allies in World War I.

In the Southern Hemisphere, British influence now dominated most of the southern part of Africa. Gold and diamonds created value, if not bulk, to South African exports. The agricultural and pastoral economy of Australia had become organized in much its present form. South American countries were well established politically. Chilean nitrates; Argentine grain, wool, hides and skins, and tanning materials; and Brazilian coffee, sugar, and rubber were moving into the world's markets in very considerable amounts. In most of these areas and these trades the United Kingdom was the major factor, and thus a presentation of Britain's shipping and trade in 1913 will show the nature of the Commercial World at the outbreak of World War I.

VII  *Problems and Controls of Shipping During World War I*

Shipping was one of the most outstanding issues of World War I. This was in harmony with the high importance of shipping in the long period of peace preceding the war.[35] Western and Central Europe had become the active heart of the Commercial World. To this area ships carried the raw materials and other exports from farming, grazing, and mining of other areas in all parts of the world. In return, they carried the output of European factories to all countries, and to some countries, as for example, Italy and Argentina, they carried coal. In simplest terms, this flow of goods to and from Western and Central Europe was the world order in 1914. To a high degree all other considerations were ancillary to this commercial structure.

In terms of ownership and control, the shipping business was a European institution. Forty-five per cent of the steam vessels of the world flew the flag of the United Kingdom, and 90 per cent of the total was controlled by European nations. Germany, with 12 per cent of the total, was Britain's only serious rival. As Germany never demonstrated ability to compete in the tramp traffic, the rivalry between these two leaders was intense in the liner traffic. This rivalry was most acute in the North Atlantic trade. The United States was involved both because it produced great quantities of exports destined for Europe and because it was the recipient of the greatest flow of emigrants from Europe. This emigrant traffic was so vital to the shipping companies operating in the North Atlantic that it became the outstanding issue in the British-German rivalry.

The rules by which the North Atlantic traffic was carried on were established in a conference of participating shipping companies. In this conference the chairman of Cunard was the spokesman for British interests and the chairman of the Hamburg-American performed the same function for the German interests (the Dutch and Belgian interests were integrated into the German sphere by membership in what virtually was a German mercantile shipping union—the famous N.D.L.V.). During 1912 and 1913 the British and German interests could not reach a working agreement, and thus by January, 1914, they practically were at war. The significance of this situation on subsequent events often is overlooked by students of international relations.

In order to show the serious situation in shipping which confronted the Allies during World War I, the distribution of world shipping by the belligerents and neutrals at the outbreak of the war is shown in the accompanying Table 5. The table shows that the Allies controlled about 65 per cent of the world's shipping, the neutrals about 20 per cent, and the Central Powers about 15 per cent.

The war opened in a period when the world was over-supplied with shipping. There were more ships than cargoes, and marine rates were so low that shipping was unprofitable. This surplus of shipping was so well known that the idea lingered in men's minds long after the situation had been reversed, namely, when there were more cargoes than ships. This in itself tended to hold back the control of shipping which subsequently became necessary.

5. WORLD SHIPPING AT THE END OF 1913.

| Country | Million Tons Net | Per Cent |
|---|---|---|
| British Empire | 12.4 | 48 |
| Allied Countries* | 4.4 | 17 |
| United States and Other Am. Republics** | 1.7 | 7 |
| Other Neutrals | 3.7 | 14 |
| Germany, Austria–Hungary, and Turkey | 3.8 | 14 |
| Total | 26.0 | 100 |

Source: Memorandum to H. Harrison Robson, Director of Emergency Shipping, U.S. Marine Commission, World War II, from Charles C. Colby, who was Special Expert, Commodity Section, Division of Planning and Statistics, United States Shipping Board, World War I.
* France, Russia, Italy, Belgium, Portugal, Rumania, Greece, Japan, and China.
** Does not include American shipping on the Great Lakes.

## CAUSES OF SHIPPING SHORTAGE

The early days of the war paralyzed trade and shipping. The uncertainty of the nature and duration of the conflict discouraged trade. Early losses from German raiders kept ships in port and made it difficult to get insurance on ships and cargoes. Exporters kept their goods at home rather than face unknown risks. Then came the great German drive toward Calais and the realization that the war was to be a war of materials. Overnight an overwhelming demand for commodities arose. This demand continued through the war, and, in large measure, was met by the control of and, in time, the skillful operation of shipping. In order to focus attention on the cause and control rather than chronology, the major factors contributing to the shortage of shipping will be reviewed briefly.

Number one was the withdrawal of the shipping of the Central Powers. It will be remembered that they controlled about 15 per cent of world shipping. Probably less than half of this was able to reach home ports at the outbreak of the war. About 1,500,000 tons net of the shipping was laid up in ports of the United States. Until our entry into the war this shipping was inactive and thus was a total loss as far as trade was concerned.

Next came the withdrawal of Allied shipping for war purposes. As soon as the Allies realized they were confronted with a long war, large amounts of shipping were withdrawn for direct or auxiliary war service. This reduced the amount of shipping available for carrying commodities.

Another cause of a shortage of shipping was wasteful use of requisitioned ships. For many months after the outbreak of the war British shipping interests complained bitterly of the way in which the requisitioned ships were employed. Some ships were held for weeks before being put into service. Others were allocated to service for which they were not suited. Still others were held up by orders from incompetent amateurs who had moved into the new agencies of control. In time (Dec., 1916) this situation was cleared in Britain by the creation of a Ministry of Shipping under Sir Joseph Maclay, a shrewd, able, and experienced shipowner. He shortly brought order out of chaos, and his success with British shipping led to the establishment of the Allied Maritime Transport Council made up of delegates from each of the Allies. All Allied merchant shipping directly connected with the war was pooled under the direction of this council.

Increased demand for commodities also added to the scarcity of shipping. The demand for food and other commodities was so great that it exceeded the diminished tonnage available for the movement of goods. Eventually this led to a rigid control of imports and exports, to the end that the essential commodities should be available and that shipping should not be used in carrying unessential commodities. This important way of saving tonnage will be told more specifically in our review of the shipping and trade of the United States.

The slow start of shipbuilding programs seriously handicapped the war effort. The low state of the shipping industry before the war, the failure of the British to realize the length and nature of the war, and the preoccupation of the leaders of the country with emergency matters delayed the development of a shipbuilding program. This delay nearly lost the war, and thus it was surprising to witness a similar delay in World War II.

War seriously interfered with the flow of goods to and from Europe. This meant that many countries had to look to the United States, Japan, or elsewhere for markets for their produce or for manufactured articles. It took much time and effort to set up the new routing, and in many cases the new routing called for more shipping than the normal routing. At the outset, moreover, much of the new routing was directed by inexperienced men, and delays and difficulties were forthcoming.

Peacetime trade moves under an international system of insurance and finance. Both matters are highly complex in their operation, and both tend to be seriously interrupted or paralyzed by war. It took time for governmental action to replace these peacetime functions.

Germany's war on shipping, especially British shipping, contributed enormously to the stringency of shipping. The attack divides into three phases. The first phase consisted of the attacks of German cruisers on British shipping. It ended in December of 1914 with a loss of about 150,000 tons net. The second phase was characterized by the gradual development of the German submarine into a vessel capable of operating on the ocean trade routes. Action in this experimental stage largely was confined to the North Sea and to small vessels. Many ships were sunk, but the total in terms of shipping was less than 150,000 tons net. The third phase was made up of Germany's supreme attempt to destroy the sea communications of the Allies. It went forward with alarming success for by the end of August, 1917, the Allies had lost 4,000,000 tons net of shipping, and Norway had lost 500,000 tons. In fact, Germany had destroyed about 5,000,000 tons net of shipping or 20 per cent of the world's shipping. This unrestricted war on shipping brought the United States into the conflict, and for our purposes transfers the field of action to this country.

## UNITED STATES TRADE AND SHIPPING DURING THE WAR

In 1914 the United States had about 4.6 per cent of the world's shipping, or an amount similar to that owned by Norway or France. Most of our tonnage was employed in coastwise trade and in a few special trades. For the most part, we were content to see our large foreign trade move in the bottoms of other nations. For a half century we had been engaged in settling and developing our great middle western and western territories and we displayed an amazing ignorance of shipping questions. At the outbreak of the war we had little or no idea how profoundly the conflict would affect our trade. It was only when marine rates climbed to the highest point in history in the early months of 1915 that we turned our attention to shipping. By this time some American shipyards had taken orders from Britain and Norway, and a revival of this industry was under way.

The first evidence of our forthcoming interest in shipping was the

Ship Registration Act passed within three weeks after the war began (Aug. 18, 1914). This permitted ships built in foreign countries to register under the American flag. Up to July, 1915, shipping to the amount of 523,000 gross tons had been registered. Most of this shipping was owned by Standard Oil Company of New Jersey, the United Fruit Company, the U.S. Steel Products Company, or other American concerns which owned tonnage registered under the British Flag. Such transfers in no way added to the carrying performance of these vessels. It is a curious fact that losses by sale following the passage of the La Follette Seamen's Act in March of 1915, exceeded the gains from transfer under the earlier act. Most of the sales were to Japan, which suggests that Japanese interests saw the great profits to be made in shipping earlier than did some American shipping concerns.

In 1915, the American press pointed out the fact that British requisitioned shipping was carrying commodities to Britain at much lower rates than unrequisitioned shipping was moving the same classes of goods to the United States. To remedy this situation President Wilson tried to pass a bill through Congress authorizing the expenditure of $25,000,000 to purchase ships for American use. Business and popular opinion were against the proposition, and it failed to pass in spite of a strong Democratic majority in Congress. Later, Mr. McAdoo advocated the construction of 500,000 tons of shipping. This highly constructive and forward looking proposal met the same fate as the President's bill.

## CREATION OF THE SHIPPING BOARD

Ships were growing scarcer, however, and shipping rates higher. Much agitation followed, and finally in September, 1916, Congress passed a bill creating a Shipping Board. More delays followed, and the Board did not become active until June, 1917, more than two months after the United States entered the war. In the following months the country as a whole became as strong in its demands for miracles of action, as previously it had been in its opposition to action on the part of the Administration. This tendency to ignore an emergency as it approaches and then overemphasize the need of action when once the emergency has arrived apparently is one of the conditions which needs correction in our democratic form of government.

The problem of creating an effective Shipping Board was nearly unsolvable. We had many able men but few of them knew the highly technical business of building and operating ships. These two phases of the shipping industry, moreover, are highly unlike. Building ships is a matter of design and construction. Operating ships is a matter of commodities, trade routes, and regions. The former probably is more quickly learned than the latter. In large measure, both types of experience and mentality were not among our national assets.

The development of the Shipping Board and the Emergency Fleet Corporation advanced through three periods. The first was the period of the statesman in which the membership of the board included a lawyer, a lumberman, a railroad administrator, and a shipping executive. The second brought naval and army engineers into the picture. They were able men but accustomed to a slow-moving routine performance. The third period introduced men long experienced in administration into the shipping puzzle. Hurley, Piez, Schwab, and others took charge and, building on what had been done by the others, finally brought order into the picture.

## STEPS IN THE ACTION OF THE BOARD

The problem of the Shipping Board was to provide shipping for all the multiplicity of war demands. The solution of the problem called for many lines of action among which the following were outstanding.

Ships were requisitioned for foreign orders. It will be remembered that American shipyards had taken orders for delivery to Britain, Norway and other countries. These vessels were promptly requisitioned by the Board.

Foreign vessels were admitted to American coastwise trades. Under our long-term policy foreign vessels cannot operate in our coastwise and intercoastal trades. Early in the war when overseas shipping rates climbed to all-time highs, about 80 per cent of the vessels engaged in our coastwise trade abandoned their normal business and went into overseas trade where the profits were greater. This threw an extra load on our railways and increased the congestion which plagued these carriers. As a result, for the only time in our history, our coastwise trades were opened to foreign flags.

The next move was to take over German shipping. It will be remembered that when the United States entered the war, nearly a million and a half tons of German shipping were tied up in our ports. The Shipping Board promptly took over this shipping and put it into service on the overseas lanes.

Ships of neutral nations plying to American ports could not take on fuel for their next voyage without permission of the Shipping Authorities. Bunker was refused unless the neutral vessel agreed to return to the United States. In this way (copied from British experience), many neutral ships were tied down to fixed routes and thus were made to contribute to the solution of our shipping problem.

In some cases the Shipping Board exchanged vessels with France. The Board took over French vessels not well suited to running the submarine gauntlet but reasonably well suited to our coastwise trade. In return the Board gave ships well adapted to the North Atlantic run.

The major business of the Shipping Board soon became the building of ships. To this end it established the Emergency Fleet Corporation with headquarters in Philadelphia. The story of this famous organization is the best known part of the work of the Shipping Board. The program advanced through the slow stages of experimentation with wooden, concrete, and other types of vessels. Finally it settled on a small steel vessel, each vessel exactly like the others. Thus came into being for the first time in shipping history an approach to the assembled ship—a practice in harmony with American experience in manufacturing. Under this plan, ships were launched in about twenty-seven days from the laying of the keel. The program gained momentum and, although the war ended before it reached its climax, it demonstrated that American yards could turn out ships faster than the submarine could sink them.

In launching their unrestricted campaign against shipping, the Germans wagered that the United States could not bring shipbuilding to the stage of quantity production. In doing this they were betting against the essential genius of a nation. Such wagering proved hazardous then, and it is hoped that it will prove equally hazardous in other times of emergency.

Upon the entry of the United States into the war, Congress promptly gave the President inclusive powers for the control of our industry and commerce. This control was delegated to several boards or administrations created for special purposes. In terms of commerce the central agency became the War Trade Board—a board made up of representatives from several government departments and administrations. Among other things, the War Trade Board turned its attention to the big question of how to direct and control our foreign trade to meet the needs of the war program and the civilian population. Planning in terms of exports was carried on by a group of the War Trade Board; whereas the import program originated in, and was developed by, the Division of Planning and Statistics of the Shipping Board. The original group in the War Trade Board did not make a success of their work, and thus in June of 1918 Messrs. Edwin F. Gay and Henry S. Dennison, who had made a notable success of the Division of Planning and Statistics of the Shipping Board, were asked to take over the planning group in the War Trade Board. At this time, therefore, part of the Shipping Board personnel was transferred to the planning group of the War Trade Board. Somewhat before this time Mr. Gay had been named as the Shipping Board's representative on the War Trade Board.

The legal framework under which our imports were brought under control was a proclamation by President Wilson in November of 1917. Subsequently, the work of planning was allocated to Mr. Gay's division in the Shipping Board but the actual decisions were made by the War Trade Board. Mr. Gay, as a member of this board, presented for the board's deliberations the recommendation of his Shipping Board division.

Control of our import trade was considered necessary for several reasons. The first idea was to guarantee the presence in this country of the commodities needed by the wartime industries, the army and navy, and the civilian population. The second idea was to save shipping by lifting these essential commodities in the nearest areas where they could be found, thus saving time and distance. The third idea was to see that no shipping space was occupied by unessentials. Luxuries were in great demand and could pay higher freight rates than many of the essentials. The fourth idea was to save shipping space by expert loading and to save time by better ship performance. All these things were accomplished, and by mid-summer of 1918 it became evident that there were 1,200,000 dead-weight tons of shipping under the American flag in excess of the amount needed to lift the essential commodities. The significance of the situation was emphasized by the fact that the Secretary of War had asked the Allied Maritime Transport Council for the loan of 1,800,000 dead-weight tons of shipping to complete the movement of our eighty-division army to France. As the loan of this shipping seriously jeopardized the flow of foods and supplies to the Allies, the importance of this program of controlled imports becomes clear.

The progress of the plan by which the imports of the country were brought under control is a long and technical story. For the present purpose it will be sufficient to sketch its major outlines. At the outset a preliminary survey was made of the entire list of imports into the country. This survey attempted to classify the imports on the basis of need. Of some commodities, such as rubber and tin, we needed all we could get. Of other commodities we needed none at all; that is, some commodities are not essential in wartime. Between these two extremes were many commodities of which we needed some, but not as much, as we imported in peacetime. We needed, for example, great quantities of the types of wool out of which clothing is made, but obviously we could get along without carpet wool. Somewhat the same is true of a large part of our imports. Of some goods, moreover, we had large stocks in the country, of others we had not even enough for immediate use.

When once the initial survey was completed, men were hired to specialize in each of the major commodities involved in the program. These "special experts," as they were called, then developed a plan for the control of the commodities with which they were concerned. Subsequently their tentative programs were criticized by men from the industry or industries which would be affected by the proposed restrictions. In many cases a hearing resulted in considerable revision of a program. In some cases the men from the industries were able to show that a larger quantity of a commodity was required than the plan estimated. In other cases they recommended restrictions more drastic than those carried in the plan. When the plan was ready, it was submitted to the War Trade Board and, if approved, went into effect.

As the work progressed it became evident that each major region of the world was a separate story. If the distance from the United States to a given region was long, the amount of dead-weight shipping in continuous service needed to lift a specified tonnage was greater than that required to lift the same tonnage from a nearby region. Australia is so far away that shipping could not be allocated to lift their wheat even though their warehouses were jammed with grain, and the Allies needed it desperately.

Different commodities stow differently. That is, it takes more ship space to stow a hundred tons of feathers than it does to stow a hundred tons of steel rails. This means that the stowage factor of every important commodity had to be ascertained and then weighed into the calculations. Only in this way could a reliable estimate be secured as to how much shipping in continuous service would be needed to lift the desired goods from a particular trade region.

Still another matter of importance in estimating the shipping requirements of our trade with each region was the question of how much could be stowed in a given ship. Under the stress of wartime demands, notable improvements in methods of stowing were developed. Bulk wheat, for example, always had been shipped with a layer of bagged wheat on the top to keep the bulk grain from shifting in a storm. The stevedores learned ways of filling the hold so full that the grain could not shift. This meant more grain delivered by each ship and thus the saving of shipping space.

As the individual programs went into effect, it became necessary to develop a complex monthly balance sheet. This sheet showed at the end of each month the progress made in bringing the essential commodities into the country from each major region, and also showed whether there was an excess or deficiency of shipping in the several trades. The twelve regions of major concern were: 1] East Asia, 2] East Indies, 3] British India, 4] Australia, 5] Hawaii, 6] Amazon, 7] La Plata, 8] West Coast of South America, 9] Caribbean, 10] West Indies, 11] Mexican Gulf, 12] Central Brazil. With the exception of Western Europe these areas are still the areas of major international concern to us.

Gradually the force of the import restrictions began to show in the balance sheet. It became necessary to allocate more shipping to some trades, whereas in others the sheet showed that there was more shipping than needed. The latter was true especially in the East Asian and Caribbean regions, and gradually it became evident that shipping could be withdrawn from those regions and allocated to the North Atlantic run. If the war had continued, the notable saving of shipping which came about through the import restrictions and the control of shipping would have become an increasing factor in the shipping situation.

VIII  *Transport and Financial Patterns of World War I*

World War I dislocated the trade, transportation, and finance patterns, first of Europe and then of the rest of the world. As J. Russell Smith wrote in 1918, "Long indeed will be the search to find the people, even the man, whose daily life has not been changed in some respect by the trade disturbances arising from this war. The world trade of 1914 is no more."[36] He points out that "within two months after the war had started 10 per cent of Buenos Aires clerks had been dismissed from their position"; that in Central America thousands of bunches of bananas were thrown into the sea because there were no ships to carry them; that Italy, Greece, Argentina, and many other countries soon suffered from a rapid decline in their imports of coal; and that wool, wheat, and other products glutted the ports of Australia and New Zealand.

Many of the dislocations of trade during the world war were only interruptions. The customary flow began again after the blockade was ended. Others were more serious, and either brought about changes in the origin or destination of the movement of commodities or left permanent dislocations in international trade. The matter may be illustrated by some of the more serious changes in trade brought about by World War I.

Before the war, Germany exported chemicals, dyes, and drugs to almost every country and had an enormous trade with the United Kingdom, France, the United States, and the other major countries. German chemistry and German chemical industries not only were the standard of comparison but the source of leadership and supply. This and other German trade was interrupted in the early days of the war by the Allied blockade and declined almost to the vanishing point as the blockade increased in effectiveness. This meant that chemical dyes and drugs of many kinds became acutely short in most markets. Under the drive of necessity, the chemical industries of other countries met this challenge, and by the end of the war a momentum had been gained in Britain, France, and America which cut permanently into Germany's former supremacy in the chemical field. This is only one illustration of the continuing penalty paid by Germany for her determination to be the supreme military power in Europe.

The grain trade of Europe furnishes another type of illustration of war dislocations. It also illustrates the power of relative nearness in world affairs. The countries of Western Europe by 1914 had become heavy importers of foods; in fact, "From Norway clear around to Greece, inclusive, no country produced all of its own bread or meat."[37] In addition, large quantities of corn, oil-coke, and meal were imported into some of these countries for stock feed. The war stopped or modified each of the six great flows which supplied grain to Western Europe, and demonstrated the commerical power of the North Atlantic Arena. The Germans promptly closed the Baltic and thus ended the movement of grain from Russia via that route. Turkey's entrance into the war on the side of the Central Powers shut off the export of grain via the Black Sea from South Russia, Rumania, and Bulgaria. This Black Sea trade had been the largest export flow of grain in the world. In peacetime ship management, this trade was highly important because it served as return cargo to Britain for vessels which on the outward voyage had carried coal to Italy, Greece, or Suez. Because of the political, social, and economic changes in Russia the Russian part of the trade never recovered its former size and importance. Of the other four sources of European grain imports, three—Argentina, Australia, and

India—were so far away that precious shipping could not be used on such long voyages. This threw upon the much nearer countries of Canada and the United States the problem of supplying the Allies with grain and flour and accounts for "wheatless days" in the United States and Canada, whereas the ports of Argentina and Australia were jammed with grain. Fortunately, the 1914 and 1915 wheat crops in North America were each the largest on record. The large demands and high price during the next three years led to a great increase in acreage, some of it on land unsuited, in the long run, for cultivation. As a result much of this land was laid waste by the high winds of the dry years which followed the war. Much the same shortage of grain in Western Europe existed in World War II, and again the enormous crops in the United States and Canada during the war years solved the situation.

World War I also effected the world's cotton trade, both during and after the war. During the temporary paralysis of trade which characterized the early months of the war, the exceedingly low price of raw cotton brought poverty and want to our Cotton Belt and led to a "buy a bale" movement to help remedy the distress. Subsequently the demand increased rapidly, and the South recovered. British exports of cotton goods declined as the war progressed, and shipping services were curtailed. Well-organized efforts led to a large increase of cotton manufacture in India and Japan, and these countries took over much of the Oriental trade. By 1917, cotton spinning had become the most prosperous industry in Japan, and Japanese cotton goods replaced British cotton in Australasia and South America.[38] After the war, though their cotton trade revived, the British never regained the dominant position in the cotton trade which they enjoyed before 1914. Like Germany, Britain paid a high price for its participation in World War I.

The foregoing illustrations only suggest the varied and far-reaching effects of a world war. The total effect probably is not known and certainly is not appreciated by many. The war not only dislocated world trade but it upset men's confidence in the world organization of trade and finance which had come into existence in the century of progress following the Napoleonic Wars.

The shortage of shipping, the inability to import the necessities of life, and the tragic losses as export commodities piled up in ports and warehouses led many nations to try for self-sufficiency during and after the war. They saw the risk of depending upon distant countries for essentials. As a result a wave of economic nationalism swept over the world. Reduced to essentials, this desire to be as independent of other nations as possible represented disillusionment regarding the ability of Western Europe to regain and hold the leadership in world trade which it held before 1914. This distrust was logical even though it surprised and aggravated Britain and the other nations of Western Europe. The United States shared in the distrust and with its Hawley-Smoot tariff act of 1930 showed its intent to live within its borders as much as possible. This high tariff, however, did not take into account certain remarkable changes in the American scene occasioned or accelerated by the war.

Before 1914 manufacturing had been on the increase in the United States both in amount and diversity. In the early months of the war, after it became clear that the war was to be a war of materials, manufactures in this country expanded rapidly under a flood of European orders. As J. Russell Smith points out "steamships and cables could not work fast enough at placing contracts for guns and shells, motor trucks, barbed wire, and explosives in the United States".[39] Later, huge orders for shipping were placed in American shipyards. In addition, importers in South America and other countries placed orders in the United States for goods which they no longer could get from Europe. Manufacturing facilities in this country were expanded, and new types of industry introduced. Skill was acquired; profits made. In short, manufacture gained momentum which, based on the huge power, raw material, and human resources of the United States, became a matter of world-wide implications.

Until the United States entered the war, finance was a major problem of the Allies. Both Britain and France were hard put to raise the funds to pay for the goods ordered from the United States and other countries. When the United States joined the Allies this financial problem largely disappeared. As Sir Arthur Salter puts it, "apart altogether from the reinforcement that she thus brought to the military forces, her accession entirely altered the whole character of the economic problem. Finance as a fundamental factor in the Allied position disappeared".[40] For the duration of the war this was true, but in the postwar years, finance became a matter of the gravest concern. What few in Europe or the United States realized at the time was that the financial dominance of Europe in world affairs had ended. The United States not only entered the war but became a new financial center in the world pattern. Never again could the producing area of the world look exclusively to Europe for markets, for credit, for manufactures, and for leadership. The present structure of the North Atlantic Arena had taken shape.

Again and again in postwar publications one meets the statement that the United States became a creditor nation. Such a statement only takes on significance for most people when it is placed in its areal perspective. Finance was the agent but the geography of resources was the cause. The New World, like a young stallion, had entered the world herd. The older stallions welcomed its help in beating off the wartime wolves, but were not ready to recognize that a new leadership was in the making. Nor did the United States realize the implications and the responsibilities of its new power. After the war the United States wanted to return to "normalcy." Its efforts in this direction were short-lived and futile because the United States was destined for a new era, not only in the North Atlantic Arena but in global dimensions.

# 7

# Lower Rhine in the Atlantic Arena

## I  *Ports and Seaborne Trade of the Narrow Seas*

Although the Atlantic coastline of Europe is characterized by bays, seas, channels, peninsulas, and offshore islands, only a few of the harbors of this long waterfront have become ports of major significance. During the centuries of development the slow processes of differentiation operated in favor of some harbors and against others. The selection was generated by the ideas and efforts of men, invited by the degree of accessibility from the sea and the land, influenced by edicts, attitudes, and conflicts of governments, and by a multiplicity of related conditions. In time the major ports of Europe localized along the arm of the Atlantic made up of the English Channel, the Strait of Dover, and the North Sea. As previously stated, for convenience this coastal waterway has been called "the Narrow Seas," and this term is used in this report. This coastal zone today is the most valuable sea frontage in the world; along it are the ports of LeHavre on the mouth of the Seine, London on the Thames, Antwerpen on the Schelde, Rotterdam on the Rhine, Bremen on the Weser, and Hamburg on the Elbe.

As Partsch pointed out at the turn of the century, even in this amazing frontage, the southeastern end of the North Sea, is the outstanding exhibit of major port localization as here have developed in close proximity London, Antwerpen, and Rotterdam.[1] Their combined trade in 1960 exceeded that of any other three ports in the world.

This Narrow Seas waterway has been called the main business street of Western Europe (*Fig. 9*). Naturally frontage on this waterway is highly prized by the nations. As Belgium and the Netherlands occupy the middle strip, they have an importance in Europe out of all proportion to their size. For the same reason they have been battlegrounds for the wars that have devastated this coveted area.

In consideration of the importance of the Narrow Seas frontage of the Atlantic countries of Europe we must again bring to mind the significance of the rivers which empty into this arm of the sea. The commerical contribution of navigation on these rivers is associated with the ports which mark the convergence of river routes and ocean highways. London, the major railway center of Great Britain, stands at the head of deep water navigation on the Thames estuary. Le Havre, on the Seine estuary, is the major Atlantic gateway into the Paris Basin. Antwerpen and Rotterdam occupy favorable positions, the former on the Schelde and the latter on the Rhine. They are now the two leading ports on the Continent. Their business, especially that of Rotterdam on the major commercial channel of the Rhine, concerns the Rhine Valley as far upriver as Basel, the port of Switzerland. Bremen on the Weser and Hamburg on the Elbe formerly handled the foreign trade of large sections of Germany; but at present, especially in the case of Hamburg, the Iron Curtain and associated policies shuts off some of their tributary areas.

Each of the major ports has river and canal connections with its tributary areas. Each network of inland waterways contributes to the economy of Western Europe. Of the rivers involved, the Rhine is the only one that rises in the glaciated Alps and thereby has the advantage of a steadier flow than the others. In addition to its waterways, each of the river ports in question have railway, highway, and airway connections with its service areas, thereby assuring some degree of competition among the several means of transport. The cooperative management of such services to the end that traffic shall move as expeditiously and efficiently as possible is not much farther advanced than in the United States. Probably here lies the responsibility and opportunity for more efficient transportation in the future.

*RHINE COUNTRIES*

As previously stated, five countries—Switzerland, France, West Germany, the Netherlands and Belgium—are known as the Rhine Countries because they are located along the navigable sections of the river. As canals connect the Rhine with most of the inland waterways of these countries, there results a regional unit of waterways on which the flags of each of the five nations may be seen (*Fig. 5*). Moreover, a system of international regulations has gained acceptance so that the flags of many other nations may be seen occasionally on these waterways. However, the five Rhine countries so dominate the traffic that together they constitute the center of interest in Rhine navigation.

*SEABORNE TRADE AT MAJOR NORTH SEA PORTS*

The seaborne trade at the major North Sea ports of the Netherlands, Belgium, and West Germany for the four years 1938, 1959, 1960, and 1961 is shown in Table 6. The table shows that Rotterdam was by far the leading port in each of the years covered by the table. In fact, the

| Port | 1938 | 1959 | 1960 | 1961 |
|------|------|------|------|------|
| Rotterdam | 42 | 70.7 | 83.4 | 90.1 |
| Antwerpen | 24 | 35.2 | 37.0 | 38.6 |
| Hamburg | 26 | 29.1 | 30.8 | 29.7 |
| Bremen | 9 | 14.1 | 15.1 | 14.9 |
| Emden | 8 | 7.1 | 10.3 | 11.5 |
| Amsterdam | 6 | 9.9 | 10.8 | 11.2 |
| Gent (Ghent) | 3 | 2.8 | 2.7 | 2.7 |
| Total | 118 | 168.9 | 190.1 | 198.7 |

6. SEA-BORNE TRADE OF THE MAJOR NORTH SEA PORTS OF THE NETHERLANDS, BELGIUM, AND WEST GERMANY FOR THE FOUR YEARS 1938, 1959, 1960, AND 1961 (IN MILLION TONS OF 1,000 KG.).

Source: *Rotterdam-Europoort,* No. 2 (1963), p. 13.

volume of trade at Rotterdam in each of the last three years of the table exceeds the combined volume of Antwerpen and Hamburg, the next two ports in order of volume.

The total seaborne trade for the seven ports listed in Table 6 increased from 118 tons in 1938 to 168.9 tons in 1959, or by 50.9 million tons of 1000 kg. for the 21 years. This figure shows the gain from the last prewar years to 1959 when trade in Western Europe had recovered after the close of World War II in 1945. Rotterdam had the largest share of the increase as its seaborne trade from 1938 to 1959 increased by 28.7 million tons or by 56.3 per cent of the total increase of 50.9 million tons for the trade of the seven ports. At Antwerpen the increase of 11.2 million tons amounted to 22 per cent of the total increase for the seven ports. The combined percentages for Rotterdam and Antwerpen was 78.3 per cent of the total for the seven ports. From 1959 to 1960 there was an increase of 21.2 million tons of traffic at the seven ports. Of this, the gain was 12.7 million tons at Rotterdam or 59.9 per cent of the total increase, and 1.8 million tons at Antwerpen or 8.4 per cent of the increase.

In the final year covered by the table 45.3 per cent of the total seaborne traffic handled by the seven ports occurred at Rotterdam and 19.4 per cent at Antwerpen. Hence, nearly two-thirds (64.7 per cent) of the 1961 seaborne trade of the seven ports was handled by Rotterdam and Antwerpen. This shows how definitely these two ports in 1961 dominated the seaborne traffic of the continental side of the North Sea.

## TRADE IN BULK GOODS

The volume of trade of the Rhine, as is true for the trade of Europe in general, emphasizes imports of bulk goods such as grain and other foodstuffs, animal feeds, and industrial raw materials including cotton and other textile fibers, metallic ores, and petroleum; whereas European exports mainly consist of manufactured products that are higher priced than the imports. The trade illustrates the dependence of Europe, and especially Atlantic Europe, on large quantities of material imports for its industrial economy, on foods for its industrial population, and on feeding stuffs for its animal industries. In recent times most of the increase of imports into Europe (1938–59) was due to increased import of petroleum to replace coal and to supply the rapid increase in the use of petroleum in automobiles and other forms of transportation.

## TRADE IN GENERAL CARGO

Although imports of bulk commodities are big business in Europe, there also is a large movement of general cargo, especially in the great North Sea ports covered in the accompanying Table 7.[2] The table shows that in 1960 and 1961 the general cargo business was considerable at each of the five ports, but that the major amounts were handled at Rotterdam, Antwerpen, and Hamburg. In the past, although the total sea traffic in Rotterdam (bulk cargo plus general cargo) has been greater than that of Antwerpen, the latter has led in general cargo. In 1961, however, for the first time the total general cargo business at Rotterdam exceeded slightly the general cargo business at Antwerpen. Moreover, the business at Rotterdam has shown a steady and continual increase, whereas both the loadings and unloading at Antwerpen have fluctuated in amount.

General cargo business is of great importance to any port because   1] it has on average a higher value per ton than bulk cargo;   2] it employs many people;   3] it involves a large number of industries in and around the port area;   4] its added value in a port is relatively high; 5] it is evident that more can be earned handling a ton of general cargo than a ton of bulk cargo. A comparison of the general cargo transshipments at Rotterdam with those at Antwerpen from 1956 to 1961 inclusive

| Ports | Year | Loaded in Seagoing Vessels | Unloaded from Seagoing Vessels | Total |
|---|---|---|---|---|
| Hamburg | 1960 | 4,433 | 6,417 | 10,850 |
| " | 1961 | 4,413 | 5,956 | 10,369 |
| Bremen | 1960 | 3,716 | 3,771 | 7,487 |
| " | 1961 | 3,672 | 3,930 | 7,602 |
| Amsterdam | 1960 | 1,729 | 2,425 | 4,154 |
| " | 1961 | 1,669 | 2,451 | 4,120 |
| Rotterdam | 1960 | 4,992 | 9,340 | 14,332 |
| " | 1961 | 5,430 | 9,205 | 14,635 |
| Antwerpen | 1960 | 10,370 | 4,783 | 15,153 |
| " | 1961 | 9,910 | 4,356 | 14,266 |

7. GENERAL CARGO TRANSSHIPMENTS AT MAJOR NORTH SEA PORTS (IN 1,000 TONS OF 1,000 KG.).

Source: *Rotterdam-Europoort*, No. 2 (1963), pp. 2–3.

is recorded in the accompanying Table 8. At Rotterdam the big business is the unloading of general cargo from seagoing vessels, whereas at Antwerpen the major traffic is the loading of general cargo in seagoing vessels. In the total trade in general cargo, Rotterdam had a marked increase from 1956 to 1961, but at Antwerpen the volume of general cargo had gained but little. As has been stated previously, the total general cargo transshipments at Rotterdam in 1961 for the first time exceeded those at Antwerpen.

In the past, Antwerpen commonly has been regarded as being the major continental general cargo port, with Hamburg and Rotterdam of somewhat less importance. It is well known that the important export via Antwerpen of metal products, originating mostly from the producing areas in Belgium and Northern France, is a big factor in Antwerpen's export business. The accompanying Table 9 shows a different status of general cargo in Antwerpen with that in Rotterdam. In the latter the arrival of general cargo from overseas is the main flow of this type of traffic, whereas in Antwerpen the main flow is the departure of general cargo to overseas countries. However, the total of imports and exports shows that Rotterdam in 1961 had the largest general cargo port in the six-nation European economic community and, in fact, on the continent of Europe.

The general cargo at the port of Rotterdam divides into two categories, domestic and international. Forty per cent of it is destined for, or originating from, the Netherlands, whereas 60 per cent originates in, or is destined for, other European countries.[3] This means that Rotterdam is on the one hand a transit port for the Netherlands, and on the other a factor in

8.  GENERAL CARGO TRANSSHIPMENTS AT ROTTERDAM AND ANTWERPEN 1956 TO 1961 INCLUSIVE (IN 1,000 TONS OF 1,000 KG.).

| Year | Loaded in Seagoing Vessels | | Unloaded from Seagoing Vessels | | Total | |
|---|---|---|---|---|---|---|
| | Rotterdam | Antwerpen | Rotterdam | Antwerpen | Rotterdam | Antwerpen |
| 1956 | 3,852 | 9,891 | 5,803 | 3,948 | 9,655 | 13,839 |
| 1957 | 4,162 | 9,906 | 6,739 | 4,072 | 10,901 | 13,978 |
| 1958 | 4,165 | 9,510 | 7,041 | 3,574 | 11,206 | 13,084 |
| 1959 | 4,807 | 10,506 | 8,189 | 4,043 | 12,996 | 14,549 |
| 1960 | 4,992 | 10,370 | 9,340 | 4,783 | 14,332 | 15,153 |
| 1961 | 5,430 | 9,910 | 9,205 | 4,356 | 14,635 | 14,266 |

Source: *Rotterdam-Europoort*, No. 2 (1963), pp. 2–3.

9.  OVERSEAS EXPORTS OF METAL PRODUCTS FROM ROTTERDAM AND ANTWERPEN 1956 TO 1961 INCLUSIVE (IN 1,000 METRIC TONS).

| ROTTERDAM | | | ANTWERPEN | | |
|---|---|---|---|---|---|
| Year | Tons | Percentage of Increase or Decrease over Previous Year | Year | Tons | Percentage of Increase or Decrease over Previous Year |
| 1956 | 1,048 | . . | 1956 | 6,461 | . . |
| 1957 | 1,092 | + 4 | 1957 | 6,568 | + 1 |
| 1958 | 1,093 | . . | 1958 | 6,482 | – 1 |
| 1959 | 1,208 | +16 | 1959 | 7,268 | +12 |
| 1960 | 1,268 | . . | 1960 | 6,905 | – 5 |
| 1961 | 1,480 | +17 | 1961 | 6,341 | – 8 |

Source: *Rotterdam-Europoort*, No. 2 (1963), pp. 2–3.

the general cargo traffic in Europe (*Fig. 10*). In both types of trade a location at the Rhine mouth is a big advantage as is knowledge of the methods and techniques of port operation. Radar, based on shore, guides ships into or out of the harbors in any weather. Ships are unloaded or loaded quickly and efficiently. This encourages shipowners to use the port in order to save time and money.

General cargo contains a great number and variety of items. The trade at both Antwerpen and Rotterdam illustrates this diversity as an amazing variety of commodities are listed in the port records. Most of this trade is carried on ships that offer regular liner services to many parts of the world. The presence of these liner services draws the merchandise that

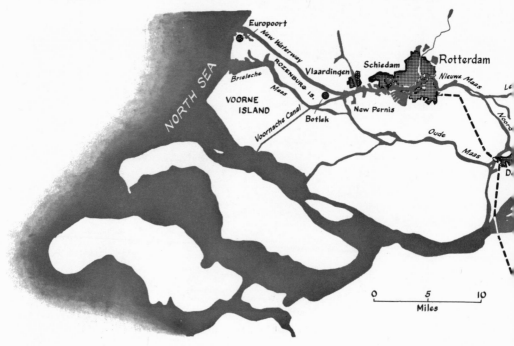

10.   *Rotterdam Gateway.*

makes up general cargo, and conversely, increasing amounts of such cargo attract more scheduled ship services. This round robin situation at Rotterdam, for example, has resulted in some 290 regular liner services with an average of 12,000 sailing a year, or about 40 each day. Much the same situation characterizes the port of Antwerpen.

## II   *Struggle for Land in the Rhine Delta*

The Netherlands and Belgium became densely peopled, prosperous countries only after centuries of struggle with the natural obstacles on the one hand and, on the other, the vicissitudes of religious oppression and governmental intervention. The never-ending struggle with nature has been associated with problems inherent in making a living on low-lying, poorly drained, nearly level land bordering the sea, whereas the struggle with religious intolerance and governmental intervention involved the desire for freedom in conducting trade and the pursuits ancillary to trade on the part of the individual, as well as of Rotterdam, Antwerpen, and other cities.

## STRUGGLE WITH NATURAL OBSTACLES

The struggle with natural obstacles has grown out of the limited quantities of usable land and the overwhelming abundance of water in the Low Countries. To increase the amount of usable land there has arisen the need of locally decreasing the supply of water. Creating usable land and water within the Rhine Delta is of vital necessity to the people of the Netherlands and Belgium, but it also is essential to the Rhine Valley, the Common Market, and to practically all of Atlantic Europe. Drainage and reclamation are technologies that underly the utilization of the best coastal frontage of Europe and prepares this area as a terminal for overseas shipping and air lanes. Moreover, this same technology of reclamation is needed in the future development of the delta region and alluvial plains of the Mississippi and of other deltaic areas.

Much of the coast of the Netherlands and all of the 42-mile coastline of Belgium fronts on the North Sea where it is so shallow that its depth does not exceed 30 feet until at least five miles from the shore. Inland, the sandy beach is bordered by a belt of sand dunes. Beyond the dunes in the provinces of Holland in the Netherlands and Flanders in Belgium the land has little or no slope and much of it is below sea level. The water table is near or at the surface so that lakes and ponds are numerous. At times swollen streams flooded the land. The solution was and is the polder, a unit of organized reclamation first developed in a big way between 1608 and 1612 in the northern part of the province of Holland.[4]

Commonly, the desire of the local people to reclaim a specific area becomes the reason for creating a polder organization. When once their reclamation unit is established, the first step is to construct a dike around the area to be reclaimed. Then the excess water is pumped over the dike wall into a canal that surrounds the dike. Originally windmills on the dike were used to pump the water, but now the work is done by diesel or electric pumps. When the water is eliminated, the land is laced by closely-spaced drainage ditches that divide it into operating units. In some situations drainage gates or sluices in the dike can be opened at low tide; then water from the polder floor drains out by gravity.

Many of the polder lands are used as pastures for the dairy cattle that are a vital element in the Dutch economy. Others are horticultural enterprises that specialize in tulip or other bulbs for export. Near the Hoek van Holland acres of greenhouses produce vegetables and fruits for the luxury market. Moreover, some of the polders in Belgium support horticultural enterprises, whereas others are used to raise grain and other farm products. Because of the great number of polder units, their maintenance must be in harmony with neighboring units and with the navigable waterways. This calls for some degree of centralized administration, and in some cases financial assistance.

The technique of polder construction is old. Through the years many problems have appeared, for storms during high tides may drive sea water over the dikes, and salt water may seep through the dikes if the water table of a polder is lowered too much. In short, the struggle with nature in these reclaimed areas is constant. Two ambitious and far-reaching reclamation plans are underway in the Netherlands. One is the Ijssel Reclamation Project for reclaiming about 60 per cent of the area of the Zuider Zee. The other is the "Delta Plan" for protecting the islands and estuaries of the delta area where the waters of the Rhine, the Maas (Meuse), and the Schelde reach the sea. These projects are underway, and the pressure of population on land is so great in this small but amazing country on the Rhine Delta, and the skill and determination of the Dutch are so well known that one can scarcely doubt that the plans will be carried to completion.

### LAND FROM THE ZUIDER ZEE

Before a plan was adopted in 1918 for its reclamation, the Zuider Zee was a shallow arm of the North Sea.[5] It was about 80 miles long from north to south and some 40 miles wide in its widest part. It covered an area of approximately 1,500 square miles and was nearly surrounded by land below sea level. As the land around its margins was productive where it was protected from the sea, nearly 200 miles of protecting dikes had been built. The cost of maintaining these dikes was a burden, and the need of more agricultural land was urgent. Hence, many schemes for reclaiming the land had been discussed before the plan of 1918 was formulated and adopted. It was estimated that if carried to completion, the plan would reclaim some 860 square miles of usable land.

Drainage was a problem as the Ijssel, a Rhine distributary, several smaller streams, and discharge of water from polders in the vicinity emptied into the Zuider Zee.[6] Under the plan several polders were to be reclaimed and the over-all water body reduced in size, but the Ijsselmeer would be left to receive the necessary drainage.

The first and probably the greatest step was the construction of a great 18-mile-long dam (Afsluitdijk across the narrow neck of the Zuider

Zee. This enormous structure, which took five years to build, constitutes one of the major engineering feats in the whole length of the Rhine Valley. The core of the dam was made of boulder clay on which enormous quantities of sand were dumped. This sand fill was covered by clay and flanked on both sides by brushwood mattresses, much like those utilized along the Mississippi levees. Both sides of the structure were riprapped (faced with rubble and stonework). Then the necessary two gaps were sealed, the sluices through which water drains at low tide installed, and navigation locks provided. The whole structure is 400 feet wide. On the inside, a level more than 100 feet wide was provided for the highway which connects Den Oever in Noord Holland with Zürich and the coast of Friesland. In the summer of 1960 sheep were being grazed on the seaward slopes.

The water in the Ijsselmeer has changed from salt to fresh water. It is said that fresh-water fish have replaced the salt-water fish and that the fresh water is used in the market gardens and the dairy industry in the polders that already have been reclaimed—one near Den Oever in Noord Holland and two on the east and southeast side of the Ijsselmeer. As yet the great sea wall has not been tested by the attack of storms during high tides, but the Dutch have invested the skill of men and some millions of dollars in the enterprise and are convinced success will mark their efforts.

In preparing the reclaimed land for agricultural or grazing uses the big problem has been to rid the clay soil of salt. This is done by pumping away all the rain water of a season and thereby gradually eliminating the salt. Calcium sulphate is spread on the soil so as to form a highly soluble compound with the salt in the soil. Then the whole area is plowed to mix the overlying sand with the clays.[7] Step by step, through the use of scientific methods and basic chemicals the land is prepared for use.

*THE DELTA SCHEME*

The entire coastal area of the Netherlands is subject to inundation from the North Sea, some sections more than others. The greatest danger is in the province of Zeeland where the islands and estuaries of the Rhine, Maas (Meuse), and Schelde deltas make the coastal area particularly vulnerable. In 1421, for example, a vast area was inundated, an estimated ten thousand people were drowned, and the Hollandsch Diep, a new arm of the sea, was formed. Moreover, in the century following 1825 nine serious floods occurred. As has been stated, sea dikes were built, but exceptionally high tides and river floods affect some 40 per cent of the total area of the country. As the years passed, various plans were made to mitigate the flood danger. In addition to the floods, tidal scour undermined the dikes, and salt water damaged the land along the estuaries and creeks. The problem was so acute that the managers of certain polder lands were given the right in 1870 to seek financial assistance from the province and the state.[8]

The pressing need of a great plan of reclamation was brought into focus by the great sea floods of 1953 when high winds, storm waves, and high tides occurring together raised the level of the southern North Sea so high that almost 600 square miles were flooded, and some 47,000 houses were damaged or destroyed, and 25,000 cattle lost.[9] As a result, a "Delta Plan" was formulated. It is estimated that construction under the plan will be finished by 1980 at a cost of 200 million dollars. Under the plan the three middle estuaries will be closed from the sea by great dikes linking the islands. They will make the estuaries into large fresh-water bodies. The mouth of the Brielsche Maas south of the island of Rozenburg already has been closed. Thus when the master scheme is completed only the New Waterway to the port of Rotterdam and the Westerschelde to the port of Antwerpen will be open to navigation.

Other features of the hydrographic struggle are 1] the maintenance of navigable diked channels in the waterways leading to the sea; 2] the construction of canals leading from one navigable waterway to another, or from one city to another; 3] the improvement of heavy clay soils by intermixing them with sand and improving their drainage; 4] the reclamation of the sandy heathlands in the higher land in the eastern part of the country; 5] the construction of heavy-duty dikes to hold back the wash of water from the sea that occurs in great storms when the tides are high; 6] the construction of causeways, railways, and improved highways across the lowlands, as for example, the highway and railway that parallel the New Waterway from Rotterdam to the Hoek van Holland; 7] the control of the inflow of salt water as the navigation channels are deepened. Hence, if the inflow of salt water goes inland, the salt may damage the pastures. These are by no means all of the triumphs of water engineering that the Dutch have developed in their struggle with nature since medieval times.[10]

The Dutch have been pioneers in hydrological engineering. They developed a national organization for the reclamation of land by controlling water and taught the techniques to the other coastal nations, especially to Belgium, France, Great Britain, and Denmark. They have made notable progress in the art and science of upgrading land and soil, and thereby have produced a prosperous country in a greatly handicapped environment.

### STRUGGLE WITH INTOLERANCE AND INTERVENTION

The long struggle of industrial and commercial interests with religious intolerance and governmental intervention characterized the development of most of the cities along the Rhine, especially during the Middle Ages, and in the North Sea ports. Religious intolerance, closely tied to governmental edicts and other forms of intervention, was especially acute in the coastal areas that were involved in the Reformation and participated in the industrial and commerical wealth that marked the growth of sea trade in the Atlantic world.

The impact of the struggle was especially acute in Flanders where both industrial and commerical enterprises made their early growth. In the fifteenth century, when the cities of Brugge and Gent declined, the struggle shifted to the rising city and port of Antwerpen. There the docks along the Schelde and the associated financial and commerical facilities probably were the most active in Europe. The effect on Antwerpen is summarized in this Chapter.

## III     *Rotterdam: Ocean Port and Rhine Gateway*

Rotterdam is a top-ranking ocean port and the major transit gateway to the Rhine (*Fig. 11*). Its basic function is transportation, a vigorous mixture of overseas, coastal, and barge service. Water transport is dominant, but is amply supplemented by rail, highway, pipeline, and airway services. For revenues it looks to commerce and trade, supported and enriched by diversified industry in the Dutch economy. Administration and financing of these basic activities are expertly handled. Moreover, through long experience in social and physical engineering the pattern and facilities of the port and the city are maintained in modern rather than historical terms.

In recent years transportation and trade with the Rhine countries, with other parts of Europe, and with overseas areas have increased until Rotterdam has become the largest and busiest port in Europe and now ranks with New York in its overseas commerce.[11] In fact, at times in busy seasons more than 200 ocean-going vessels are in port.

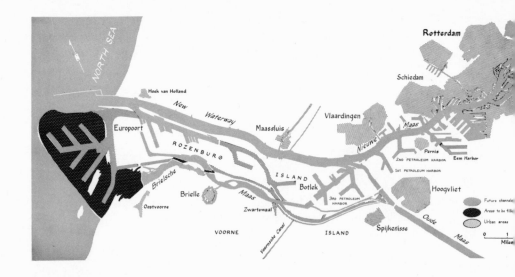

11.  The Port of Rotterdam with its subports and outriders.

## LOCATION AND PATTERN OF THE PORT

Rotterdam is on the north side of the estuaries and islands that characterize the south flank of the Rhine Delta and has the shortest channel to deep water of any of the major North Sea ports (*Fig.* 11). The tidal range helps to scour the channel and also provides a period of high water during which vessels of deep draft can enter and leave the port. The port is open to navigation throughout the year even though it lies in latitude 51°55′ north. The city proper spreads over the right bank of the river, whereas the major portion of the port with its display of docks, transit sheds, warehouses, refineries, and factories make up the well-organized pattern on the left bank. Bridges and a tunnel connect the two parts of the city.

The pattern of the port on the left or south flank of the waterway is developed in functional terms with many channels and harbors. The latter vary from a fourth of a square mile to plans for a harbor nearly five square miles in size. Incoming grain formerly was the major bulk cargo and still is important, but petroleum and its products now lead in value and volume of bulk cargoes.[12]

At the end of World War II, about 40 per cent of the port's facilities and overseas quayside and much of the center of the city were destroyed. By now, however, a new city built on modern plans has appeared

in the center of the old city. The port pattern and facilities on each side of
the river have been rebuilt according to an expert plan so that in 1961
more than 24,000 ocean-going ships and 200,000 river crafts were handled efficiently. About 90 million tons of cargo were transferred, and some
600,000 passengers moved through the port.[13] The overseas trade included both bulk and general cargoes and came from and went to most of
the countries of the Commercial World. Traffic on the Rhine and associated waterways was heavy, and although it reached all the Rhine countries,
as might have been expected, it was largest on the Lower German Rhine.

The port of Rotterdam is served by more river barges than any
other port in the world. Estimates were made that in 1962 the barges
would handle about fifteen times as much of the port's freight traffic as
railroads and trucks together.[14] Rotterdam is one of the shipbuilding centers in the Netherlands. The 850 shipbuilding yards in the country built 7.2
per cent of the world's total in 1961. This included 165 ocean-going vessels, of which more than half were for foreign countries and eight were for
British accounts.

### FORMULATION AND EFFECTUATION OF PLANS AND DESIGNS

Since Rotterdam's origin in the thirteenth century, the development and maintenance of the port on the shifting channels of the deltaic
plain of the Rhine River has necessitated almost continuous formulation of
plans and designs implemented by the associated engineering skills and
crafts. The city and its several ports are built on a structure of wooden and
concrete piles driven deep into the underlying silt, sand, and mud. Earth-
moving machinery digs the channels that lead to the slips where the ships
berth. Even told in brief fashion, the story demonstrates the livelihood
struggle of an intelligent and courageous people. It is an object lesson in
riverine economy and in fluviomarine geography under the changing conditions which may appear during long periods of time.

### SETTLEMENT AT ROTTERDAM

The low-lying, water-drenched terrain on which Rotterdam is built
must have hindered rather than fostered the beginning of a city. The first
settlement at Rotterdam was at the junction of the Maas and the Rotte
rivers. The latter drained out of great marshes north of Rotterdam and
gave its name to the early settlement. In 1250 a dike or levee constructed
on the north bank of the Maas blocked the flow of the Rotte and created a
drainage problem. The difficulty was solved when a system of locks to

carry water from the Rotte into the Maas was planned and built. Subsequently, a small settlement localized on the dike; and in 1299, and again in 1328, requests for certain sovereign rights or charters were granted by the sovereign, Maximilian of Austria. Today, the Haag Straat built on the dike divides the city into two parts.[15]

## SPANISH ANNEXATION

When Charles v of Spain separated the Low Countries from German rule and annexed them to Spain, the Netherlands included Belgium and the present province of Holland. Peace was established, and under liberal rule a degree of prosperity resulted. Under his son, Philip II, the power of the state and the Church were emphasized, and the Netherlands were merged with Spain and Austria in a vast and discontinuous empire. Then in 1572 Antwerpen on the Schelde was devastated by Spanish troops, and all of the Netherlands occupied. After a few months the Spanish withdrew from Holland and Rotterdam, and the northern Netherlands came under the leadership of the Prince of Orange.[16] Antwerpen and Flanders, however, remained under Spanish authority, and after the Treaty of Münster (Westphalia) in 1648 the Schelde was closed to navigation until 1792, or for nearly 150 years. Antwerpen, as a result, declined in commerce, whereas Rotterdam moved into a period of prosperity, in part, because some textile artisans and merchants, unable to work under the despotic rule in Belgium, moved from Antwerpen to Rotterdam where they began the production of textiles. This represented a loss for Antwerpen but a gain for Rotterdam.[17]

## COMPREHENSIVE PLAN IN THE SIXTEENTH CENTURY

In the last quarter of the sixteenth century a plan for the development of Rotterdam was formulated. This involved digging a harbor on the mud flats of the delta. It is said that the plan was so comprehensive that for the next two and a half centuries the city was provided with adequate plans for expansion.[18] This is an illustration of the value of long-range planning in port development.

## TRANSIT TRADE WITH RHINE VALLEY

During the early years of the nineteenth century Rotterdam became increasingly concerned with the transit trade of the Rhine Valley and connecting waterways. At that same time business and industry was moving into the inland or continental areas. Rotterdam's situation at the mouth of the best water route into the back country led to rapid growth, especially when Bismarck, after 1870, organized the German Empire and increased the industrialization of the Ruhr. This period witnessed the growth of Rotterdam under a program planned by Pieter Coland. It called for the construction of a "New Waterway," planned to provide a better channel to the sea. The execution of this plan took from 1866 to 1872 and involved the construction of harbors along the New Waterway that helped to make Rotterdam one of the most modern and efficient world ports.[19]

## THE NEW WATERWAY

Under the Coland plan the 18-mile-long direct channel now used was cut from Rotterdam to the North Sea just south of the Hoek van Holland. (*Fig.* 11). This project was carried to completion in the period from 1866 to 1872. It is called the New Waterway, and Kuipers in his recent study describes it as "lock free, bridge free, and sand free."[20] At first it was only 10 feet deep, but after being enlarged from time to time it attained a depth of water that is sufficient for seagoing vessels with a draft up to thirty-three feet. The channel requires constant dredging helped by tidal action directed by special walls constructed for this purpose. Safety of ship operation along the New Waterway is helped by a shore-based radar network that in periods of fog or snow helps to guide vessels to or from the docks in the several divisions of this great port.

## GROWTH OF COMMERCE AND INDUSTRY

The organization of the German Empire in 1870 and the construction of the New Waterway so that Rotterdam could serve the industrial development at the junction of the Ruhr River and the Rhine threw into relief the great growth of industry and commerce in the latter part of the nineteenth century. In sea trade, steamers replaced sailing vessels. Next iron and then steel were substituted for wood in the construction of seagoing vessels, thereby increasing the life of a vessel. Steel was first used in a Cunard liner in 1881.

A series of inventions reduced the size of the engines and boilers in a ship and made available two-thirds of the ship space for cargo or passengers. This meant increased carrying capacity, increased profits, and led to scheduled sailings. For the first time ocean transport became regular, fast, and efficient. In fact, for the first time the Atlantic world began to profit from low cost transport.

On the land, industrial inventions facilitated the development of manufacturing and increased the industrial output enormously. Railroads were built in Europe and America, and transportation and industry prospered. Both sides of the Atlantic grew in population and wealth, and the ports of Western Europe increased their services to their industrial hinterlands. Time was of the essence.

The construction of the New Waterway gave Rotterdam direct access to seagoing vessels and, conversely, gave seagoing vessels direct access to Rotterdam and to the Rhine waterway (*Fig. 11*).[21] In large measure it made Rotterdam a seaboard city that became a real gateway to the Rhine.[22] Until the middle years of the eighteenth century, vessels to and from Rotterdam used the Brielsche Maas route to the North Sea. This route constituted the principal line of water flow from the Lek. Gradually, however, so much mud was deposited in this waterway that mud flats formed, eventually becoming the present island of Rozenburg. This island divided the Maas into a north and a south channel. As a result, this direct channel to the sea was abandoned for another nearly twice as long via the Noord. Under a plan to shorten the route, the Voornsche Canal was dug from the Brielsche Maas across Voorne Island in 1830. This channel was utilized for more than a third of a century before it was obstructed by banks of mud and sand.

## COMPETITION WITH OTHER NORTH SEA PORTS

Although by 1900 Rotterdam had become one of the major European ports, its preeminence among these ports has been attained since World War II. Before World War I, Rotterdam was somewhat overshadowed by Hamburg on the Elbe and Bremen on the Weser, but by 1938 Rotterdam led in sea-borne goods traffic (*Table 6*). Today Hamburg and Bremen are cut off from some of their tributary areas by the Iron Curtain —a sad comment on modern civilization.

Amsterdam, the largest Dutch city in population, was another active competitor with Rotterdam before the First World War (*Fig. 9*). although Amsterdam's early route to the high seas was via the Zuider Zee, in 1876 the North Sea Canal was dug from Amsterdam to the North Sea.[23] Amsterdam had developed industrial activities and far-flung commercial, financial, and administrative functions to the point that it had the qualities of a capital city, even though The Hague is the seat of the Netherlands' government. This meant that it commanded much of the profitable relations with the Netherlands East Indies and other ports of the East Indies region, especially in their exports of sugar, rice, rubber, coconut oil, and petroleum—commodities that the world uses in huge quantities. However, in the recent splurge of nationalism in tropical areas the Dutch lost most of their overseas possessions and their control over the trade of their colonies.[24]

The Rhine has become so important in the transportation structure of the Netherlands and the Lower German Rhine that, for many years, Amsterdam has wanted a direct canal connection with this major artery. Hence, after many years of effort the New Amsterdam-Rhine Canal was opened in 1952.[25] It shortens the distance from the German-Dutch border by 25 miles. This means a saving of about twenty hours in barge traffic.[26] However, as yet it has had little effect on the growing leadership of Rotterdam in Rhine traffic.

## PLANS AND PROGRESS SINCE WORLD WAR II

Although Rotterdam suffered during the First World War and the following depression, it was the Second World War that really devastated the city and the port. As has been stated, some 40 per cent of the port's facilities and the overseas docks were destroyed.[27] Within a few days after the air attacks, clearing of the destroyed areas began, and the city architect was instructed to prepare a plan for redevelopment. Under the plan all of the devastated area was expropriated to facilitate central planning. Shortly, a second and more comprehensive plan was adopted. It is said that the reconstruction of the port facilities was completed by 1949, and that by January, 1957, some 65 per cent of the devastated area was redeveloped.[28]

As is true of the great ports of New York and London, Rotterdam is the center of a conurbation of municipalities, i.e., it's a metropolitan area. Down river on the north bank are the industrial and port suburbs of Schiedam, Vlaardingen, and Maassluis, whereas on the south bank is the oil port of Pernis, with the first and second petroleum harbors, and the new port of Botlek with the third petroleum harbor (*Fig. 11*).

As might be expected, the principal industrial developments are associated with the quays along both banks of the Nieuwe Maas, and more especially with the harbor basins opening from the river without locks. Railways, highways, and airways reach the port areas, and thus increase the business of the port and the city. The built-up business and financial and residential areas of Rotterdam are divided into two parts, the larger area being north of the river. The over-all pattern confuses the casual visitor but in fact functions efficiently for such a major conurbation. The great developments at the port of Rotterdam since the Second World War indicate that a penchant for the effectuation of plans through engineering still characterizes the people of Rotterdam and the Netherlands. For example, two new ports are being built on the island of Rozenburg, Botlek on the east and Europoort on the west.[29]

BOTLEK PROJECT

The Botlek section of the port of Rotterdam is under construction along the Botlek waterway between the Nieuwe Maas and the Brielsche Maas (Fig. 11).[30] The harbor with its channels, docks, and quays will be along the river but will be flanked by land areas reserved for industry. The project as planned includes about five and a half square miles and lies west of the oil port of Pernis. To facilitate access by land a new bridge has been built across the Oude Maas west of Pernis. As might be expected, in view of the increasing demand for petroleum and petroleum products in Western Europe, Botlek promises to become another oil port, as witness the localization in the port of an Esso refinery unit of Standard Oil of New Jersey. In nearby Pernis the Royal Dutch Shell organization has a large oil refinery, as has the Caltex Petroleum Company.

Botlek already has attained some diversification in its industrial activities. These include chemical installations, shipbuilding yards, storage facilities for Canadian iron and other ores, and other warehouses.

EUROPOORT

Another illustration of forward-looking enterprise is the construction of Europoort at the North Sea end of the island of Rozenburg.[31] This port is under development across the New Waterway from the Hoek van Holland, and in 1962 is expected to be the major port of the Western Europe Common Market. At this new port bulk cargoes of coal and ore for a new steel mill and a major inflow of crude oil will be featured. Pipelines and a large tanker fleet will carry the crude oil to Dutch refineries, and it is planned that eventually these pipelines will be built up the Rhine Valley as far as Köln.

Under the development as planned Europoort may become a major port not only for the Rhine Valley, but for Western Europe. The plan, in its present dimensions, calls for construction on an area of about eight square miles. The developments will include new channels, new dock basins, new quays, and designated sites for new petroleum establishments. Several dock basins will be built for vessels up to 730 feet in length and a draft of about 47 feet, and three huge tankers are being built for Standard Oil of New Jersey. To reach these basins a newer and deeper channel than the New Waterway is planned.

At the outset emphasis will be placed on the handling of petroleum brought by large tankers. Huge storage facilities will be provided in order to aid transshipment by river tankers and by pipelines to Duisburg and the Ruhr. Refineries and petro-chemical industries also are to be developed. Hence, Europoort will be a seaboard refining center as well as a great transit center. Throughout the vast area tributary to the port of Rotterdam, the two major oil companies, the Royal Dutch Shell and the American Standard Oil of New Jersey, compete energetically for the oil business.

In addition to petroleum, iron ore from Canada, Sweden, and elsewhere will come by sea to the projected blast furnaces and steel processing units. Sites for other industries will be available, and residential and shopping areas are under construction. All these will take the place of the agricultural and horticultural enterprises which formerly were the characteristic activities of Rozenburg Island.

ROTTERDAM IN 1960

As viewed in 1960, Rotterdam impressed the visitor with its vigorous cultivation of new enterprises and new ideas. It has the largest oil refineries in Europe; its shipbuilding yards are active in terms of both maritime construction and craft for the Rhine and other inland waterways. It has automobile assembling plants, engineering works, and processes foodstuffs received from overseas such as coffee, cacao, tea, tobacco, coconut oil, and grain. Clothing, paper, railway equipment, and a great variety of chemical products are produced, and the port has breweries and distilleries. It shows the activities of an ocean port, as it imports raw materials from overseas and manufactures or processes them into usable items for the national and international economies.

As we have tried to point out, municipal, port, financial, and other types of planning have characterized the evolution of this great Dutch port. Planning in terms of both physical and social planning has characterized the thought and action of Rotterdam since the early settlements in the thirteenth century. It is the Dutch way of meeting the challenge presented by its natural liabilities and assets. Certainly it demonstrates that in the utilization of a river valley and its delta there is much to learn, much to plan, and much to be done.

Rotterdam, among the ports of the North Sea, has the geographic advantage of its situation at the outlets of the Rhine and Maas rivers. These rivers and their associated canals and waterways provide efficient services to the industrial and commercial centers in West Germany, the Netherlands, Belgium, Luxembourg, France, and Switzerland. The low-lying sites on which the several sections of the port of Rotterdam are built present never-ending difficulties. These sites are below sea level, and the soft ground tends to sink. The dikes (levees) must be built higher and wider. The buildings of the ports must rest on wood or concrete pilings sunk deep into the land. These foundations are difficult and expensive to build and maintain, but their service of the buildings and other installations at this great traffic center more than offset the cost. The battle with this low-lying complex of land and water emphasizes the technological significance of planning and engineering in an industrial and commercial economy.

IV    Antwerpen

Antwerpen, Rotterdam, and London are the three great ports at the narrow southern end of the North Sea. Antwerpen and London lie practically in the same latitude, both cities being crossed by the 51st parallel north. Antwerpen's situation on the Schelde River 55 miles from the North Sea corresponds to London's situation some 46 miles up the Thames. Moreover, the estuary of the Schelde and the estuary of the Thames face each other across the North Sea, the one leading into and from the Continent and the other into and from the great offshore island. Antwerpen and Rotterdam, however, are delta ports, the one associated with the south flank and the other with the north flank of the estuaries through which the Rhine, Meuse (Maas), and Schelde rivers drain to the North Sea. The estuaries break the low-lying deltaic plain into numerous islands and marshes. Hence, it scarcely is an exaggeration to say that before modern transportation, travel across the deltaic plain from Antwerpen to Rotterdam was more difficult than that from Antwerpen to London across the Strait of Dover.

In early times Rotterdam and Holland probably were more difficult to reach from the Continent than were Antwerpen and Flanders. The full-flowing Rhine, the marshy North German Plain, and the channels and marshes of the delta must have been more difficult to negotiate than the land approaches to Antwerpen and Flanders. According to Mackinder, in

Roman and even in later times, the downward Rhine trade for the most part left the river at Köln to pass overland into Flanders along the landway at the border of the higher land and the plain, necessarily through the narrow interval between the marshes and the hills, between Antwerpen and Liége.[32]

## THE CITY AND THE PORT

The site of the city and the port of Antwerpen is on the right bank of the Schelde about 12 miles upstream from the point where the Schelde opens into the West Schelde estuary, the first deepwater inlet that breaks the European coast north of the Strait of Dover (*Fig. 12*). The boundary between Belgium and the Netherlands crosses the head of the Schelde estuary. Hence, of the 58 miles from Antwerpen to deep water, 34 miles lie in Dutch territory. Extensive drying banks and shoals occupy a large part of the river from its mouth to Antwerpen. The main channel has a winding course and in some places is so narrow that extreme caution must be exercised in reaching the port.

## DIVISION OF THE PORT

The port of Antwerpen includes two separate divisions. The first is along the river front of the city where vessels with a draft up to 35 feet may dock during high tide, whereas the second consists of a large dock system down river from the city, and connected with the river by six locks. The water area of the dock basins covers 1,235 acres for seagoing navigation and about 90 acres for river craft. The quays have a length of 32 miles for seagoing vessels and four miles for barges. The total area of the port covers 3,460 acres. The installations include oil refineries, shipyards, sawmills, scrap iron yards, food and chemical industries, and also breweries, sugar and flour mills, soap factories, and assembly plants for American automobiles.[33]

Antwerpen illustrates the advantage of a seaport at the head of a navigable arm of the sea. The city and the riverside docks are located at the great bend of the lower Schelde where the river changes from a northeast to a northwest course. The Schelde is navigable upriver from this curve but not for ocean-going vessels of great size and draft. This landward penetration makes Antwerpen the nearest deep channel port to the Ruhr, industrial areas along the Meuse (Maas) River, and to more remote industrial sections. From Antwerpen, railroads, highways, and airways fan out to reach Duisburg, Düsseldorf, Köln, Aachen, Liége, Bruxelles, and many

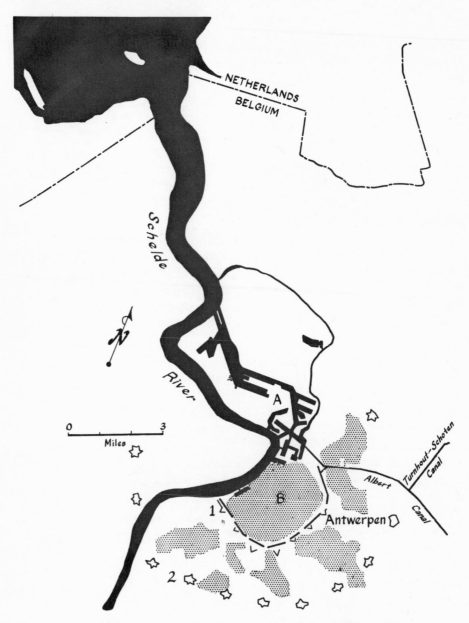

12. The port of Antwerpen on the Schelde.   a] The industrial port;  b] the city frontage on the Schelde with the barge
port. Under the ten-year redevelopment plan,   1) indicates the
inner circle highway over sites of former inner fortifications
and  2) shows contemplated outer circle route over sites of the
outer fortifications.

other points. In fact, Antwerpen is the chief outlet for goods requiring railway transport. This fact has given impetus to the installation of modern loading and unloading machinery, both in the railway yards and in the port areas.[34] There are 30 miles of quays and 1,000 acres of docks equipped with cranes and other cargo handling apparatus.

## ADMINISTRATION OF THE PORT

Antwerpen, the capital of the province of the same name, is the commercial center of Belgium. Both governmental and private agencies are concerned with the responsibilities and problems of harbor and port administration at Antwerpen. At the municipal level, the maintenance, improvement, extension, and operation of the docks and ancilliary facilities for seaboard shipping are the responsibility of the city administration. This agency operates the municipal port equipment, hires out the municipal dry docks, provides towing service on the slips and channels, and arranges for electric current to offices, transit sheds, and other port installations. The Belgian government provides for the maintenance and lighting of navigable channels in the Schelde, polices the river and the roadstead, manages the sea and river pilotage service, collects the customs duties, and looks after the sanitary facilities and needs of the several parts of the port. The Belgian National Railways Company owns and operates the railway installations in the port. This company's services are essential to the smooth transfer of goods to and from the ships.[35]

Private firms and enterprises manage the handling and guarding of goods and ships on the quay and their storage in transit sheds and warehouses. They also look after the repairing of ships and provide pilot service on the Schelde and in the docks. The ships agent, who represents the owner, takes steps to ensure that the services to the ship are promptly executed, including the provision of pilots, tugs, and berths. He also takes the necessary documents to customs and pays the expenses incurred by the ship. The dockers (stevedores) discharge the cargo. They have a fine reputation and are known and respected for their skillful work in loading or unloading cargoes with a minimum of damage. Such a reputation constitutes an asset of first importance in the operation of a port.[36]

## RIVERS OF BELGIUM

The Schelde, on which Antwerpen is located, enters the plain at the junction of the Schelde and the Lys where the city of Gent lies, at the southeastern end of the historic Flemish textile district. The Schelde fol-

lows a winding course to Antwerpen through the highly productive reclaimed land, much of which specializes in the production of flower seeds
and bulbs for both local and foreign markets.

The small, densely peopled, and highly productive country of Belgium is traversed by two rivers which enter Belgium from France and flow,
in general, from south to north across Belgium to enter the Netherlands
enroute to the North Sea. The Meuse (Maas) crosses the coal fields in the
eastern part of Belgium, and from Liége on the Meuse the Albert Canal
connects the coal fields with Antwerpen, the great industrial and commercial center on the Schelde.

Although descriptive treatment of the cost and benefits of inland
waterways are numerous, attempts to measure them in statistical terms are
few and far between. However, in the *Geographical Review* for January,
1955, Henry Madison Kendall reviews an expert study of the Albert Canal
in Belgium by Professor Alexandre Delmer, professor emeritus of the University of Liége. The Albert Canal is about 81 miles long and connects
Liége in the Meuse Valley with Antwerpen on the Schelde River. The drop
from the Meuse to Antwerpen is 184 feet and necessitates six locks. The
time required varies from fifteen to thirty-two hours depending on the
speed of the barges. The construction on the canal began in 1930, and it
was severely damaged during World War II. Since 1953 the canal has been
usable throughout its length, and traffic has come to make up 7.7 per cent
of the total volume of railroad and water transport within Belgium. The
canal also serves as an aqueduct to increase the water supply of metropolitan Antwerpen.

Although there were unforeseen problems of construction, changes
in value, and damages occasioned by World War II, the Albert Canal has
proved to have benefits beyond the hopes of those who planned and built
it. Its worth to the national economy far exceeds the cost. It has created
traffic, industries, and employment. Moreover, it leaves with those who use
it the greater part of the produced revenue. Kendall notes that it has been
of particular value to the port of Antwerpen, the coal field of the Campine,
and the Liége industrial area.

*CENTURIES OF STRUGGLE*

Antwerpen attained its present status as a world port after centuries of struggle with natural obstacles on the one hand and, on the other,
with the vicissitudes of religion and government. The historic development
of Antwerpen witnessed striking fluctuations. For example, its economic

development, based on its river position, was overshadowed by its political significance growing out of its protection from invasion because of surrounding marshes. However, its advantage for shipping and trade included its site 55 miles up the Schelde from the North Sea which gave it almost an immunity from storms and its tides which were sufficiently marked so that at high tide large vessels could reach the port. Furthermore, Antwerpen is as near as London to the center of the sea trades, and it is near the canals, railways, and land routes that focus on the Atlantic from Central and Northern Europe.[37]

## PROSPERITY IN THE FIFTEENTH AND SIXTEENTH CENTURIES

Antwerpen prospered in the fifteenth and sixteenth centuries after Charles the Fifth of Spain, elected emperor of Spain in 1519, severed the ties between the Netherlands and the German Empire and united the former to the Spanish domain.[38] Previously, Flanders and neighboring sections had attained prosperity from the weaving and other crafts and the associated trade with England and Europe. It also profited when Venezia sent trading vessels through Gibraltar, around the coast of Spain and Portugal to trade with London, Brugge, Antwerpen, and other outposts on the European frontier. This sea trade foreshadowed the shift of shipping leadership from the Mediterranean to the Atlantic after the discoveries of Columbus and Henry the Navigator led to profitable trade with the Americas, India, and the East Indies. Moreover, for a time after the union with Spain, Antwerpen participated to some extent in this trade with the New World. When silting in its channel to the North Sea led to the decline of Brugge, Antwerpen, with excellent connections with European trade routes, developed into one of the outstanding commercial and financial areas of Europe. This position was favored by the liberal view of the city in regard to religion, foreign merchants, and taxes. In the beginning of the sixteenth century at least 1,000 business houses were located in Antwerpen, and over 500 vessels docked at the waterfront every day. Its busy docks were the marvel of the time.[39] By the peak period of its early economy Antwerpen surpassed Venezia (Venice) in European commerce and enjoyed a high degree of wealth and culture.

## DECLINE TO OBSCURITY

Antwerpen's period of prosperity ended in 1576, following local disturbances, when the Spanish garrison plundered the town and massacred six thousand citizens.[40] In the next year Antwerpen threw off the

Spanish control, destroyed the Citadel, and the city came under Calvindish control. However, the Spanish under Philip II, a despotic king who was a religious fanatic, regained control in 1585 and in the following war the Netherlands was divided into a northern section that attained independence, whereas Antwerpen and the southern section remained under Spanish rule. The struggle continued, but in 1648 the Treaty of Münster (Westphalia) stipulated that the southern Netherlands be separated from the northern Netherlands and that the Schelde be closed to navigation. As a result of this governmental and religious intervention, the port business was lost. Then for nearly a century and a half—from 1648 to 1792—the city, having lost its greatest asset, its outlet to the sea, declined into obscurity and poverty.[41]

REVIVAL IN 1795

The revival of Antwerpen as a port began in 1795 when Napoleon made Antwerpen his chief military harbor and his point of threat against England. The Schelde was reopened to shipping, channels were cleared, docks and a naval arsenal were built, and the shipyards were busy building a fleet with which Napoleon planned to invade England.[42]

The struggle to develop the port continued in one form or another after the Belgian revolt of 1830; then the Schelde was opened to navigation, and in 1831 a liberal constitution was adopted. Finally, in 1863 Antwerpen moved into a period of rapid growth when the Dutch rights to levy tolls on Antwerpen's ships in the Schelde estuary were redeemed by purchase.[43] As was true in Rotterdam, Antwerpen prospered with the development of the Ruhr industrial area after the unification of the German Empire in 1870. As in Rotterdam, Antwerpen also suffered in World War I and World War II. However, as has been stated, it now is one of the great world and inland waterway ports. At long last it is in a position to take advantage of its geographic assets. Its story illustrates the principle that freedom in the flow of commerce comprises one of the great avenues to prosperity, and that state interference with freedom of thought and action inevitably leads to a decline in commerce and the welfare of a people.

EMPLOYMENT STRUCTURE

As might be expected, transportation is the fiber of which the employment activities of Antwerpen are woven. Its port facilities accomodate the vessels of 200 seagoing lines and some 170 lines operating on inland waterways. Antwerpen interests are said to control about 90 per cent of the shipping under the Belgian flag. In 1961, 17,000 vessels with a total of 46 million gross shipping tons called at the port of Antwerpen. This doubled the tonnage of ten years before. These ships loaded and unloaded 40 million tons of merchandise. During the same year 53,000 barges of which 17,000 came from foreign countries strengthened Antwerpen's ties with the interior. In recent years this business on the waterways has exceeded 20 million tons a year.[44] Antwerpen's three railway stations serve systems providing direct freight and passenger service to Amsterdam, Bruxelles, Paris, Duisburg, Düsseldorf, Köln, Basel, and other centers. For some of these centers, including the cities on the Lower Rhine, Antwerpen is the nearest port, and considerable high grade traffic goes from the port by rail to these points. Moreover, Antwerpen has a busy international airport. Although Antwerpen's labor force finds varied employment, emphasis is placed on transportation. For example, in a recent year 24 per cent of the total labor force was employed in transportation and shipbuilding. In addition to this group, 15 per cent was employed in metallurgy and 19 per cent in the diamond industry.[45]

IMPORTS AND EXPORTS

In the port of Antwerpen in 1959, 16,022 seagoing vessels brought 16.4 million tons (1,000 kg) of general cargo plus 3.7 million tons transit freight. Some 9.9 million tons of outgoing cargo was augmented by 5.3 million tons of transit cargo.[46] The major incoming cargoes were of three groups: 1] minerals, including petroleum, iron ore, coal, phosphate, and copper; 2] foodstuffs, such as cereals, oil-seeds, and fruit; 3] cotton, wool, rubber, and other colonial products.

The exports were iron and steel, machinery, railway materials, cement, chemicals, fertilizers, coal and coke, and textiles—all reflecting the diversified output of Belgian industry. In fact, manufactured products, including machinery, account for about 75 per cent of the exports. It has been claimed that Antwerpen, drawing on Belgium, Luxembourg, Lorraine, Saar, and their steel work has been at times, the largest steel-exporting port in the world.

RHINE TRAFFIC

Antwerpen is both a loading and an unloading port for Rhine traffic. In the 1959 upstream traffic passing Emmerich, the border point on the Rhine between the Netherlands and West Germany, Antwerpen handled only 7.2 per cent of the total as against the 66.9 per cent contributed by Rotterdam. In contrast, the downstream traffic in 1957 at Emmerich was more widely distributed among the Dutch and Belgian unloading harbors, with 28.8 per cent going to Rotterdam and 29.3 per cent to the other Dutch harbors. Antwerpen handled 19.9 per cent of the downstream traffic and the other ports of Belgium 14.4 per cent of the total.[47]

*PORT REDEVELOPMENT*

The port of Antwerpen is working on a ten-year program of port development (1956–65). The depth of water at the new docks is to be 39 feet at high tide. The building space for seagoing vessels and river craft will be increased from 32 to 47 miles, and large areas are planned for indus-trial plants. There are to be added another harbor dock and adjoining industrial basin with modern equipment and an extension transport bridge plant. The whole program involves expenditures amounting to 5.1 billion Belgian francs.[48]

*COMPETITION WITH ROTTERDAM*

Present and potential competition between Antwerpen and Rotter-dam is always a matter of concern. It will be remembered that throughout the seventeenth and eighteenth centuries the Dutch kept the lower Schelde closed to traffic, thus causing great damage to Antwerpen. Two problems are of acute interest in the controversy; namely, 1] a canal through Dutch territory to connect the port of Antwerpen more effectively with the Rhine and 2] Belgium's payment of subsidies to attract Rhine barges through the southwestern part of the Netherlands to Antwerpen in prefer-ence to the more convenient Rotterdam. Settlement of these and other controversial matters constitutes a major task for the Benelux Economic Union.[49]

# 8

# Transport Structure of Atlantic Europe

It is self-evident that for the long run in the battle of competition, traffic carriers can only maintain themselves when they adapt at the right time to the march of technical progress, and make use of all innovations in the forwarding, transfer, and, above all, the building of vehicles. In the beginning, inland navigation only hesitantly followed the results of modern technical development.[1]

## I  Over-all Transport Structure

Rhine navigation and traffic constitute a part of the whole transport structure of Atlantic Europe much as navigation and traffic on the Mississippi and Ohio rivers are a part of the over-all transportation in the United States. In Europe, although the utilities and activities of the transportation pattern were seriously disarranged in World War II, recovery after the war came rapidly, much more rapidly on the railways and highways than on the inland waterways.

During the recovery decade from 1950 to 1959 transport by air and pipelines increased, thereby adding to the complexity of the over-all transport structure. This complexity was increased also by  1] changes in fuels for motive power;  2] by improvements in rolling stock on the railways;  3] by increased electrification of the railway lines where the traffic is heavy;  4] by the greater use of motor vehicles associated with the reconstruction of roads and highways;  5] by a general improvement in incomes;  6] by the construction and use of self-propelled barges and tankers on the inland waterways. Moreover, better methods and techniques of organization and operation made for increased efficiency in the transport plant. Probably these changes in technology would have occurred in this mid-century decade even if destruction and damage during the war had not necessitated reconstruction of the transport plant. Although some attention has been given to the integration of the several means of transportation in order to better serve the needs of the country, not much more has been accomplished toward the solution of that problem in the Rhine countries than in the Mississippi Valley. One concludes that the solution of the over-all transport problem awaits the ideas and effectuation of the future.

According to the United Nation's Economic Commission for Europe, the mid-century decade was "one of expanding economy in Western Europe and in most countries of full employment." National economies expanded steadily. Deliveries of coal and petroleum products to the Rhine countries increased greatly in number, and their use increased where they were available; whereas in areas where the number of private cars in relation to population was low, increased use of buses and trucks was the rule. As restrictions on international travel such as visas, customs requirements, and currency regulations were eliminated, international travel doubled or tripled. Much of this travel was by highway in summer. In 1958 in Italy, for example, 70 per cent of the tourists entered in this manner. It is estimated, however, that in most countries railway revenues per passenger-kilometer increased during the decade.[2]

A working idea of relative magnitude of the major three means of inland transport in the Rhine countries may be gained from estimates that in 1959 in West Germany the percentages for rail, inland waterways, and road were 58, 26, and 16 respectively; whereas in the Netherlands the percentages were 9, 49, and 42. In the latter the road figures included only carrier by road for hire or reward, whereas in the former the total road transport was covered.[3] In the case of Germany the high percentage of rail transport is in harmony with the relatively long land distances; whereas in the Netherlands, on the Rhine Delta, canals and roads completely overshadow rail facilities.

## MOBILE EQUIPMENT

During the decade from 1950 to 1959, steam power on the railroads of the Rhine countries gradually declined and was replaced by electric powered or diesel traction equipment. In fact, the acquisition of steam locomotives is of the past on most railway systems. In this decade the large numbers of obsolete or overage passenger vehicles characteristic of 1950 were replaced either by new or by completely rebuilt and modernized equipment.[4] Moreover, refrigerator cars (wagons), tank cars, and other cars of special types increased in number and use.

In reviewing the number of employees on the railway, the Economic Commission for Europe points out that in general there was a reduction in staff despite increases in railway traffic during the middle century decade. This was attributed to improvements in labor productivity and the general increase in operating efficiency resulting from capital investments. Comparisons of systems cannot be made because of "differences in national transport policy, in the scope of the activity of railway administrations, in internal organization, and in conditions and hours of work."[5] These differences remind one of prevailing conditions in the United States in spite of the efforts of the Congress and the Interstate Commerce Commission to standardize the service of our common carriers.

In the Rhine countries the numbers of private automobiles increased steadily during the decade under consideration, some cases being three times greater in 1959 than in 1950. Likewise the number of buses increased steadily, as did the fleets of trucks (goods vehicle fleets), especially in the fleets of large vehicles.[6] The foregoing statements for railway and highway vehicles serve as a background for the situation in inland water craft—the subject of consideration in this study.

II    *Length of Inland Waterways*

The length of the inland waterways of the Rhine countries is shown in the accompanying Table 10.[7] In Belgium and the Netherlands the length of canals exceeds the length of the river waterways, whereas in France and West Germany the opposite holds true. In the Rhine Delta, especially in the Netherlands, canals are a part of the way of life, whereas in France and West Germany canals connect navigable rivers or serve as extensions of river navigation. Switzerland has only 21 kilometers of the Rhine in regular use for transport. As will be shown later, this Swiss waterway is the 21 kilometers in use at the port of Basel. The total length of the inland waterway as shown in Table 10 is 20,636 kilometers or approximately 12,815 miles. Since World War II, except in the U.S.S.R., only slight changes have been made in the total length of navigable waterways. In West Germany, for example, differences from 1951 to 1959, in most cases, were due to changes in definition or to the reclassification of some rivers. The decrease of some 28 per cent in France was due to the fact that navigation was closed on some canals and rivers where little, or no, traffic was carried.[8]

10.  LENGTH OF INLAND WATERWAYS.

| Country | Canals km | Rivers km | All Waterways km | Length of Waterway in Regular Use for Transport km |
|---|---|---|---|---|
| Belgium | | | | |
| Total Length 1950 | 894 | 879 | 1,773 | . . |
| Total Length 1959 | 947 | 872 | 1,819 | 1,618 |
| France | | | | |
| Total Length 1950 | 5,295 | 7,934 | 13,229 | . . |
| Total Length 1958 | 4,745 | 5,671 | 10,416 | 7,854 |
| West Germany | | | | |
| Total Length 1949 | 1,332 | 3,103 | 4,435 | . . |
| Total Length 1959 | 1,526 | 4,129 | 5,655 | 4,375 |
| Netherlands | | | | |
| Total Length 1950 | 5,838 | 1,140 | 6,978 | . . |
| Total Length 1958 | 5,654 | 1,114 | 6,768 | 6,768 |
| Switzerland | | | | |
| Total Length 1950 | . . | 21 | 21 | . . |
| Total Length 1959 | . . | 21 | 21 | 21 |
| Five-country Total | | | | 20,636 |

Source: *Annual Bulletin of Transport Statistics for Europe, 1959* (Geneva: United Nations Economic Commission for Europe, 1960), Table 1, p. 2; 54–56.

In the Rhine countries the construction or further development of certain waterways is underway. By 1959 canals linking Amsterdam to the Rhine, the Nimy River to Blaton in Belgium, and some work on the Main had been completed. Recent canalization of the Neckar from Heilbronn To Stuttgart added new dams, locks, and port facilities to that river (*Fig. 5*). Hence, Stuttgart has become a distributing point for the coal, petroleum and other mineral products, grain, and heavy foodstuffs that move up the river in barges. Most of the barges return empty as the finished products are shipped by rail or truck. Canalization of the Moselle from Coblenz, where it joins the Rhine, to Thionville in France is underway. Moreover, developments in West Germany are indicated by the fact that the length of inland waterways navigable by craft of 1,500 tons increased from 987 km. in 1954 to 1,075 km. in 1958, while that navigable by craft of over 1,500 tons rose from 1,104 km. to 1,335 km.[9]

The closely spaced pattern of inland waterways in the Netherlands in relation to the area of the country is in harmony with the land-water conditions in its deltaic terrain. Belgium has somewhat the same character in the low, northern section of the country. The inland waterways of Switzerland are confined to the section of the Rhine in Basel-Town and Basel-Country. The inland water pattern of West Germany shows only 23 kilometers for each 100 square kilometers of area (*Table 11*). This country has most of the navigable Rhine, the most valuable and most used river in Western Europe. France, with 7,854 kilometers of inland waterways in regular use, has the most kilometers of navigable river of any of the Rhine countries.

11.  LENGTH OF INLAND WATERWAYS IN RELATION TO AREA
AND POPULATION IN THE RHINE COUNTRIES IN 1959.

| Country | km. of Inland Waterways | sq. km. of area | km. of Inland Waterway for ea. 1,000 sq. km. | Population 1959 | km. of Inland Waterway for ea. 1,000,000 People |
|---|---|---|---|---|---|
| Belgium | 1,819 | 30,507 | 60.0 | 9,104,000 | 199 |
| France (1958) | 10,416 | 551,208 | 19.0 | 44,970,000 | 23 |
| West Germany | 5,655 | 245,322 | 23.0 | 51,800,000 | 11 |
| Netherlands | 6,768 | 40,893 | 166.0 | 11,346,000 | 597 |
| Switzerland | 21 | 41,288 | .5 | 5,235,000 | 4 |

Source: *Annual Bulletin of Transport Statistics for Europe, 1959* (Geneva: United Nations Economic Commisssion for Europe, 1960), Table 1, p. 2; Table 31, pp. 54–56; Chart III, p. 43.

In addition to its frontage on the Upper Rhine, the navigable rivers in France include in the north the Seine with its tributaries the Oise, Marne, and Yonne; in the west center the Loire; and in the southwest the Dordogne and the Garonne. For a considerable part of their courses these streams flow through plains and valleys presenting only minor obstructions to navigation. In the southeast, although the Rhone is mapped as navigable from Lyons, abrupt irregularities in its gradient means that its course is impeded by sand deposits and other obstructions.

## III   *Motorization of the Rhine Fleet*

In recent years much progress has been made in the introduction of technical improvements in Rhine navigation. An outstanding feature has been the increasing motorization of freight carriers and tugs. The trend to motorization was in evidence before World War II. However, according to Dr. Eric Schwoerbel of Duisburg only 10 per cent of the German inland navigation was motorized in the prewar years.

The Economic Commission of the United Nations for Europe, in its studies of the inland waterways, recognizes five groups of canal and river craft in their tables: 1] self-propelled barges, 2] self-propelled tankers, 3] dumb barges, 4] dumb tankers, and 5] tugs. The dumb barges and dumb tankers have no motive power of their own, and they are pushed or hauled by tugs built for that purpose. The self-propelled craft are increasing in number, whereas the dumb craft are decreasing. Clearly the trend is for an increasing emphasis on self-propelled boats.

The mobile equipment on the inland waterways of the Rhine countries for 1950 and 1959 is presented in Table 12. As a general rule, load-carrying craft increased in the Rhine countries both in numbers and in carrying capacity. As has been stated, this held true especially in the number and over-all carrying capacity of self-propelled barges and tankers as compared with dumb barges and tankers. The big fact in the operation of barges is that gradually the self-propelled barges replaced the dumb barges in the more important trading sectors. Although with the rising traffic in

| | Country | Year | Self-propelled Barges | | | Self-propelled Tankers | | |
|---|---|---|---|---|---|---|---|---|
| | | | Number | Carrying Capacity (tons) | H. P. | Number | Carrying Capacity (tons) | H. P. |
| 12. MOBILE EQUIPMENT ON THE INLAND WATERWAYS. | Belgium | 1950 | 3,374 | 1,060,760 | 275,509 | 100 | 20,847 | 7,352 |
| | | 1959 | 4,792 | 1,806,092 | 626,884 | 304 | 94,595 | 38,994 |
| | France | 1950 | 2,150 | 696,000 | 164,000 | 385 | 128,000 | 39,000 |
| | | 1959 | . . | . . . . | . . | . . . | . . . |
| | West Germany | 1950 | 1,650 | 508,699 | 249,573 | 130 | 59,686 | 34,471 |
| | | 1959 | 3,853 | 1,861,071 | 1,041,958 | 519 | 354,655 | 215,321 |
| | Netherlands | 1950 | 6,443 | 872,139 | 386,216 | 338 | 68,852 | 34,991 |
| | | 1959 | 9,442 | 1,994,129 | 886,913 | 729 | 261,124 | 148,971 |
| | Switzerland | 1950 | 202 | 145,856 | 86,494 | 58 | 42,632 | 26,441 |
| | | 1959 | 250 | 210,272 | 134,377 | 87 | 84,263 | 56,801 |

Source: Annual Bulletin of Transport Statistics for Europe, 1959 (Ge

petroleum and its products the number of dumb tankers increased slightly, the fleet of self-propelled tankers more than doubled in numbers and tripled in carrying capacity.[10]

After 1945 the technical advances were accelerated because of the interest of the international commission appointed to deal with the problems of Rhine navigation (Federated Traffic Ministry). The commission is made up of representatives of the Rhine countries, Great Britain, and the United States. This commission considered the introduction of modern technology as a major phase of its program. In this connection it should be remembered that shipyards and port facilities as well as financial resources had been severely decimated during the war. However, with help of the commission after 1949 it is reported that, of the intra-Rhine ships, 65 per cent of Swiss navigation was motorized, 19 per cent of Dutch navigation, 13 per cent of the Belgian Rhine navigation, and 9 per cent of the French Rhine navigation. At this time there was only an 8.5 per cent motorization of the average German ships employed on the Rhine. Schwoerbel points out that by 1951/52, after the currency reform, conditions for the first time encouraged new and larger construction.[11]

At the outset, it was thought that the motorized freight ships, because of their savings in time, would be used mainly in transporting piece goods, or as we say package goods. However, it soon became apparent that because of their freedom of operation, their greater turn-around speed, and their better over-all performance on longer trips and in exchange traffic between the Rhine and its tributaries and associated canals, the motorized ships have penetrated into the traffic of bulk commodities. By 1958 the total inland fleet was 40 per cent motorized, and in 1960 the self-propelled

| Dumb Barges | | Dumb Tankers | | Tugs | | All Craft | | |
|---|---|---|---|---|---|---|---|---|
| Num-ber | Carrying Capacity (tons) | Num-ber | Carrying Capacity (tons) | Num-ber | H. P. | Num-ber | Carrying Capacity (tons) | H. P. |
| ,857 | 1,303,812 | 12 | 5,383 | 369 | 39,619 | 6,712 | 2,390,802 | 322,480 |
| ,254 | 681,152 | 24 | 13,981 | 187 | 24,644 | 6,561 | 2,595,820 | 690,522 |
| ,700 | 2,350,000 | 208 | 113,000 | 472 | 167,000 | 9,915 | 3,287,000 | 370,000 |
| . | .... | .. | ... | .. | ... | .. | .... | ... |
| ,285 | 2,372,224 | 167 | 108,965 | 913 | 320,375 | 6,145 | 3,049,574 | 604,420 |
| ,325 | 2,502,999 | 176 | 103,723 | 847 | 323,072 | 8,720 | 4,822,448 | 1,580,350 |
| ,263 | 3,234,037 | 178 | 115,957 | 2,506 | 340,664 | 19,728 | 4,290,985 | 761,878 |
| ,272 | 2,590,187 | 217 | 141,723 | 2,136 | 353,766 | 20,796 | 4,987,163 | 1,389,658 |
| 75 | 64,731 | 6 | 6,895 | 24 | 29,830 | 365 | 260,114 | 142,769 |
| 47 | 50,403 | 11 | 13,770 | 17 | 23,935 | 412 | 358,708 | 215,115 |

ited Nations Economic Commission for Europe, 1960), Table 43, pp. 90–93.

crafts were so much in evidence that barges towed or pushed by diesel-powered tugs were matters of special notice.

Motorized freight space was obtained in two ways. From 1945 to 1957 a total of 610,000 tons of motorized freight space was newly built. Moreover, another 644,000 tons were gained through the motorization of barges. Hence, the self-propelled space under the West German flag increased in that period approximately 1,250,000 tons through new construction and modeling. In the same period only about 4,000 tons of barge space was built.

Of the 157 newly constructed motorized freight ships put into service in 1957, some 139 with 121,000 ton capacity were standardized craft, and almost 25 per cent of the new motorized ships were tankers. There also has been real interest in creating a motor ship type on a smaller scale which might be especially serviceable in working the waterways of middle Germany and the French canals connecting with the Rhine. The type known as the "Theodor Bayer" is less then 400 tons loading capacity, whose smaller size and lower cost is intended for the German equivalent of "small business."

By 1958 the total carrying capacity of the German inland fleet reached about 4.4 million tons. The total carrying capacity of barges amounted to about 2.6 million tons with about 1.8 million tons of motorized vehicles. The engine performance of the tugs towing or pushing barges was about 309,000 horsepower, with the motor tugs gaining on the coal-burning steam tugs. Modern tankers in the number of 250 with a 150,000 ton capacity were in service on German inland waterways in a recent year. By 1958 the motorized tanker space in the Federal Republic grew to over 225,000 tons; "almost 25 per cent of the motorized new ships were motorized tankers. Naturally . . . the builders of modern tankers discovered strong incentives in the last years."[12] New construction of all kinds continued in 1958, but the emphasis was on motorized vehicles—freight ships, motor tugs, and tankers. At this time the orders for motorized freight ships for German accounts amounted to 195,000 tons; for foreign accounts about 84,000 tons. Barge orders for German accounts consisted of 48,000 tons; for foreign accounts about 33,000 tons. "From this the irresistible trend to motorized freight ships is clearly visible."[13]

"The rising modernization of inland navigation and especially the advancing motorization have made possible the mastery of great traffic performances in the postwar period. Considering the strained situation of over-all inland navigation and in view of the unforseeable future development, a slower tempo in new construction is awaited."[14] Apparently Schwoerbel thinks that the period of rapid construction is about over, and that maintenance and repairs may be the rule until the present construction is worn out, or some new demands appear. The construction and use of craft of small draft and carrying capacity on the rivers and canals is a characteristic of the Rhine countries that is not repeated in the United States. For example, tables are available that show the number of craft in Western Germany in 1959 with carrying capacity for canals as follows: 620 with a carrying capacity up to 250 tons, 672 with a capacity of up to 1,000 tons, and 223 with a capacity of up to 1,500 tons or over. For use on rivers the figures are 934 up to 250 tons, 101 up to 1,000 tons, and 2,253 up to 1,500 tons or over.[15] The smaller craft are generally used on the quiet water and shallow depths of the canals, whereas the larger craft, for the most part, are held for river navigation. In many cases the small barges are owned and operated as a family enterprise.

As one viewed the amazing display of craft on the rivers and canals of the Rhine countries in 1960, the differences in the age of the craft in use was striking—the old as compared with the new. Obsolescence was in evidence as it is along the Mississippi and Lower Ohio rivers. Old warehouses and other structures along the rivers and canals were almost as conspicuous as they are along the Mississippi. Changes in methods of handling river commerce and advancing technology in river transport have outmoded some features and increased the use of others in Europe as well as in America. For example, the method of pushing rather than pulling barges has lowered the cost of power and personnel.[16] Finally, the combined fleets of the Rhine countries—Belgium, France, West Germany, the Netherlands, and Switzerland—in which inland navigation plays an important part in the transport structure were used much more intensively at the end than at the beginning of the period. The same held true on the Lower Mississippi, the Ohio, and the Illinois rivers.

## iv    *Freight Traffic at the Borderstation Emmerich*

A view of almost any section of the Rhine offers convincing evidence that the Rhine is a busy waterway. Passenger traffic is heavy on daytime excursion boats and on modern craft that offer regular service through the Rhine Gorge and other scenic segments. Moreover, the Rhine is a major tourist attraction, and special luxury service has recently been established on weekly round trips from Rotterdam at the mouth of the river to Basel, Switzerland, at the head of navigation. These services add variety to the craft that ply the river, but this study is focused on the freight movement that characterizes the Rhine and its associated waterway at present.

The period under review is from the close of the Second World War to the present. However, in large measure the statistical evidence available covers the decade from 1949 to 1959 inclusive. This period witnessed considerable economic activity and full employment in most countries of Western Europe. Production increased markedly, more especially in areas where in the immediate postwar years war destruction and dislocation retarded recovery. Commonly, exports increased and helped to maintain a favorable balance with the dollar. Moreover, after 1952 intra-European trade was strengthened by the increasing demand by manufacturers for raw materials and other basic commodities. On the inland waterways this demand was especially noteworthy as the waterways commonly carry a substantial volume of such materials. It should be appreciated, however, that increases were relative, for in 1949 inland waterway tonnage in Germany was only 56 per cent of that handled in 1936. Rail transport, however, had recovered more rapidly than water transport as the rail tonnage in 1949 amounted to 82 per cent of the 1936 total.

As much of the traffic on the Rhine, especially on the lower reaches of the river, must cross the boundary between West Germany and the Netherlands, records are kept at the borderstations Emmerich on the German side and Lobith on the Dutch side. More complete records are available from the former. Hence, Emmerich becomes the pivot point in our first approach to Rhine traffic. A second approach is made by a consideration of the major commodities moving in the traffic of the Lower Rhine. For the Middle and Lower Rhine, recourse also is made to a brief consideration of traffic at the major river ports.

Records from the borderstation Emmerich deal with all traffic that crosses the border there (*Table* 13). However, it should be understood that the Netherlands and West Germany lead overwhelmingly in Rhine statistics and Rhine navigation. In large measure the Rhine, with its commerce and industries, constitutes the bread and butter of these two countries. With only the Rhine they would still be important in Europe and the world; without the Rhine and its auxiliary waterways and resources, in all probability, they would be reduced to areas of small interest in the world's economy.

At Emmerich, the last German city on the Rhine, the volume of traffic on the German Rhine reaches its greatest dimensions. Annually about 150,000 ships pass this border. Moreover, in 1958 some 59.0 million German tons of freight were dispatched through the border customs.[17]

The total tonnage of the freight recorded at Emmerich for selected years and also the upstream and downstream traffic is shown in Table 13. In the two right-hand columns the quantitative relationship of upstream to downstream traffic is shown.

In 1929 and 1937, in the depression period between both wars, the total volume of traffic was nearly equal, i.e., 54 to 59 million tons. In this period the quantitative relationship of upstream to downstream traffic amounted to the ratio 44 to 56. After the last war, however, the upstream traffic exceeded the downstream. For example, in 1957, the peak year with 60,753,000 German tons, the quantity of freight in upstream and downstream traffic was in the ratio of 70 to 30. The preponderance of upstream movement was due to large imports into West Germany of flour and other

13. FREIGHT AT BORDERSTATION EMMERICH (IN 1,000 TONS [GERMAN TON=1.1023 U.S. TONS]).

| Year | Upstream Traffic | Downstream Traffic | Total Up and Downstream Traffic | % Up-stream | % Down-stream |
|------|------------------|--------------------|--------------------------------|-------------|---------------|
| 1929 | 23,850 | 30,158 | 54,008 | 44 | 56 |
| 1937 | 25,768 | 33,246 | 59,014 | 44 | 56 |
| 1956 | 39,970 | 18,154 | 58,124 | 69 | 31 |
| 1957 | 42,491 | 18,262 | 60,753 | 70 | 30 |
| 1958 | 40,760 | 18,262 | 59,002 | 69 | 31 |
| 1959 | 35,440 | 19,886 | 55,326 | 64 | 36 |

Source: *Wirtschaftliche Mitteilungen*, Vol. 16, No. 14 (15 July 1960), 273.

foodstuffs, fertilizers, other basic commodities in a recovering economy, and to shipments of coal amounting to 23,758,000 German tons. Of this huge volume, 8,800,000 tons consisted of imports of American coal. Downstream traffic after 1957 was augmented by shipments of raw steel, rolled steel, fertilizers, flour, sand, gravel, and other goods. In 1959 this "unfavorable" balance of trade began to be corrected with a decline in the imports of American and other foreign coal and by the increasing use of petroleum.

The total of 55,326,000 German tons of commodity movement at borderstation Emmerich in 1959 illustrates the flow of traffic on the Lower Rhine (*Table* 13). This traffic includes the commodity groups that are characteristic of river transport. Some of these groups are so heavy in weight as to stow in a small space. Iron ore, for example, is so heavy that if an attempt were made to fill all the space in a barge with this ore, the barge would be unmanageable and probably would sink. Other groups are sufficiently bulky in relation to weight as to require careful methods of stowage. Careful stowing, therefore, is a factor in successful management of traffic.

The energy fuels—coal, coke, and petroleum—made up about 30

per cent of the upstream flow in 1959, as shown in Table 14.[18] Coal and coke are commodities of long standing in Rhine traffic, whereas petroleum and its products are newcomers. Through the years coal and coke have moved primarily downstream as, for example, in 1937 when they made up 72 per cent of the downstream traffic. However, British coal moved up the Rhine as far as Köln in 1913, and for a time after the last war large quantities of American coal moved upstream. By 1960, in large measure, West Germany's coal shortage was over, and the practice of using petroleum was on the increase. Such changes in direction of movement of the energy fuels are occasioned by new demand and by new discoveries of resources. Petroleum, now in second place in volume on the Rhine, has become of increasing significance throughout the whole Rhine country.

14. FREIGHT TRAFFIC AT BORDERSTATION EMMERICH IN 1937 AND 1959 BY TYPE.

| Commodity | Upstream | | | | Downstream | | | |
|---|---|---|---|---|---|---|---|---|
| | 1937 in 1,000 t. | 1959 in 1,000 t. | 1937 % | 1959 % | 1937 in 1,000 t. | 1959 in 1,000 t. | 1937 % | 1959 % |
| Coal, Coke | 2,423 | 2,829 | 9.4 | 8.0 | 23,758 | 4,734 | 72.0 | 23.2 |
| Ore | 13,139 | 13,009 | 51.0 | 36.7 | 55 | 41 | 0.1 | 0.2 |
| Grain, Flour, Sugar, Legume | 3,148 | 2,854 | 12.2 | 8.1 | 46 | 482 | 0.1 | 2.4 |
| Gravel, Sand, Stone | 34 | 692 | 0.1 | 1.9 | 3,354 | 4,397 | 10.0 | 22.1 |
| Petroleum | 1,728 | 7,872 | 6.7 | 22.2 | 290 | 728 | 0.8 | 3.7 |
| Fertilizer | 590 | 139 | 2.3 | 0.4 | 1,432 | 2,900 | 4.2 | 15.1 |
| Wood | 582 | 1,007 | 2.3 | 2.8 | 45 | 37 | 0.1 | 0.2 |
| Raw Iron & Steel | 101 | 342 | 0.3 | 1.0 | 102 | 542 | 0.3 | 2.8 |
| Scrap Metal | 592 | 564 | 2.3 | 1.6 | 9 | 72 | . . | 0.4 |
| Others | 3,431 | 6,132 | 13.4 | 17.3 | 4,155 | 5,953 | 12.4 | 29.9 |
| Totals | 25,768 | 35,440 | 100.0 | 100.0 | 33,246 | 19,886 | 100.0 | 100.0 |

Source: *Wirtschaftliche Mitteilungen*, Vol. 16, No. 14 (15 July 1960), 274.

By 1959 ore in the amount of 13,000,000 tons moved upstream. Currently this is the largest tonnage item transported on the Rhine (*Table 14*). Most of it is destined for mills in the Duisburg port district, with smaller amounts to the Rhine-Herne Canal, the Lippe-Seiten Canal, the Middle and Upper Rhine, as well as to Switzerland and Alsace. Piles of these ores are to be seen on the unloading piers of the industrial docks in the Ruhr and other heavy industrial areas. The almost black iron ore imported from northern Sweden via the Norwegian port of Narvik is one of the high-grade ores that move up the Rhine. Of the long-standing upstream traffic, grain, legumes, flour, and sugar move into the densely peopled industrial Ruhr in a steady flow by rail, highway, and waterway.

Four groups of commodities bulked large in downstream traffic on the Lower Rhine in 1959: 1] coal and coke, 23.2 per cent; 2] gravel, sand and stone, 27.1 per cent; 3] fertilizers, 15.1 per cent; 4] miscellaneous, 29.9 per cent. This last group includes a greater diversity of commodities than holds true on most inland waterways. For example, a wide range of chemicals is included and, with the increasing use of powered craft, the variety appears to be increasing. As will be noted presently, the revival of heavy industry in the western zone of Germany effected a substantial increase in upstream traffic, the finished products in the industrial areas moved to market largely by rail and highways.[19]

## ORIGIN AND DESTINATIONS OF GOODS THAT PASSED BORDERSTATION EMMERICH

Freight traffic on the Rhine, as recorded at Borderstation Emmerich in 1959, was predominantly with Germany. In that year 89.6 per cent of the upstream traffic had its destination in Germany and 88.8 per cent of the downstream traffic had its origin in that country. These figures help to demonstrate the high importance of navigation on the "German Rhine."[20] From Table 15 it becomes evident that more than half the

15. FREIGHT TRAFFIC AT BORDERSTATION EMMERICH BY DESTINATION AND ORIGIN IN 1959.

| Upstream Traffic | | | Downstream Traffic | | |
|---|---|---|---|---|---|
| Destination | in 1,000 t. | in % | Origin | in 1,000 t. | in % |
| To Germany | 31,765 | 89.6 | From Germany | 17,650 | 88.8 |
| Of that: | | | Of that: | | |
| Lower Rhine | 18,248 | 51.4 | Lower Rhine | 10,339 | 52.0 |
| West German Canals | 5,342 | 15.1 | West German Canals | 3,629 | 18.3 |
| Middle Rhine | 1,406 | 4.0 | Middle Rhine | 1,399 | 7.0 |
| Main | 1,661 | 4.7 | Main | 793 | 4.0 |
| Upper Rhine | 3,857 | 10.9 | Upper Rhine | 1,362 | 6.8 |
| Neckar | 1,251 | 3.5 | Neckar | 128 | 0.7 |
| Switzerland | 2,826 | 8.0 | Switzerland | 223 | 1.1 |
| France (Alsace) | 849 | 2.4 | France (Alsace) | 2,013 | 10.1 |
| All Destinations | 35,440 | 100.0 | All Origins | 19,886 | 100.0 |

Source: *Wirtschaftliche Mitteilungen*, Vol. 16, No. 14 (15 July 1960), 274.

goods that passed through Emmerich upstream or downstream came from or were enroute to the Lower Rhine district of West Germany. This district includes Duisburg-Ruhrort and the twenty-one harbors in the "Duisburg Chamber District" (*Table 15*). Continuous round-trip freight service with the Rhine mouth ports is maintained. Other points to which traffic is routed, or from which it is dispatched, are the West German canals, the Middle Rhine, the Main Valley, the Upper Rhine, the Neckar Valley, Alsace, and Switzerland (*Table 15*).

The upstream traffic to West Germany amounted to 31,765,000 tons. Of this, 51.4 per cent went to the Lower German Rhine ports, 15.1 per cent to the West German canals, 4 per cent to the Middle Rhine, 4.7 per cent to the Main River ports, 10.9 per cent to the Upper German Rhine ports, 3.5 per cent to the Neckar River ports, 2.4 per cent to Alsace (France), and 8 per cent to Switzerland.

Of the downstream traffic past Emmerich in 1959, in addition to the 88.8 per cent originating in Germany, 10.1 per cent came from Alsace and 1.1 per cent from Switzerland. Of the points within Germany, 52 per cent came from the Lower Rhine, 18.3 per cent from the West German canals, 7 per cent from the Middle Rhine, 4 per cent from the Main, 0.7 per cent from the Neckar, and 6.8 per cent from the Upper German Rhine. Again, the Rhine traffic to a large extent is confined to the Lower Rhine which is the major waterway of the Ruhr region.

## LOADING AND UNLOADING HARBORS FOR THE FREIGHT TRAFFIC PASSING EMMERICH

According to Table 16, the freight traffic on the Rhine that is recorded at the Borderstation Emmerich in large measure comes from or goes to the Netherlands and Belgium. Only 2.8 per cent of the upstream freight traffic and 7.6 per cent of the downstream traffic involves areas other than the Netherlands and Belgium.

16. FREIGHT TRAFFIC AT BORDERSTATION EMMERICH BY LOADING AND UNLOADING HARBORS IN 1959.

| Upstream Traffic | | | Downstream Traffic | | |
|---|---|---|---|---|---|
| Loading Harbors | in 1,000 t. | in % | Unloading Harbors | in 1,000 t. | in % |
| From Rotterdam | 23,710 | 66.9 | To Rotterdam | 5,668 | 28.8 |
| From Amsterdam | 2,385 | 6.7 | To Amsterdam | 870 | 4.3 |
| From the other Dutch harbors | 3,636 | 10.3 | To the other Dutch harbors | 4,979 | 25.0 |
| From Antwerpen | 2,573 | 7.2 | To Antwerpen | 3,973 | 19.9 |
| From the other Belgian harbors | 2,158 | 6.1 | To the other Belgian harbors | 2,869 | 14.4 |
| From France | 319 | 0.9 | To France | 644 | 3.2 |
| From Germany | 375 | 1.1 | To Germany | 624 | 3.1 |
| From other ports | 284 | 0.8 | To other ports | 259 | 1.3 |
| All Loading Harbors | 35,440 | 100.0 | All Unloading Harbors | 19,886 | 100.0 |

Source: *Wirtschaftliche Mitteilungen*, Vol. 16, No. 14 (15 July 1960), 274.

Of the upstream freight traffic at Emmerich 83.9 per cent was loaded at Dutch harbors, and 58.1 per cent of the downstream traffic was unloaded in these same harbors. Of the downstream freight traffic crossing the German-Dutch border, slightly more than a third was unloaded at Belgian harbors, with 19.9 per cent of this traffic handled at Antwerpen. The loading and unloading harbors for both the upstream and downstream traffic at Emmerich in 1959 are presented in Table 16.

In 1959, although some of the Rhine import and export traffic was handled at Antwerpen, Amsterdam, and lesser ports, 67 per cent of the upstream business and 29 per cent of the downstream traffic was handled through Rotterdam. In large measure this is due to free and effective communications with the German hinterland, with its energy resources, and with its energetic people. Moreover, this position is in harmony with the fact that the southern part of the Rhine delta divides into a number of islands too small to be suitable for port development.

Connecting canals feature Rhine navigation, and therefore the Rhine is the central artery of a system of canals and other waterways. Nowhere is this system more in evidence than in the Netherlands where the total length of navigable waterways amounts to 4,817 miles. This network of rivers and canals feeds Dutch products to the ports and distributes imported commodities to all parts of the country. The result is a fluvio-marine economy of the first order of importance.

This deltaic country lies north of the fiftieth parallel of latitude and thus is north of the source area of the Mississippi and in the latitude of Southern Canada. However, the rivers are open throughout the year although the shallow quiet water in the canals freezes over in the winter. The Rhine as a water route leads southward into Western Europe and is navigable to the border of Switzerland. The utility of the Rhine in its inland sections is affected by irregularities in the surface configuration and by the increasing severity of the inland winters. Along the Rhine, only a relatively few points possess the combination of land suitable for a port with a productive capacity which justifies the great cost of port development and operation. By 1900 more than 50,000 tons of commodities were brought up annually to Strasbourg, some 480 miles from the North Sea. Today, modern engineering has made it possible to follow a channelized route to Basel at the border of Switzerland. Costs of construction and maintenance are great but as Partsch pointed out long ago, "It is precisely, however, in extensive inland districts where distances (from the sea) are very great that the cheapness of water carriage for heavy goods is most fully felt."[21]

Orsoy Harbor
Walsum Harbor
River
Homberg Harbor
Ruhrort Harbor
Duisburg Harbor
Hochfeld Harbor
Rhine

0  1  2  3
Miles

13.  *Harbors in the I.H.K. district Duisburg.*

Of course, he ignores the cost of river and canal improvements and the question of rates on rail and highway transport.

v    *Freight Traffic in the Duisburg Industry and Trade Chamber*

From Emmerich to Duisburg-Ruhrort, the major Rhine ports of the Ruhr mining and industrial area, is a river distance of 62.5 miles. This stretch of the Lower Rhine is organized as the Duisburg Industry and Trade Chamber and includes twenty-one harbor-ports spaced at irregular intervals, with only seven on the left bank (*Fig. 13*). This district maintains continuous circulating traffic with the harbors at the mouth of the Rhine. Of the twenty-one ports, seventeen are factory harbors, i.e., industrial ports, whereas four are public harbors. In 1959 the twenty-one harbor-ports handled 39,031,960 German tons of freight. Of this, 22,882,703 were incoming and 16,149,257 tons were outgoing according to Table 17.[22]

The harbor-ports of the Duisburg Chamber for statistical presentation are divided into four groups as summarized in Table 17. The first group includes nine harbor-ports of which Duisburg-Ruhrort are by far the most important (*Fig. 13*). It will be noted in most of the groups that the incoming traffic exceeded the outgoing, a natural situation in this period of active redevelopment in the economy of West Germany. Only in the Walsum group did the outgoing traffic exceed the incoming.

More than half of the commodities that passed upstream at the borderstation Emmerich were sent to the Lower Rhine, especially the

17. HARBORS IN THE I.H.K. DISTRICT DUIS-BURG—FREIGHT TRANSSHIPPED IN TONS IN 1959.

Source: *Wirtschaftliche Mitteilungen,* Vol. 16, No. 14 (15 July 1960), 277.

I.H.K. means Industrie und Handels Kammer, or Industry and Trade Chamber.

| Harbors | Incoming | Outgoing | Total Traffic |
|---|---|---|---|
| Duisburg Harbors Together | 15,456,663 | 11,826,066 | 27,282,729 |
| Harbors in Rheinhausen-Homberg | 2,232,108 | 2,096,896 | 4,329,004 |
| Harbors in Walsum | 1,962,433 | 2,136,393 | 4,098,826 |
| Harbor in Wesel and Emmerich | 3,231,499 | 89,902 | 3,321,401 |
| All Harbors in the IHK District Duisburg | 22,882,703 | 16,149,257 | 39,031,960 |

twenty-one harbors in the Duisburg Chamber district. In order of importance, goods transferred in 1959 were ores and residual metallic oxides, followed by coal, coke, and briquettes. Other items included rolled steel, petroleum, sand, gravel, and other building materials, grain, wood, mineral salt, chemicals, and similar items.

VI   *Duisburg-Ruhrort Ports and World Traffic*

The Duisburg-Ruhrort ports are the largest river ports in Europe, not only in traffic handled but in the extent of their combined physical pattern (*Fig. 14*). They constitute the Rhine frontage for the Ruhr Industrial District and, in fact, constitute the most important traffic center of the Rhenish-Westphalian Industrial Region. Moreover, two-thirds of all the goods that move via German river navigation are handled in these Rhine River ports.

*ELEMENTS OF LEADERSHIP*

Many conditions have contributed to the outstanding record of the Duisburg-Ruhrort ports. Their leadership reflects 1] the long run significance of the Rhine River in Western Europe, 2] the growing importance of the Rhine as a river arm of the Atlantic Ocean, 3] the international trade of the Ruhr with many parts of the commercial world, and 4] more recently the importance of the Rhine in the affairs of the

Common Market. As has been stated, Rotterdam and other Rhine ports have and will continue to share in the advantages of the Rhine waterway, but none more effectively than the dual port display at the junction of the Ruhr River and the Rhine.

Of the Duisburg-Ruhrort complex, the former is old in its origin, whereas the latter came into prominence with the growth of coal mining in the Ruhr Valley. Duisburg began as a castle place some 1200 years ago and was a Franconian royal court frequented by many German kings. In the Middle Ages Duisburg became a Hanse town and participated in the activities of the Hanseatic League, thus foreshadowing its present commercial importance. Today it is the retail, financial, and management center of the port patterns. It supports parks, playgrounds, theaters, railway terminals, and many cultural activities.

Ruhrort has most of the port basins and other port facilities, is the terminal of the Rhine-Herne Canal leading into the Ruhr Industrial District, has a great display of railway freight yards, and has roads and highways leading to the several parts of the port. Although the major development of the port of Ruhrort has occurred in modern times, the town was established in 1373 on an island in the Ruhr Delta. Its great growth began in 1715 when a port basin of 2,471 acres was constructed in an old branch of the Ruhr. At this basin coal from the Ruhr boats was loaded on the Rhine vessels. Other parts of the port were completed from 1820 to 1825, and in 1837 to 1842 the Lock Port of 29,652 acres was constructed. Later, further extensions were added as the port grew to its present importance.

*ADMINISTRATION*

The Duisburg-Ruhrort ports are administered under a uniformly managed port system. The two ports were organized into their present form as a joint-stock company when Duisburg, Ruhrort, and Meiderich were amalgamated in 1905-6. Then, the stock was jointly held by the city of Duisburg and the Prussian State, but at present it is held in equal parts by the Federal Republic, the country of North Rhine-Westphalia, and the city of Duisburg.

As has been true of many river ports, Duisburg has had trouble in maintaining contact with the Rhine. In early times Duisburg occupied a site on the river's bank. However, when the river bed was cleared in 1275 after a devastating flood the river shifted its course on the flood plain, and Duisburg was separated from the main channel of the river by more than a mile. Centuries passed before the widespread waters on the flood plain could be harnessed and canalized. Only then was the so-called "Bort-shipping" between Duisburg and other river ports of Holland reestablished. Still later, access to the center of town was restored by the construction of the Outer Harbor, the Inner Harbor, and the Parallel Harbors.

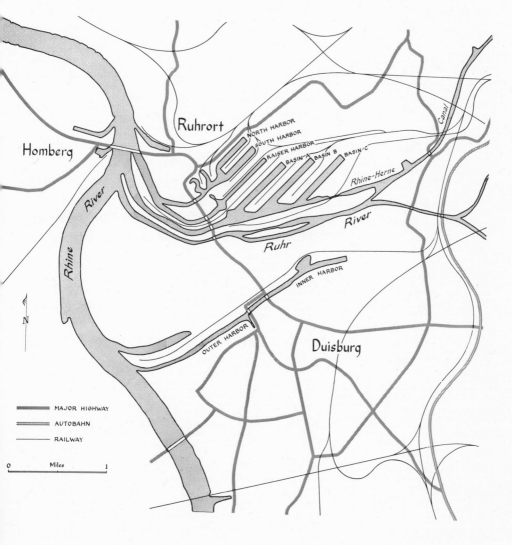

14. *Duisburg-Ruhrort harbors.*

EQUIPMENT AND FACILITIES

The Duisburg-Ruhrort ports include some twenty port-basins (beckens) with 27 miles of banks (*Fig. 14*). Of this length, 15 miles serve the traffic of the ports. In times of medium water level the separate port-basins have a navigable width from 60 to 130 meters. The ports together have 130 modern cranes with a lifting capacity of from one to 100 tons, four electric coal tippers with a daily output of 14,000 tons, one big loading plant and coal bunker, tanks for the storage of minerals with a capacity of 210,000 cbm., 14 granaries and silos equipped with 14 grain lifts, and ample general cargo warehouses. In addition, duty-free storage is possible, and there is an area of 224 acres for the storage of bulk goods. Moreover, 16 miles of roads serve the road traffic in the ports and lead to the Autobahn east of the city. There are three port railway stations in Duisburg with standard equipment and a 153-mile network of highways.

The terrain of the Duisburg-Ruhrort ports is leased to the firms operating in the port area, but the tenants build their own plants, mills, and warehouses. The rent charges vary with the qualities of site. Favorable sites with access to water, rail, and roads are still available.

TRAFFIC

A review of the traffic in major commodities for 1936, 1950, 1956, 1957, and 1958 is shown in Table 18. This was compiled from graphic

18. TRAFFIC AT DUISBURG-RUHRORT PORTS IN MAJOR COMMODITIES IN 1936, 1950, 1956, 1957, AND 1958.

| Commodity | 1936 | 1950 | 1956 | 1957 | 1958 |
|---|---|---|---|---|---|
| Coal Carbon | 12,200,000 | 3,300,000 | 3,600,000 | 4,300,000 | 3,900,000 |
| Erz (iron ore) | 1,250,406 | 1,406,003 | 3,100,000 | 3,200,000 | 2,700,000 |
| Eisen (steel) | 363,079 | 540,885 | 890,000 | 1,180,000 | 1,116,000 |
| Schrott (scrap metal) | 367,356 | 1,381,843 | 930,000 | 1,280,000 | 540,000 |
| Gravel and Sand | 1,529,455 | 1,501,384 | 1,700,000 | 1,400,000 | 1,330,000 |
| Wood | 223,229 | 54,155 | 61,920 | 69,953 | 73,817 |
| Oil | 208,617 | 425,574 | 2,495,379 | 2,890,584 | 2,303,850 |
| Fertilizers | 193,841 | 271,280 | 663,520 | 556,030 | 411,288 |
| Salts and Other Minerals | 259,287 | 449,611 | 473,250 | 497,715 | 466,056 |
| Grain | 294,844 | 266,353 | 285,445 | 264,961 | 270,395 |
| Victuals and Luxurio | 187,089 | 111,249 | . . . . | . . . . | . . . . |
| General Cargo | 17,400,000 | 10,000,000 | 14,900,000 | 16,300,000 | 13,700,000 |

Source: *Die Duisburg-Ruhrorter Häfen* (Duisburg, 1956).

materials in a bulletin showing the development of transshipment at the Duisburg-Ruhrort ports in those years. Note that the traffic in all commodities except coal, gravel and sand, wood, grain, and general cargo have increased.

Traffic in the Duisburg-Ruhrort ports amounted to a turnover of nearly 15 million tons in 1956. There are favorable services by water, rail, and roads. The major commodities handled are coal, ore, gravel, mineral oil, iron, fertilizers, salts, cereals, and wood. In prewar time more than 80 per cent of the traffic in the Duisburg-Ruhrort ports was with foreign markets. A large part of this was coal. As the coal trade has declined, the percentage to foreign countries is not as large as formerly.

Traffic on the Rhine and connecting waterways in 1936 and 1955 was as follows: 1] Traffic to Holland, Belgium, France, and the Lower Rhine area was in round numbers 12,400,000 tons in 1936 but was reduced to 9,300,000 in 1955. 2] Traffic to the Middle and Upper Rhine area was 4,400,000 tons in 1936, whereas in 1955 it reached 5,000,000 tons. 3] The traffic with the Rhine-Herne Canal showed an increase from 630,000 tons in 1936 to 694,000 tons in 1945. The great output of the Duisburg-Ruhrort ports is shown in the figures of ship and rail traffic. The number of incoming ships in 1955 was 52,983 for which 366,949 railway wagons were necessary.

The Duisburg-Ruhrort ports are still the large collecting base of Ruhr coal. The share of coal in the total traffic, however, has declined from 70 per cent in prewar time to 36 per cent of the total at present. The turnover capacity is still large, and a daily output of 50,000 tons might be obtained if the demand for coal warranted. The decline is due in part to high bundesbahn transport tariffs for short distances. This tariff caused a shift from canal transport to work-railways to turnover points belonging to the mining companies on the canals.

## OVER-ALL TRADE AT DUISBURG-RUHRORT HARBORS

Six commodity groups make up about 80 per cent of the traffic at the leading transfer center on the Rhine. These groups for 1936, 1952, and 1957 are shown in Table 19. These are heavy, bulky commodities well-suited to water transport. Moreover, they are basic items in the industrial life of the Ruhr Industrial District. Changes in the relative position of individual commodity groups in the transfer traffic include the decline of coal from 70.5 per cent of the total traffic in 1936 to 33.8 per cent in 1952 and 26.4 per cent in 1957. Coal is still the leader, but it no longer has as great a significance.

Changing technology in water transport, amazing growth in the use of automobiles, buses and trucks, and a multiplicity of other demands for gasoline, lubricants, and other petroleum products have moved mineral oils from almost nothing in 1936 to third place in 1957. Gasoline of good quality is made from coal and is distributed through well-managed service stations (Aral). The Rhine country produces but little petroleum. Hence,

19. MAIN TYPES OF GOODS ON A TONNAGE BASIS AND THEIR RANK IN THE TOTAL TRAFFIC ON THE DUISBURG-RUHRORT HARBORS.

| 1936 | Per Cent of Total | 1952 | Per Cent of Total | 1957 | Per Cent of Total |
|---|---|---|---|---|---|
| Coal | 70.5 | Coal | 33.8 | Coal | 26.4 |
| Sand and Gravel | 8.5 | Ore | 20.7 | Ore | 19.6 |
| Ore | 7.5 | Sand and Gravel | 14.0 | Mineral oil | 17.8 |
| Scrap metal | 2.2 | Scrap metal | 6.8 | Sand and Gravel | 8.6 |
| Mineral oil | 1.2 | Mineral oil | 4.3 | Scrap metal | 8.0 |
| Remaining goods | 10.1 | Remaining goods | 20.4 | Remaining goods | 19.6 |

Source: *Stadt und Häfen,* Vol. 9 (November 5, 1958), 967.

in this respect the Mississippi River Valley, rich in oil and gas, has the advantage not only of a large production of oil and gas but huge reserves for future use. Sand and gravel, much in use and in evidence along the Rhine, have become essentials in modern construction. As in the United States, the sources of supply are varied but quantities once thought inexhaustible are no longer regarded in that manner.

Ores include iron ore from the Kiruna District in northern Sweden, from German resources, from Brazil, Venezuela, and other countries. They are essential to the high standing of German iron and steel and other metal products. "The remaining goods include a diverse list some amounts of which are needed in the industrial complex."

# 9

# The Ruhr Generates Commerce

Unashamed, the giant river has removed a mask of medieval romance
to serve as the main artery of transportation to one of the most densely
populated and most heavily industrialized regions of the world: The
Ruhr District of West Germany.—Gordon M. Fair

THE RUHR INDUSTRIAL DISTRICT generates, by far, more traffic for
the Rhine than any other district of West Germany. In world markets the
Ruhr is the best known of all the heavy industrial districts (*Fig. 15*). This is
due to the quality, diversity, and quantity of its output and to the fact that
it has pioneered the production of basic products and has demonstrated
leadership in the organization, the financing, and the marketing of its
products. In terms of heavy industry, the Ruhr has been the standard of
comparison not only in regard to output but in appearance. To a visitor
accustomed to the drab appearance of the heavy industrial districts of the
United States, it looks remarkably clean and orderly.

The Duisburg-Ruhrort harbors are the points of contact of the
Rhine River and the world famous Ruhr Industrial District. Steinhauer in
his *The Reviere: Portrait of an Unusual Landscape* calls the Ruhr District
the one European economic landscape that occupies public opinion
throughout the world more than any other landscape. Chauncy D. Harris,
writing in 1944, noted that "this German district is of world concern primarily as the greatest center of steel and coal production in the Eastern
Hemisphere and that the use to which the Ruhr is put after this war

171

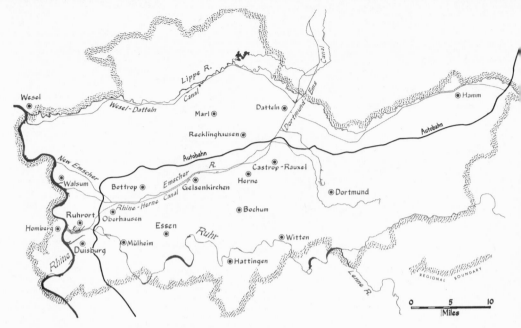

15.   *The Ruhr Industrial District.*

(World War II) may determine the character and duration of peace in the next generation."[1] In the summer of 1960, as viewed for the first time, the Ruhr was booming with production, alive with new technology organized by efficient management, and employed almost to the capacity its labor force.

Wilhelm Helmrich in his fine study of the economy of the Ruhr District points out that, in comparison to other heavy industry districts in Europe and the rest of the world, the Ruhr District is distinguished by its geographical compactness, that is, through the large accumulation of people and industries in a small space.[2] According to Steinhauer, on its surface area of 1,776 square miles—or 2 per cent of Germany—live 5.5 million people. In fact, in the heart of the area the population density is 6,500 to a square mile, or thirteen times the national average. The district has a west-east length of about 110 kilometers and an average north-south width of about 30 kilometers. This narrow belt is almost completely urbanized, with its numerous cities closely spaced as the links of a chain, each touching the next in line (*Fig.* 15).[3] Bituminous coal mining and iron and steel producing industries stamp its face and determine its borders; the district extends until its mining towers and blast furnaces are replaced by the green, rolling hills of rural Westphalia. In many places the change from urban to rural landscape is surprisingly abrupt.

1    *The Ruhr in the Transport Pattern*

The Ruhr Industrial District is in touch with the Duisburg-Ruhrort ports by modern means of transportation and communication. The railway network operated by the Federal Railways in the Ruhr has a track length of 3,430 miles. To it is linked privately owned railways having a track length of 2,735 miles. About 40,000 goods wagons are handled every day in the Essen area alone. Moreover, the Ruhr has the fastest service operated by the Federal Railways.[4] The major autobahn enters the area from the southwest, bypasses the ports from south to north, and enroute to Hannover and Berlin curves eastward across the northern border of this densely peopled area (*Fig. 15*). Lesser highways and railroads form a compact network over the entire area; pipelines, gas and water mains, telegraph, telephone lines, and radio are almost everywhere. The Ruhr is well equipped for its active participation in mining, manufacturing, and trade.

In the navigation of the Rhine River and its associated waterways, an evaluation of traffic on the connecting canals which serve the Ruhr region was made (*Fig. 5*). The busy Rhine-Herne Canal leads from the lower Ruhr River and the Duisburg-Ruhrort ports eastward, dividing the industrial district into two unequal parts (*Fig. 15*). The southern part exceeds the northern in volume and diversity of industrial production. At the east, the Rhine-Herne Canal joins the Dortmund-Ems Canal, forming the all-German water route to the North Sea. Farther north, the Wesel-Datteln Canal follows the irregular route of the Lippe River across the northern fringe of the Ruhr District. The Rhine-Herne and the Wesel-Datteln Canals are Class iv waterways, whereas the Dortmund-Ems Canal is Class iii. The canal classes range, by size and character of channel and locks, from Class v, the best, through classes iv, iii, ii, and i.

The coming of motorized ships with their variations in size and draft has increased the significance of many of the canals and decreased the usefulness of others. In considering the attitude of people in regard to canals and their place in the over-all transport pattern, it should be remembered that canals were in use long before railroads and modern highways were introduced. It may be presumed that, in many cases, the cost of construction of many canals has been forgotten. At least the question of construction cost is not discussed with such acute diversity of opinion as it is in the United States.

EMPLOYMENT IN INDUSTRY

In 1958 the manufacturing and mining industries plus the building trades in the Ruhr employed 1,100,000 people.[5] Since then the employment in these industries has increased, and the Ruhr has enjoyed a period of almost full employment. The active demand for labor since World War II has encouraged a steady inflow of nationals from other parts of West Germany and also from East Germany. Moreover, many of the expellees and refugees from Poland and other Soviet satellites have found jobs in the Ruhr industries. To a considerable extent, these immigrants represented skilled labor and were industrially experienced. They constituted an asset in the expanding industries. Their needs for housing brought on a shortage and stimulated the building industries. In the employment structure of the Ruhr 64.2 per cent of the employees worked in coal mining and iron and steel production; 21.6 per cent in the iron and metal processing industries; and 14.2 per cent in other industries. In addition, there was auxiliary employment in retail and other trades, as well as in service, professional, agricultural, and transport occupations.


II  *Coal and Coke in Trade*

Coal mining is the basic activity of the Ruhr. Moreover, coal is the major commodity shipped on the Rhine. In 1959 coal made up 8 per cent of the upstream traffic at Emmerich, the German station at the Dutch-German border, and 23.2 per cent of the downstream traffic.[6] These percentages have changed notably with the passing years, but coal always has been the leader or among the leaders. In 1957 coal mining in the Ruhr District provided employment for about 494,000 workmen. This was 47 per cent of the total employees in mining and industry in the area. Of those employed in mining, approximately 310,000 worked underground. In 1959 the output of coal declined somewhat, and employment declined accordingly.

In the Ruhr there has been an increasing diversity in the use of coal. This depends in part on the several types and qualities of coal mined in the Ruhr. The coal of the Ruhr District, according to Helmrich, is distinguished from the coal of other European coal basins because of the wealth of coal types.[7] He states that, taking advantage of coal at all mining depths, all types can be obtained, and that the reserves are divided as shown in Table 20. Group 1 has the highest gas content and is the steam coal and the most important raw material for coal chemistry. Group 2 is the sought-after coal for the iron foundries, as in the degasification process it results in a compact and brittle coke that withstands the pressure of the ore mass. Group 3 is used as fuel, and Group 4 is the coal with the largest carbon content and a gas content of only 7 to 12 per cent. Because it burns

20. COAL RESERVES BY TYPES.

| Group | | Per Cent |
|---|---|---|
| 1 | Free-burning, free-burning gas, and gas coal | 22 |
| 2 | Fat or cannel coal (bituminous) | 59 |
| 3 | Forge coal | 15 |
| 4 . | Semi-bituminous | 4 |
| | | 100 |

Source: Wilhelm Helmrich, *Wirtschafts-kunde des Landes Nordrhein-Westfalen* (Düsseldorf: August Bagel Verlag, 1960), p. 73.

21. COAL OUTPUT IN THE RUHR AREA BY TYPES IN 1957.

| Type of Coal | Output Million Tons | Per Cent |
|---|---|---|
| Free-burning, free-burning gas, and gas coal | 24.3 | 19.7 |
| Fat or cannel coal (bituminous) | 82.6 | 67.2 |
| Forge coal | 7.0 | 5.7 |
| Semi-bituminous (non-coking) and anthracite coal | 9.3 | 7.4 |
| Total | 123.2 | 100.0 |

Source: Wilhelm Helmrich, *Wirtschaftskunde des Landes Nordrhein-Westfalen* (Düsseldorf: August Bagel Verlag, 1960), p. 74.

without smoke and with a short flame it is the coal for slow-combustion stoves in households. These several types of coal are to be found in the areas drained by the Mississippi and Ohio rivers but not in a single district. Hence, juxtaposition of types in the Ruhr is one of the assets of that area. The output of coal in 1957 in the Ruhr by types is presented in Table 21. Approximately two-thirds of the production in that year was in bituminous coal, and that together with the first two types made up almost 87 per cent of the total. Both types are available in the drainage basin of the Ohio River.

Comparing the thickness and stratification of coal seams, the coal districts tributary to the Ohio and Mississippi rivers have an advantage over Ruhr coal. In the United States, mining conditions are more favorable as a fourth of the coal comes from open-pit mines, and in the underground workings the greater thickness and continuity of the seams than those in the Ruhr mean more use of mining machinery. Hence, an average output per man per shift is about ten tons. On the average in all the collieries of the Ruhr District the output per man per shift in July of 1959 amounted to 1.9 tons. However, in the Pattberg shafts of the Rhine Prussian Company on the left bank of the Rhine the output per man per shift was more than three tons. In discussing this matter, Helmrich states that in the United States "coal can be mined substantially cheaper and a high freight expense borne, even to the extent of exporting coal to Europe." Such export, however, is abnormal rather than normal business, but it does open the question as to the ways and to the extent the cost of coal transport in the United States can be reduced. No conclusion in this matter can be reached at present, but one can advance the theory that appreciable lowering of transport costs probably must await the efficient integration of rail, highway, and waterway transportation. Experiments in the control of barge service by certain of our railroads might be of help in this matter. In the Ruhr much of the coal shipped out of the area moves on the Rhine and connecting waterways.

To the coal industry of the United States, Ruhr coal is especially interesting because it is both a source of energy and a raw material to be processed and finished. In fact, according to Helmrich, two-thirds of the coal utilized in the home market is subject to finishing. In 1958 around 48 million tons of coal were converted into the metallurgical fuel, coke. Helmrich summarizes this situation in Table 22.

22. PRODUCTION OF COAL BY-PRODUCTS AND CURRENT IN THE RUHR INDUSTRIAL DISTRICT.

| Product | Unit | 1938 | 1958 |
|---|---|---|---|
| Raw tar | 1,000 tons | 1,263 | 1,653 |
| Crude benzene | 1,000 tons | 364 | 507 |
| Sulphate of ammonia | 1,000 tons | 95 | 105 |
| Fuel and illuminating (coal) gas | | | |
| Available quantity | billion cu. m. | 16.4 | 20.0 |
| Foreign market | billion cu. m. | 6.8 | 10.1 |
| Current | | | |
| Generated quantity | billion kw. hr. | 3.4 | 13.4 |
| Foreign deliveries | billion kw. hr. | 1.2 | 7.5 |

Source: Wilhelm Helmrich, *Wirtschaftskunde des Landes Nordrhein-Westfalen* (Düsseldorf: August Bagel Verlag, 1960), p. 75.

The increases from 1938 to 1958, shown by the table, reflect advances in technology and recovery from the effects of World War II. The increase in crude benzene as it is processed into carburetor fuel benzene and technical benzene rose by more than a third. Motor fuel, derived from coal, is sold through a chain of filling stations, and in 1960 it was as satisfactory as regular gasoline. Moreover, this chain of stations had the added attraction of distributing the best highway maps available. Also noteworthy is the increased production of fuel and illuminating gas from coal. Of the available quantity in 1958, half went to foreign markets. Other products are made from coking plant gas, as for example, the manufacture in Dortmund of gas soot, a necessary ingredient in rubber tire manufacture, and the output of polyethylene, a raw material for the production of synthetic products.

In West Germany, as in the United States, there has been a great increase in the amount of coal utilized in the output of electrical current. Gas and forge coal and "ballast rich and otherwise unmarketable coal" are utilized in this growing use of coal. In addition, the Essen-Karnap of the Rhine-Westphalia-Ems daily burns 700 cubic meters of sewage sludge from the filter plant of the Ems Cooperative Society.[8] This production of electricity, of course, calls for large quantities of water needed in the conversion of steam power to electrical power. In all probability, the use of coal as a raw material will increase in the future as new technological discoveries are made and in view of the increasing competition of petroleum products and nuclear energy. The Ruhr, with its four types of coal under production and its leadership in the technology of coal use, is almost certain to lead the search for new uses for coal as a raw material.

Bituminous coal ranks as the greatest mineral asset in Germany. The Ruhr contains the outstanding coal field in West Germany. This field is about 110 kilometers long from east to west, and the Rhine cuts the field into a large east segment and a smaller segment west of the river. The eastern segment is drained by the Ruhr, and the river gives its name to the area. The bituminous coal of the Ruhr has a gas content of 19 to 30 per cent, and a compact, brittle coke results in the degasification process in the coke ovens. More gas was obtained from the Ruhr cokeries in 1960 than from the entire German Empire in prewar times. A 1,475-mile pipeline system, the largest grid gas system in Europe, distributes gas to other enterprises. Moreover, of the electric power utilized by public power supply stations in the Federal Republic, 45 per cent is generated from Ruhr coal.[9]

In 1957 about 50 million tons of coal were converted into metallurgical coke. This coke production was the bridge between coal mining and the output of iron and steel. It constituted a condition that promoted output from the furnaces, as will be seen presently. In addition, the gases from the coke ovens are a basic factor in the chemical industries.

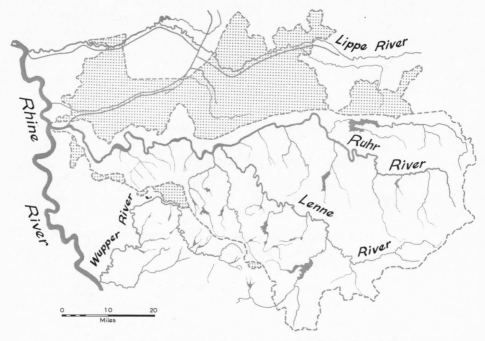

16. *Energy and water supply regions of the Ruhr Association and the Ruhr Valley Dam Association. The broken line indicates the border of the rainfall region. The stippled pattern shows areas beyond the watershed supplied with Ruhr water.*

III     Water Problems in the Ruhr District

Areas as industrially developed and as densely peopled as the Ruhr face the ever-increasing demands for potable water and equally urgent needs for sewage disposal. In the Ruhr the major supply of water comes from the Ruhr River which margins the southern border of the area for more than 44 miles (*Fig.* 16). Fifty water recovery plants have been built along the river's course, and the length of the distributive pipes totals 9,500 miles. About 220 billion gallons of water a year are distributed, mainly to the Ruhr industrial area where the need of water for domestic, municipal, and industrial purposes is great. For most of its length the Ruhr flows through rolling terrain, partly farmed and partly forested. From some vantage points on the upland slopes castles built in an earlier era look down on the river with its dams and reservoirs. Hence, this attractive landscape contains evidence of functional structures of the past in close proximity to functional structures of the present.

As long ago as 1600 the Emscher River and its valley was a sanitary problem to the people who lived or worked in this coal mining and industrial area. The ground over some of the underground workings caved in, thereby creating undrained depressions.[10] Marshes formed, and the wastes of a growing population polluted the valley. Improvements began about the turn of the century under the direction of the Emscher Association, and the Emscher River has been deepened for 50 miles of its course and the banks of its tributaries stabilized. Many square miles of area have no free outlet. The area is kept dry by forty co-operated clarifying plants, and some twenty-five dephenolizing plants recover 7,000 tons (German) of crude phenol for industrial processing. The heavy cost is borne by the local Association. Except for war-damaged structures, the funds are raised entirely by the Association. The results are most gratifying. At present, the visitor to the Emscher valley finds little or no unsightly waste or neglected land and swamps. In financing the work of the Association that controls the operations, the guiding principle is that both the cost of pollution abatement and the value of direct, as well as indirect, benefits derived by a member from the execution, maintenance, and operation of the different installations are accessible.

## IV   *Manufacture and Sale of Iron and Steel*

In large measure, the fame of the Ruhr depends on its leadership in the production of iron and steel and of the manufacture and sale of iron and steel products. Historically this leadership was displayed in the application of chemical methods and techniques in the development of the blast furnace and other sections of industry. This leadership has continued into modern times, as the Ruhr is one of the areas that contributed significantly to the huge output and use of steel in all previous years.

According to Gerhard Steinhauer, "Metallurgical coke from the Ruhr's coking plants was responsible for making the Ruhr the focal point of the iron and steel industry." He also stated that at the end of 1958 there were sixty-six blast furnaces in operation in the province of North Rhine-Westphalia and that with a few exceptions all were located in the Ruhr. From the blast furnaces the molten iron passed directly into the steel plants which mass-produced heavy rolled products such as rails, sheet steel, beams, and plates. The Ruhr furnaces supplied in 1958 a third of the output of pig iron in the countries belonging to the European Coal and Steel Community. Moreover, steel production included 18.4 million tons of crude steel, 7.4 million tons of basic Bessemer steel, 9.2 million tons of open hearth steel, 67,000 tons of acid Bessemer steel, 1.7 million tons of electric and other steels, and 12.3 million tons of rolling mill products.[11]

Next to coal mining, the iron and steel industries lead in employment with 37.6 per cent of the total. In 1957 the production of iron and steel employed 17.1 per cent of the employees engaged in industry in the Ruhr, and the iron and steel processing industries employed 20.5 per cent, as shown in Table 23. Because the range of skill is great, there commonly

23. NUMBER OF EMPLOYEES IN IRON AND STEEL INDUSTRIES IN THE RUHR IN 1957.

| Branch of Industry | Employees | |
|---|---|---|
| | Total | Per Cent |
| Iron and Steel Production | | 179,005 | 17.1 |
| Iron and Metal Processing Industries of which the divisions were: | | | |
| Iron, steel, and metal casting | 19,216 | | 1.9 |
| Machine and vehicle building | 66,200 | | 6.3 |
| Shipbuilding | 3,009 | | 0.3 |
| Iron and steel construction | 57,001 | | 5.4 |
| Iron, lead, and metal goods | 15,099 | | 1.4 |
| Iron and steel molding | 25,552 | | 2.4 |
| Electrotechnical industry | 28,145 | | 2.7 |
| Precision tool industry | 1,572 | | 0.1 |
| | | 215,794 | 20.5 |
| Total | | 394,799 | 37.6 |

Source: Wilhelm Helmrich, *Wirtschaftskunde des Landes Nordrhein-Westfalen* (Düsseldorf: August Bagel Verlag, 1960), p. 79.

is an inflow of labor into the Ruhr from other sections of Germany, an inflow interrupted somewhat by the Iron Curtain and other restrictions.

The full range of the iron and steel industries, from basic production to finished products, spread broadly but in an irregular pattern over the Ruhr mining and industrial district. There are, however, four areas of concentration: 1] along the Rhine in the Duisburg section, 2] at Dortmund in the eastern part of the Ruhr, 3] in the Bochum, Witten, and Hattingen in the south central section east of Essen, the administrative center of the coal mining centers, and 4] in Gelsenkirchen in the neighborhood of the Rhine-Herne Canal.[12]

To a notable extent, basic iron and steel production is localized along the Rhine in the Duisburg area. Originally the iron plants were scattered over the Ruhr Valley, but after 1860 the change from local to imported ores led to increasing production in the Duisburg area where water transport is available. Hence, between 1855 and 1939 the plants at Rhine side increased their share of Ruhr iron production from 30 to 60 per cent of the total output of the Ruhr.

In 1957 six centers directly at Rhine side produced more than half of the pig iron and 48 per cent of the crude steel output. With the production of the foundry at Oberhausen, along the Rhine-Herne Canal not far from the Rhine, and two mills at Mülheim, along the lower Ruhr River, there is produced in the area of the lower Rhine about 66 per cent of the pig iron and 60 per cent of the crude steel and finished steel output of the Ruhr District. In this general area along and near the Rhine there were in 1958 some 47 of the total of 70 blast furnaces under fire in the Ruhr.[13] In addition to a site along the river, a mill needs to be at a point where land transport focuses on the river as it does in the Duisburg-Ruhrort area.

Helmrich points out that a single blast furnace with an output of 1,000 tons daily needs iron ore in the amount carried by two or three freight trains and an amount of coke that could be carried by one and a half freight trains. Of course, some of the needed iron ore and coke actually reach the mills by canal and river transport. The iron foundries also follow the principle of the utilization of the worthless, as for example, slag from the Thomas process became Thomas Meal, a phosphate fertilizer.

Dortmund, the second center of the iron and steel industries, is the southern terminal of the Dortmund-Ems Canal (*Fig.* 15). This canal was completed in 1899, taking seven years to build. Its purpose was to give the Ruhr District an outlet to the North Sea entirely through German territory. It is 165 miles long and reaches the North Sea at the port of Emden. It transports coal to the sea and Swedish iron ore from Emden to the mills in Dortmund. Of the output of the Ruhr District in 1958, the Dortmund area produced 24 per cent of the pig iron, 25 per cent of the crude steel, and 26 per cent of the finished steel. Dortmund was also a member of the Hanseatic League. At present it is a rail and highway center and, in addition to its coal mining and steel producing activities, is a brewing, petroleum, and synthetic oil center.

The Bochum, Witten, and Hattingen centers are distinctly detached one from the other, but they have common interests in coal mining and steel manufacture. Bochum, famous as a center of steel casting for bells, produces coke and coal tar products. Witten, at the head of navigation on the Ruhr River, produces steel, coal tar products, and glass. Hattingen is a rail center and has coal and iron mining, and some steel production.[14]

Several specialized plants form a fourth group in or near Gelsenkirchen. Since the opening of the first coal mine in 1853 this area has become increasingly important.[15] For example, Gelsenkirchen became world-famous through its centrifugal castings.[16] Its iron and steel industries are somewhat integrated as it has blast furnaces, coke ovens, foundries, and steel-rolling and wire mills. Coal tar products are obtained as by-products of the coke works. Machinery and the manufacture of machinery and various other products associated with heavy industry are among the major activities of Gelsenkirchen. It is also a center of the German glass industry, specializing in the making of window panes.[17] In recent times a clothing industry has developed, in part to utilize women as employees.

As stated previously, second only to coal, the iron and steel industries are of major importance in the economy of the Ruhr region and, in fact, of West Germany. During World War II great damage was inflicted on the iron and steel plants; nevertheless, the plants have been rebuilt, and with modern installations their potential production is as great and, in most cases, considerably greater than before the war. The industry is again so diversified and so well organized that, in general, efficient management is characteristic, as it has been since 1870 when large scale production came into existence.

The Krupp enterprises in the past were a major factor in the Essen war industries and to a degree became a symbol of the Ruhr. Their ascendancy resulted from hard effort, bold venture, engineering achievement, and government support. Today, the Krupp's works, with their payroll of some 50,000, are devoted to production for peaceful purposes and are among the largest enterprises in the Federal Republic.[18]

Efforts have been made to arrange the pattern of the industry so that the several phases of production are closely integrated and yet so localized that advantage is taken of the inherent qualities of the areas such as: 1] the large output of coke for energy and heat, 2] the presence of abundant water supplies, 3] the concentration of skilled workers, 4] the momentum of long-range experience, and 5] the facilities of transportation, especially of access to navigation on the Rhine and associated waterways.

In selling and marketing their numerous products, management in the iron and steel industries has been alert and progressive. Government cartels with adequate finances and active management have been organized to gain control of distribution. Cartel is the European term for a trust, and it now commonly implies an international organization of industrialists and businessmen. German firms, for example, have organized cartels with firms in Belgium, Great Britain, Luxembourg, and France to control and direct the production and marketing of products in which there is active international competition. According to Gottmann, cartels have been particularly active in the fields of metallurgy and chemicals.[19]

## v    *Technological and Mechanical Industries*

As presented herewith, the technological industries include enterprises that owe their modern development to scientific discoveries applied to the processing of materials into new products, or of upgrading materials into a form or substance that increases their utility. Hence, in the processes of production it may be argued that the applied technology takes on values greater than the utilized materials. However, the assemblage of the great variety of utilized materials on sites and in situations that promote production and facilitate distribution of finished products is of prime importance, more especially under highly competitive conditions.

In view of the recognized achievements of German science it is not surprising that the Rhine section of the Ruhr has a broad panel of technological industries. Helmrich lists them in terms of employment but does not provide a title for the group. In Table 24 they are arranged in seven categories under the convenient heading Technological Industries. Although their combined employment of 149,000 in 1957 is small when

| Industries | Employees | Per cent All Industries |
|---|---|---|
| Technological Industries: | | |
| Chemical Industry | 40,909 | 3.9 |
| Synthetics, Rubber, Asbestos | 2,754 | 0.3 |
| Stone, Earth, and Glass | 20,846 | 2.0 |
| Wood Working, Wood Pulp, Paper and Printing | 24,157 | 2.3 |
| Textile, Clothing, and Leather | 30,522 | 2.9 |
| Food and Luxury Stuff | 27,789 | 2.6 |
| Remaining Industries | 1,628 | 0.2 |
| Total | 148,605 | 14.2 |
| ALL INDUSTRIAL EMPLOYEES | 1,049,097 | 100.0 |

24. EMPLOYEES IN THE TECHNOLOGICAL INDUSTRIES AND THE RELATION OF THE EMPLOYEES IN EACH INDUSTRY TO THE TOTAL EMPLOYMENT IN THE RUHR IN 1957.

Source: Wilhelm Helmrich, *Wirtschaftskunde des Landes Nordrhein-Westfalen* (Düsseldorf: August Bagel Verlag, 1960), p. 79.

compared with the 494,000 in Ruhr coal mining or with the 395,000 for the iron and steel industries (*Table 24*), in many cases they offer employment to more skilled technicians and have a greater seasonal and annual continuity than prevails in the basic industries. Little or no information is available as to what extent these technological industries provide traffic on the Rhine and associated waterways. However, it may be assumed that, although much of the output is shipped by rail or truck, some shipments are made up or down the Rhine, especially in view of the increasing use of powered craft and faster schedules on the river. Of the technological industries, the chemical group is outstanding in the economy of the Ruhr and along the Rhine. In large measure the chemical group owes its early development to German enterprise, and it illustrates the application of scientific methods and techniques in industry.

## CHEMICAL INDUSTRY

The chemical industry in the Ruhr region commonly employs about 41,000 workers, or nearly 4 per cent of the employees in the technological industries. The industry is both old and young. Old because 140 years ago in Duisburg the first German sulphuric acid factory began production. Some twenty-four years later an alkalai plant and an ultramarine factory were built. Later the calcination of sulfur-bearing ores was undertaken. Eventually, according to Helmrich, the Duisburg copper foundry (Duisburg Kupferhutte) was developed. This large and unique enterprise not only produces half of the West German output of sodium sulphates but also "high value pig iron, copper, lead, zinc, cobalt, cadmium, silver, and gold."[20] Many developments followed, and by the first decade of the present century chemical production had localized in each of the four major industrial districts of prewar Germany. Germany had become the acknowledged world leader in dyes, medicines, potash fertilizers, and other commercial chemicals. Furthermore, German success in the iron and steel trade depended largely on the use of newly discovered chemical processes.

In addition to supplying energy and heat, coal is the parent of many useful substances. In 1957 nearly 14,000 workers found employment in the chemical enterprises associated with the coal production of the Ruhr, more especially with the output of coke. By-products recovered from the cokeries have contributed to the economic operation of the plants. Included in these products are tar, benzole, ammonia, curamon resins, and rich gas. Under the magic of applied science, the coke oven plant is the cradle of the coal tar industry. Coal tar, one of the by-products in making coke, yields a long list of valuable substances, including dyes, medicines, photographic chemicals, perfumes, and flavors.[21]

From the waste gas of the cokeries, research and experimentation developed a high grade product from which the new man-made fibers are obtained. The coking process also contributes to the output of fertilizers and explosives. Some of these and other products were discovered and are produced at Duisburg-Ruhrort and other points along the Rhine.[22] More than a third of the hard coal mined in the Ruhr is utilized in the cokeries, and the by-products recovered contribute notably to the economy of the coking plants.

The early success of the chemical industries in Germany depended 1] on the advanced status of the chemical sciences, and the application of scientific methods and techniques to industrial processes, 2] on the organizing and administrative abilities of the leaders in production and marketing, 3] on the skill and experience of available labor, and 4] on the presence of resources of water, coal, potash, salt, and sulphur.[23]

Basic materials and industrial chemicals are generally bulky, heavy, and low priced commodities. Hence, the manufacturers choose plant locations at which the raw materials are assembled readily and cheaply, and from which the finished or partially finished products can be shipped to market at relatively low cost. In all these essentials Germany demonstrated leadership in each of its four major industrial areas, but nowhere more definitely than along the Rhine and associated waterways. Hence, centers of chemical enterprise became established at the Rhine cities of Duisburg-Ruhrort, Düsseldorf, Köln, and Mannheim-Ludwigshafen.

The processes of chemical manufacture are, in general, various combinations of those employed in chemical laboratories, such as grinding, mixing, roasting, distilling, compressing, and crystallizing. In many cases substances are produced that bear little or no resemblance to the raw materials. There is, however, no sharp boundary between chemical manufacture and some industries not classed in the chemical group. Two closely related types are the coal-chemical and the petro-chemical industries. The latter will be mentioned under petroleum traffic on the Rhine.

186 / NORTH ATLANTIC ARENA

VI   Secondary Activities

GLASS, STONE, AND EARTH

Coke oven gas encouraged the development of an important glass industry. Production of flat glass, hollow glassware, mirror glass, glass brick, glass liters, and other glass products employs about 11,000 people. It is said that "each second window pane produced in West Germany comes from a Gelsenkirchen factory." The output of the stone and earth industries comes from many installations in the Ruhr. Along the Lower Rhine large excavations produce sand and gravel for building operations and road construction, molding sand for foundaries, quartz sand and gravel for roofing-paper and for filtration plants. "A plant of the Portland Cement Industry is located in Essen-Kupferdreh, where plaster for facing overhead construction also is produced."[24]

WOOD WORKING, WOOD PULP, AND PAPER AND PRINTING

This loosely integrated group of technological and mechanical industries provides employment to some 24,000 workers. These industries are widely, though unevenly, distributed in the Ruhr and in the Rhine Valley. They are produced by the application of a wide range of mechanical methods and techniques. However, they have in common both direct and indirect relations to forest resources and the output of forest products.

Traffic in forest products has featured the Rhine for many years. From time to time the products shipped changed, and the volume changed accordingly. According to Elkins, in early times deciduous forest predominated in the west, with a mixture of deciduous and coniferous in the east. At the turn of the century, even in the west, coniferous softwoods found preference as they grew more rapidly, produced straighter timbers for construction, and did better on poor soils than the deciduous varieties. Today the demand for a variety of forest products has re-emphasized the value of the deciduous plantations.[25]

The demand for forest products changed during the great wars. The demand since the wars has remained constant, however, and today half or more of the forest lands are held by the State or other public bodies. Laws protect these forest holdings, many of which are enclosed or otherwise protected from intruders. Cutting is confined to mature trees. Hence, the output is relatively steady. In fact, Elkins states that West Germany is fourth in timber production and second in timber imports. The demand for wood products, in large measure, comes from urban localities, and the principal production is in rural areas. Along the Rhine, the forest-clad hills and lower mountain slopes are as conspicuous as the Rhine cities. Shipments by waterways, railways, and highways connect the producing and consuming areas.

The harbors on the Rhine Delta figure in the imports of timber from America, Norway, and the Baltic forests. Today the upstream movement of wood products to the mining centers in the Ruhr is probably twenty times as great as the downstream traffic in forest products. The importance of wood-using industries in the Ruhr is shown by the fact, previously stated, that these industries employ over 24,000 workers (*Table 24*).

### TEXTILE, CLOTHING AND LEATHER INDUSTRIES

Textile manufacture employs 6,000 people, whereas the clothing industry in 1957 employed 20,000. The employees mainly are women, and thus this type of manufacture is ancillary to the basic iron and steel and coal mining industries. Around 2,000 persons are employed in the Duisburg-Rheinhausen District. The leather industry is small and employs about 4,700 persons.[26]

### FOOD AND LUXURY INDUSTRIES

Seven large grain mills import wheat and other cereals and supply the flour requirements of the Ruhr. Most of these mills are in Duisburg and Homberg where their output also includes bread, feed grains, oil imports for the margarine industry, and coffee imports. Slaughtering, meat packing, and brewing are other features in the food division of the technological and mechanical industries.

### COAL-CHEMICAL AND PETRO-CHEMICAL INDUSTRIES

Coal and petroleum, the major energy resources, are important sources of raw materials in the chemical industries of the Ruhr. For example, the coal-chemical and the petro-chemical industries are linked in the manufacture of starting products for plastics based on hydrocarbons, such as polyvinyl chloride, polyester resins, and polyethylene. Moreover, according to Steinhauer, the synthetic buttadiene natrium is under development at the present time.[27]

Technical integration occurs in many branches of industry in the Ruhr. The Ruhr sulphuric acid industry cooperates with the mining industry. Their products go to the coking plants where they are utilized in the manufacture of fertilizers. Still further, the residual gases of the atmospheric nitrogen plants are utilized in the large scale chemical industry.[28]

## TECHNICAL INTEGRATION

Technical integration characterizes many industrial operations in the Ruhr, more especially in the western or Rhine section. Coal constitutes the basic element in the integration, with the production of coke serving as the connecting link between coal mining and the production of iron and steel. More than a third of the bituminous coal is processed in the coke ovens. The annual production averages about 40 million tons (German). Ruhr coal helps to create trade and commerce. Gas from the coke ovens is piped long distances through the countryside to installations were it is needed. The grid system extends over 1,475 miles. In some cases it is stored in high tanks or in porous underground layers of rock in order to provide for seasonal and other varying requirements. Moreover, 45 per cent of the electric power utilized by public power supply stations in the Federal Republic is generated from Ruhr coal.[29]

A few examples will illustrate the extent and character of integration: 1] The coking plants use the products of the sulphuric acid works for the production of fertilizers. 2] Some divisions of the chemical industry utilize the residual gases of the nitrogen plants. 3] Gas from the coke ovens stimulated the growth of the glass industry, and some of the glassworks are owned by the mining corporations. Moreover, as the glassworks use much gas, in most cases they are in close proximity to the coking plants. It is reported that after the war some glassmaking craftsmen expelled from Silesia found new jobs in the Ruhr industry. 4] The waste from coke ovens yields a high-grade product from which man-made fibers are produced.

Steinhauer points out that integration has made great progress in the large-scale chemical industry. He sites as an example "the production plants in the Chemische works at Hüls."[30] He states that, "Centralized control is obtained from electronically and pneumatically operated control stands. . . . Substances are created from ethylene gas and air, for instance, which are used in the textile, paint, soap and pharmaceutical industries." The over-all pattern is presented in the following paragraph.

## UTILIZATION OF THE WORTHLESS

An illustration of regional organizations in "the principle of the ultilization of the worthless" is the utilization of waste materials as provided by the chemical establishments at Marl five miles northwest of Recklinghausen—a city of 100,000 people with coal mining, coke works, and coal tar extraction. Marl lies between the Emscher Valley at the south and the Lippe Valley at the north. The chemical works in the area employ about 15,000 people. In terms of raw materials the factories have a dyadic emphasis in that they operate partly in the domain of coal chemistry and partly in petroleum chemistry (petro chemicals).

The industries at Marl receive, as a raw material, gas and benzine from nearby coking plants. They also obtain, as a raw material, refinery gas through pipelines from crude oil refineries in Gelsenkirchen. These refinery gases otherwise would be waste products. A third valuable raw material is natural gas brought by a gas trunk line from the natural oil and gas fields in Emsland, between the Dortmund-Ems Canal and the Dutch border. These gas fields were discovered in swampy terrain north of Bentheim in 1940. Extensive drainage systems were needed to make the area accessible, but now the three fields produce a third of Germany's petroleum.

Ethyl, still another basic material, is obtained by a 90-kilometer pipeline from the great Esso refinery near Köln to use in the Marl chemical plants. This source of supply makes possible a larger output of ethyl than hitherto had been possible.

The Marl chemical plants give as well as receive. For example, they deliver hydrogen and other waste products to neighboring nitrogen refineries. They also furnish waste products to the Persil factory in Duisburg, via a 70-kilometer pipeline, for the manufacture of detergents. The major output at Marl consists of raw materials for varnish, water softeners, synthetics, textile auxiliaries, washing raw materials, preservatives, and synthetic rubber.

The functional pattern that spreads out from Marl is based on natural resources of land, water, and minerals that lie in reasonably close proximity. These constitute an asset when recognized, described, organized, planned, and engineered by men who possess leadership in concept, knowledge of the necessary technology, accessibility to finances, and the power to implement materials and processes into realities. Hence, from the Ruhr and Lower Rhine, where men and nature have teamed for many decades, there is much to be learned.

VII   *Leadership in Business, Finance, and Culture*

In addition to the industrialized Ruhr and the twin ports of Duisburg-Ruhrort, the Lower Rhine has two major ports and business, financial, commercial, and cultural centers. Villages are closely spaced and each major city lies within 25 miles or less of another city or cities in the same size group. For example, Düsseldorf lies 15 miles upstream from Duisburg, and about 23 miles by highway from Köln.

## DÜSSELDORF

Düsseldorf is a river port and a commercial, financial, and fashion center. It is a beautiful city with impressive shopping areas, wide boulevards, and attractive parks and residential areas. As in the case of Köln, Düsseldorf bankers helped finance early enterprises in the Ruhr; today it is the fashion mecca of this section of West Germany. Its major harbor is at the upper end of the great curve of the river as it approaches the city. Another harbor is the "Rheinhafen" west of and farther up the river.

In the major harbor where seagoing vessels dock, grain and flour are handled in eight grain elevators and ten granaries with a total capacity of 156,000 tons. Cattle and hogs also are brought in and processed. Chicken feed is prepared in special facilities much as it is in the United States. As might be expected, the chemical industry is represented in Düsseldorf, with sulphuric acid as a major product. Iron and steel products, including finished steel and pipe, plate and industrial glass, ceramics and textiles, are included in the livelihood structure of this prosperous metropolitan area astride the Rhine. The port has a water area of 532,300 square miles, quayage of 12,000 square miles, and the customary equipment of cranes. Rail and highway connections with the harbors facilitate transshipments from and to these agencies of transport.

## KÖLN

At Köln, in latitude 50° 57′ north, there is a significant addition to Rhine navigation; seagoing craft of small dimensions—drawing less than 12 feet—regularly ply to the city on the left bank of the river and to the neighboring towns of Mülheim and Deutz on the right bank (*Fig. 5*). The developed river front extends for about 9.3 miles and is divided into five sections or ports—three on the left bank and two on the right. Each section has a distinct function or functions. For example, Köln's oil harbor is at Niehl, down river from the city. One section of the oil harbor has special facilities for loading and unloading tankers at the Esso oil refinery. Another section of this harbor handles and stores grain and other bulk cargoes. In 1960 two extra basins, each 400 meters long, were under construction. All of the port sections are reached by rails and highways. Hence, goods can be loaded directly from ships to trucks or railway cars, or vice versa.[31]

Köln's situation at the crossing of the Rhine Valley route and the west-east land route favored its rise as the commercial and financial center of the region stimulated into industrial activity by the development of the Ruhr coal field.[32] According to Shackleton, much of the capital needed in the development of the early mines and associated industries was provided by the financial institutions of Köln.[33] Moreover, it became a manufacturing outpost of the Ruhr, the greatest region of German industry. Fuel and some electrical power for its establishments are derived from large open-pit lignite deposits west of the city.

Köln was an ancient commercial center. During its long history it has witnessed times of prosperity and times of impoverishment, depending in large measure on the prevailing conditions of transport and trade in Europe and the Mediterranean. Köln joined the great league of Rhenish cities founded at Mainz in 1254, which in time included free and fortified towns from Basel at the head of the Rhine Rift Valley to Köln in the North German Plain.[34] Köln became an influential member of the Hanseatic League, and its trade with England began as early as the eleventh century.[35] It flourished in Medieval times with the overland trade in Eastern and Mediterranean commodities. Its site at the head of seagoing transport enabled it to become a transshipping point for goods moving in smaller craft further up the Rhine and associated waterways.[36] Moreover, through the centuries Köln was the river crossing point for a west-east route which followed the border of the Rhenish Plateau; a route utilized by a major railway from Paris eastward to Russia. The importance of this route is suggested by the construction at Köln of the first railway bridge across the Rhine. Partsch says of Köln: "As the port of the German Rhine country, it spread the net of its communications as far eastward as the lands extended which had been colonized by Germans, and southward over the Alps as far as Milano and Venezia, distributing not only foreign wares, but also the products of its own industry, and especially of flourishing spinning, weaving, and dye works."[37]

After two centuries of prosperity Köln lost its trade with the Rhine Delta because the Protestant power in the Netherlands blocked upriver traffic from the sea. Moreover, it lost its trade with England on account of discrimination against the Protestants.[38] In time Köln began to recover, but its prosperous modern growth began after Bismark had established the Ruhr in 1870, taking Germany into the industrial age.

Köln suffered great damage to its industrial and commercial structures during World War II. It was an early target for Allied raids, and most of the old town was destroyed. Since the war much of the damaged areas have been rebuilt, especially in the industrial and port sections. Shipping and trade have revived, as evidenced by the 6 million tons of cargo handled in 1960. In general, the inbound freight is made up of raw materials and partly finished goods, whereas high-grade processed commodities feature the outbound traffic. Some direct freight and passenger services are maintained to London, Bremen, Hamburg, and Scandinavian ports. Basic to the trade by river and land is an industrial structure whose output includes iron, steel, and other metal foundries; vehicles and railway cars; diesel motors, cranes, cables, and machine tools; chemical products, including dyes, pharmaceuticals, and perfume; and a great variety of textiles and clothing.

As Köln has both river and seagoing traffic, it offers a variety of port services. All kinds of fuel are supplied from shore stations or bunkering boats. Water and provisions are also available. Harbor dues are levied under the provisions of the official tariff of the Association of Rhine Ports. Pilotage and towage services are available. In these and other ways Köln justifies its large population and its leadership in culture in the Lower Rhine country.

# 10

# Motivation of Petroleum Traffic

IN 1961 the free world consumed a total of 20 million barrels of crude petroleum a day. Informed sources predicted a consumption of an additional million barrels a day in each of the next two years. This means that there is a truly dynamic growth in the demand for petroleum and of the products that can be made from it. This increasing consumption of oil is an indication of the continuing effort to gain a higher level of service from the domain of transportation.

## 1    Traffic on the Rhine

In no part of the world has the consumption of petroleum and petroleum products been more marked than in the North Atlantic nations of Europe. For example, in the decade ending in 1960 industrial production in the six Common Market countries grew at a 7 per cent rate, whereas in the United States the rate was 3 per cent; but in the latter there was a much broader base on which to grow.[1] In this period, product sales of Standard Oil of New Jersey increased 10 per cent. Much of the increasing use of oil in the North Atlantic nations of Europe has been in the Rhine countries. In recent years, increasing imports of petroleum and petroleum products have featured Rhine navigation, and many of the refineries and petro-chemical industries have localized along or near the river.

About 90 per cent of the petroleum imports into Western Europe came through the Benelux ports of Rotterdam and Antwerpen. Before the First World War much of the relatively small oil imports were petroleum products. At that time Europe was only entering the oil age. After the first war, imports of crude oil became the rule, and European markets were supplied by tankers—some small enough to go upriver to Duisburg-Ruhrort. Other tankers transferred their oil to barges at Rotterdam or Antwerpen, and the barges were hauled upriver to four inland harbors from which it was transferred to markets by canal, rail, or highway. These inland harbors were Duisburg-Ruhrort on the Rhine; Gelsenkirchen in the Ruhr Industrial District; Wesseling on the west bank of the Rhine at the first big bend of the Rhine above Köln; and Basel, the Swiss port at the head of the Rhine Rift Valley. The relative position of these petroleum harbors has changed notably. In 1953 Duisburg-Ruhrort harbors were in last place; but from 1953 to 1954 they moved from last to first place. Meanwhile the other three maintained their relative rank. In large measure, the petroleum traffic on the Rhine has been postwar business. The upstream oil traffic from the Benelux ports to the Duisburg-Ruhrort harbors has consisted of crude oil and processed products in about equal quantities, but with the latter having a slight preponderance. Shipments upstream from Duisburg-Ruhrort consisted almost exclusively of finished products for destinations along the Rhine.

The rapid growth of the oil transfer business at the Duisburg-Ruhrort harbors is shown in Table 25. The capacity at the end of 1957 in tank storage space of about 270,000 cubic meters (1 cubic meter = 1.3079 cubic yards or 35.3156 cubic feet) has increased sevenfold since 1939. Probably it will be continuously expanded, as an end of the needed storage space is not in sight. The progress in the construction of tank storage space created much activity in the transfer of petroleum products in the Duisburg-Ruhrort harbors. Such transfer was strengthened by initiation of deliveries of crude oil via pipelines to some of the large refineries in the neighboring industrial area. By May, 1955, these pipelines also served the manufacturing work of the Gelsenberg Gasoline Company in Gelsenkirchen, the Scholven Chemical Company in Gelsenkirchen-Buer, and the Ruhr Chemical Company in Holten. The success of petroleum transfer in the Duisburg-Ruhrort harbors resulted from systematic promotional action. In the entire Ruhr in 1955 there were only six plants engaged in the processing of crude oils. These plants together employed about 6,000 persons.

| 25. TANK SPACE DEVELOPMENT IN THE DUISBURG-RUHRORT HARBORS. | Year | Number of Firms | Number of Tanks | Holding Capacity Cubic Meters |
|---|---|---|---|---|
| | 1939 | 6 | 156 | 41,298 |
| | 1950 | 7 | 156 | 55,798 |
| | 1955 | 16 | 390 | 206,738 |
| Source: *Stadt und Hafen,* Vol. 9 (November 5, | 1956 | 16 | 396 | 227,738 |
| 1958), 965. | 1957 | 18 | 423 | 269,392 |

The Duisburg-Ruhrort harbors have striven for promotion of the petroleum traffic by water and by connection with rail and highway facilities. For example, in the rail station in Duisburg the Wagon Repair Company has a specialized works for tank car repairs and for official inspection of tank cars and brake equipment. Its large capacity has made it one of the leading workshops of its type in the Duisburg area. In Ruhrort, at the mouth of the harbor canal, as well as in the upper Kings Harbor (Kaiserhafen), there are two different installations. One serves as a collection station for the wash water containing diesel oil which accumulates from the rinsing of tank space on the inland ships; the other makes possible the cleaning of vehicles used in transporting crude oil. In addition, tankers, tank cars, and highway vehicles can be freed of gas here or be completely cleaned so that they are usable for forwarding refined oil.

At the end of 1957 a decisive change occurred. From this time on crude oil deliveries for the refinery of Gelsenberg Gasoline Company came from the new oil harbor at Wesel, at the mouth of the Lippe River on the east side of the Rhine. Wesel is a highway and railway center at the Rhine end of the Wesel-Datteln Canal. Deliveries from this port may cause a realignment in the near future—the Duisburg-Ruhrort ports will deliver less, and Wesel more, of the crude oil needed at Gelsenkirchen in the Ruhr Industrial District. Such is the effect of competition.[2]

As consumption of crude petroleum increased in the Atlantic countries of Europe following World War II, the crude oil tankers increased in size to the point where only the major ports could handle the larger tankers. Hence, the crude oil was refined at many of the major ports from Scandinavia to Italy.[3] This practice meant cheaper oil, and as a result, coupled with increased use of fuel and diesel oils in automobiles, the consumption of petroleum and petroleum products from 1956 to 1960 increased by 31 per cent in France, by 43 per cent in Switzerland, and by 120 per cent in West Germany.[4]

The increase in the demand for oil and its products in the Atlantic countries of Europe over-taxed the carrying capacity of the barges, railroads, and trucks and increased the cost of the products to consumers. Consequently, pipelines were built from selected ports to refining centers where the demand was sufficient to justify the great cost of the pipelines. An early example was a 240-mile-long pipeline extending from Wilhelmshaven, a small port on the German North Sea coast, to the Ruhr and to Köln. Later another line was built to Köln from Rotterdam.

A pipeline of considerable promise is under construction from the French port of Lavera on the Mediterranean up the Rhone Valley and over the Belfort Gap to Strasbourg and Karlsruhe on the Rhine. It is scheduled for completion in 1963. The contruction is a major engineering project. The line will be 475 miles in length and will have a capacity of 200,000 barrels of crude oil a day. The project is being financed by, and will be owned by, Belgian, British, Dutch, French, German, and American oil companies. Standard Oil of New Jersey is an important shareholder as it owns 28 per cent of the Societe du Pipe-Line Sud-European.[5]

About 90 per cent of the Rhine imports in 1961 came through the Benelux ports of Rotterdam and Antwerpen. At the former, petroleum is the largest single commodity handled. In fact, Rotterdam has become the greatest oil center of Europe. About 225 million barrels of crude petroleum and refined petroleum entered the port in 1961.[6] The source of these imports was largely from the Middle East, with smaller amounts from Venezuela, North Africa, and other producing areas. In 1960 an estimated 180 million barrels were processed in the three refineries then operating in Rotterdam. Approximately half of the imported and locally refined products went to local markets in the Netherlands. The other half moved by tanker and barge to Germany, Great Britain, Belgium, Scandinavia, and lesser European markets, with some to Africa and the Far East.[7] Hence, Rotterdam is both a domestic market center and a seaboard distributing center.

At Antwerpen the early distribution of petroleum products was facilitated by the dense network of railways and canals that connect this port with the Rhine Valley and other interior points. By 1951 a petroleum dock had been brought into use, and by ten years later a petroleum harbor had been developed on the right bank inside a meander of the Schelde.

Berths for extra large tankers are under construction. Modern express highways from Antwerpen to Köln and other points now provide additional means of rapid distribution of oil and other products. Antwerpen, with its oil harbor and refineries, has the business of a seaboard oil port, a seaboard refinery, and a domestic supply center. Oil tankers now account for 10 per cent of tonnage arriving in Antwerpen. This is one reason why the inward shipping traffic at the port of Antwerpen has increased steadily since 1946. Another reason is that there has been a continuing growth in the importance of ore carriers, and, of course, by the rise in the average tonnage per ship.

## II   *Discovery of Natural Gas in the Netherlands*

In 1959 the Netherlands and, in fact, all Western Europe became excited by the announcement that a great natural gas field had been discovered in the northeastern part of the Netherlands. This discovery of the Slochteren Field containing a reserve of forty trillion cubic feet of natural gas in Groningen Province created an active interest in Dutch exploratory drilling and focused attention on the possibility of further discoveries in the general area.

The new field was discovered by the Netherlands Petroleum Company, commonly called the N.A.M., jointly owned by Royal Dutch Shell and Standard Oil of New Jersey.[8] Gas will be sold by the Netherlands Gas Union of which State Mines holds 40 per cent; Esso (Standard Oil of New Jersey) 25 per cent; Royal Dutch Shell 25 per cent; and the Netherlands State 10 per cent. The field will be developed on twenty-five locations with eight wells on each location, and it will be operated from a conveniently located sales center. Complete developments with automation is predicted for 1970.

The Slochteren Field is said to be the second field in size in the world, ranking below only the Hugoton Field in the mid-continental area in the United States. The high significance of the Slochteren discovery can be seen when it is realized that this large gas supply is in the midst of one of the most active and densely peopled areas of the world. How will it affect the pipelines now in use and others under construction? Today it not only has stimulated interest, but also great activity among the major oil companies of Europe and America.

*NORTH SEA POSSIBILITIES*

So much international interest in oil and gas exploration has been created that active exploration has begun in the coastal and other areas of the North Sea. A gas blowout occurred in the first German offshore wildcat. This is taken to indicate favorable geological trends and has spurred gas and oil exploration of some fifty companies, including most of the powerful American organizations. Commonly the American companies, which command the funds and the oil drilling equipment, have joined with European national organizations.

The section of the North Sea over which each of the national units have jurisdiction has reached an international agreement.[9] Britain has all of the west side; but the east side is divided among Belgium, Netherlands, Germany, Denmark, and Norway, with Norway, Denmark, and Netherlands having the larger areas. The problems of exploration are enormous as to costs, technical equipment, and knowledge; but if success attends the efforts the results should be staggering both in national and international terms.

The strong position of Royal Dutch Shell and Standard Oil of New Jersey illustrates many aspects of petroleum and marketing. The two organizations pioneered in some of the same areas, and both contributed to the development of methods, equipment, and techniques. Both companies competed in many markets, working alone in some areas and in combination in others. At times they combined finances where costs of exploration were high.

The Standard Oil Company of New Jersey is one of the largest industrial and commercial organizations in the world. Its principal affiliates number forty-seven, and they are distributed in the United States, Canada, Latin America, Middle East, Far East, Europe, and Africa. Europe has twenty-two units, most of which are in Western or Atlantic Europe.[10] To a certain extent the organization is a family of companies, all of which are engaged in one or more functions of the oil business. However, the success of this great company is due in part to the momentum of an early start, to its early operation via the high seas to the world's major markets for oil and oil products, to top-flight management throughout most of its history, to command of capital in an activity that requires huge amounts of capital, to recognized ability to work and prosper under international conditions, and to command the proper equipment and skills. For example, witness its position in the divisions of the port of Rotterdam, its operation with Royal Dutch Shell in the new Slochteren Field in the Netherlands, and its ownership of 28 per cent of the new pipeline from the Mediterranean up the Rhone Valley to the middle of the North German Rhine.

In addition to its basic enterprises of producing and marketing oil and gas in Western Europe, Standard Oil owns refineries, port facilities, pipelines, and petro-chemical plants in the British Isles, France, Belgium, the Netherlands, Germany, and the Scandinavian countries. Back of all these activities is the basic fact that it owns or controls more reserves of petroleum than any other corporation.

Although the activities of the Royal Dutch Shell and the Standard Oil Company of New Jersey are almost world-wide in scope, the emphasis in terms of volume and value of their businesses has been in the North Atlantic Arena. Historically, big production of petroleum and petroleum products has been in North America with heavy shipments across the North Atlantic to Western Europe and the Mediterranean. Hence, the production and marketing aspects of the oil industry illustrate the validity of recognizing the North Atlantic Arena as the most promising area for leadership in the world in the coming decades.

# 11

# Ports of the Upper Rhine Valley

IN THE LOWER RHINE this study deals with the river as an arm of the sea. Hence, it has both maritime and riverine qualities. Rotterdam and Antwerpen serve as the major sea ports with the Rhine as the major river route to the industrialized Ruhr where Duisburg-Ruhrort are the principal ports and Düsseldorf and Köln are the major trading and financial centers.

In the Upper Rhine or Rhine Rift Valley, Basel, Strasbourg, Mannheim, and Mainz are the major river ports, with Frankfurt am Main as the principal transportation and financial center of West Germany (*Fig. 17*). These ports have been and still are tied to the river, but with their rail, highway, and airway connections into the interior they possess both riverine and continental qualities. They are presented, in order, from south to north, thus conforming to the flow of the Rhine (*Fig. 5*).

## I   *Port of Basel*

The growth of Basel, Switzerland, as a Rhine port illustrates many of the problems and values associated with the development of ports on

17.  The Upper Rhine Valley.

inland reaches of major rivers. As the Rhine River constitutes a waterway
between the seaport of Rotterdam and the city and country ports of Basel,
the Swiss think of Basel as their water gate to the North Sea and the
Atlantic. Moreover, Basel as a port is of relatively recent origin, hence its
plan and facilities illustrate modern design and construction. In addition,
its ownership and administration are constructively unique. For these reasons the port of Basel is given particular attention.

According to a recent release of the port authority, the Rhine docks are still under development. Their capacity and characteristics in 1961 were summarized as follows:

"According to recent releases of the port authority, the Rhine docks still under development comprise the docks of St. John, Kleinhüningen and Klybeck Quay in Basel-Town and the Birsfelden and Au docks in Basel-Country. Altogether they occupy an area of 1,433,000 sq. yds. and have 3.7 miles of usable quayage. Fifty miles of railway line have been laid down in the dock railyards and along the quays.

The 28 grain silos and warehouses can accommodate 220,000 metric tons of grain and some 130,000 metric tons of piece goods of every kind. There is open storage space for 500,000 tons of coal and other non-perishable goods. Tanks with a capacity of approximately 130 million gallons are available for the ever increasing volume of liquid power and heating fuel imported. For handling cargoes there are 47 modern cranes, 2 pneumatic grain elevators, 1 discharging plant for bundled briquettes and 15 pumping stations for the storage of liquid fuels."[1]

Basel lies slightly upstream from the point of contact of the boundaries of France, Germany, and Switzerland. Here the Rhine, having gathered most of the runoff of the Swiss Alps and the Swiss Plateau, turns from its east-west course and, entering the Upper Rhine Valley, begins its northerly course to the sea. Through skillful engineering Basel has become the port at the head of the commercial Rhine and provides 550 miles of navigable waterway between the Swiss frontier at Basel and the North Sea.

The site of Basel is 900 feet above sea level and is only 7.5° east of the prime meridian and is the same number of degrees north of the 40th parallel of latitude. It was inhabited as far back as the pre-Roman period of antiquity. In fact, in 1957 the city celebrated the 2000th anniversary of its founding. It became an episcopal see about the year 400. At the end of the fourteenth century the citizens took over temporal power and transformed Basel into a free city. The new status encouraged its use as a center of industry and trade; a use in harmony with its geographic position.[2] Hence by early Middle Ages, the Rhine Valley had a flourishing civilization based on trade, mineral wealth, and agriculture. Today, Basel not only lies at the head of a waterway but is also a major point on the rail and highway routes from the North Sea to the Mediterranean.

The first steamer, the "Stadt Frankfurt," arrived at Basel in 1832, and shortly afterward there was regular steamship service from Basel to Strasbourg and Mannheim. This continued until the building of railways put the shipping services out of business. Hence, until the first train of barges ended its experimental and adventurous journey on arrival at Basel on June 2, 1904, the Upper Rhine Valley between Strasbourg and Basel was devoid of traffic.[3] In this connection it should be understood that Strasbourg is the natural head of navigation on the Rhine. The river above Strasbourg is characterized by rapids and meanders which made navigation difficult, especially in late summer when the upper river is low in volume.

Although the arrival of barges at Basel in 1904 ushered in the era of river transport in Switzerland, the idea of navigating the Rhine above Strasbourg still had to win adherents among influential people in the three countries concerned; namely, Switzerland, Germany, and France. At the outset there was little or no preparation for trade. The cargo of the first barges consisted of few hundred tons of coal and was unloaded with sacks and baskets on the left bank of the Rhine below the Dreirosen Bridge, the last bridge over the Rhine in Switzerland.[4] For many years there were only temporary wharves and little or no unloading and discharging equipment. Moreover, the barges and tugs were small in size and decrepit in appearance. In fact, many thought that the rapids and other difficulties in navigating the Upper Rhine never could be overcome. To them, navigating difficulties, obsolete vessels and equipment, and the absence of docks and cargo-handling equipment appeared as unsurmountable difficulties.

Each problem, in its turn, has been solved: Port areas have been selected and laid out; piers and ships with cargo handling equipment constructed; canals dug around the rapids and shallows; general improvements of the Upper Rhine for better shipping.[5]

A major part of the development has been directed to the design and construction of river craft suited to navigation of this part of the river. Sturdy shallow draft barges of two types have been built. Some are equipped with self-propelling machinery; others are "dumb" barges with no power of their own. The latter, known as Rhine barges, have a capacity of from 1000 to 3000 metric tons and are towed to their destination by low-draft tugs. The powered barges are always smaller with a capacity that varies between 400 and 1800 metric tons.

All the foregoing progress has been strengthened by joint federal and internatonal efforts. Switzerland has done all in her power to preserve the principles of free navigation on the Rhine embodied in the Mannheim Acts of 1868. For example, the Central Rhine Bridge in Basel (Fritte Rheinbrucke) marks the upper limit of the segment of the Rhine that is under the jurisdiction of the International Legislation for shipping.[6] These achievements coupled with efficient management have enabled Basel to handle more than 40 per cent of Switzerland's foreign trade.

## PORT DEVELOPMENT

Well-managed ports, equipped with modern facilities, characterize the major centers of Rhine navigation, in no place more conspicuously than in Basel. The old wharves along the river's bank and the crude loading and discharging equipment have been replaced by five port areas, three down-river under the authority of the Canton of Basel-Town, and two up river under the jurisdiction of the Canton of Basel-Country (Fig. 18). In each case private interests have taken a constructive part.

## PORTS OF BASEL-TOWN

The port areas down river from the city lie below the Dreirosen Bridge. On the left bank the Rheinhafen St. John (St. John's Harbor) occupies a small area between the bridge and the French border. Opposite, on the right bank, is a complex of buildings belonging to CIBA, the largest chemical firm in Basel. Continuing on this bank is the Klybeck Quay, the second port area. It is used chiefly for unloading and storing liquid fuels, making it the major oil port of Basel. Vessels which transport liquid fuels can be recognized by pipework on their decks and by a blue band around the hull. Adjacent to the Klybeck Quay are the railway yards where every year more than 150,000 "goods wagons" are made into trains and dispatched to interior points in Switzerland.[7] This fact illustrates the close integration of river and rail transport in handling traffic.

The Rheinhafen Kleinhuningen (Kleinhuningen Harbor) is the third and largest of the port areas under the authority of Basel-Town. It is separated from the Klybeck Quay by the channelized mouth of the Wiese River. The two port areas, however, are connected by seven closely spaced bridges, all of which carry rail traffic and three of which also carry street vehicles. The Rheinhafen Kleinhuningen has three divisions, the Rheinquai used as a berth for ships and for ship repairs, and enclosed basins I and II. The entrance to the two basins is only a few rods above the "Three Countries Corner" in the middle of the river. This is the point where the boundaries of Switzerland, Germany, and France meet.[8]

At the entrance to basin I is a small towerlike building which houses the harbor master's office where inward and outward bound vessels are recorded and where visual traffic signals regulate the traffic in the dock

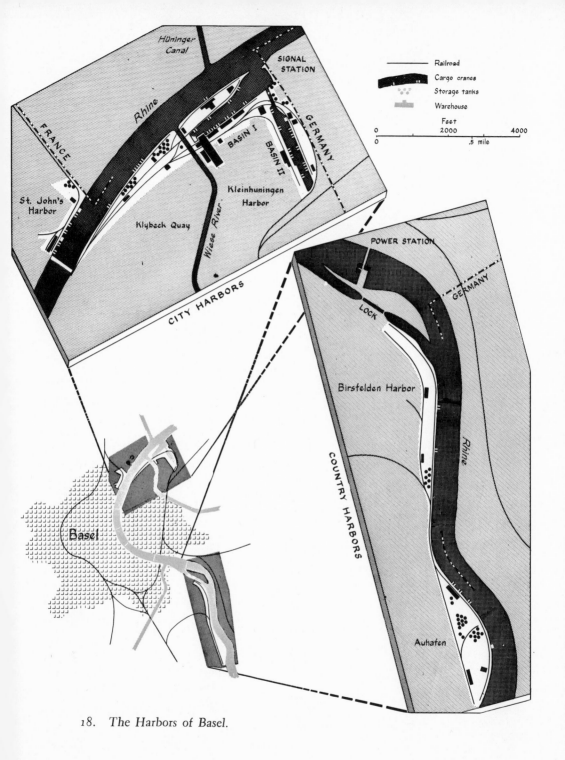

18. The Harbors of Basel.

basin. Dock basin I is 808 yards in length.[9] The silos and warehouses of the east quay handle the storage of grain and feeding stuffs as well as piece goods of great variety. At the southern end of dock basin I is the modern cargo-handling equipment for discharging and dispatching piece goods. The roof of the transit shed where piece goods are unloaded projects far out over the water so that goods susceptible to moisture can be unloaded from three ships at a time and then transferred, via overhead traveling cranes, to railway trucks, to the storage sheds, or into a special lorry loading ramp. On the west quay are storage sites for coal or other solid fuels.

An approach canal leads to basin II (760 yards in length). It was dug and equipped by 1939 and thus came into service before the outbreak of the Second World War.[10] A part of the town's gas works gets its coal directly from its storage yard adjoining the south quay. The water area in basins I and II taken together is 156,739 square yards and, allowing for daily variations in the water level, can take vessels with a draft up to 8 feet 9 inches. The basins can accommodate 130 ships with an average carrying capacity of 1,000 metric tons. Including St. John's dock on the left bank of the river, there is usable wharfage of about 2.2 miles. These docks handle some 1,000 tons of goods per year for every meter of quayage—an absolute record for all inland ports on the Rhine.

The Canton of Basel-Town is the proprietor of the whole dock area, including the dock basins, quays, railway yards, and station buildings.[11] The storage sites in the docks are let to private organizations operating in the docks on the basis of building leases of fifty or more years. It should be understood that the construction and operation of Rhine ships, the cargo-handling plants, and storage are entirely in the hands of private companies. The total capital invested in the Basil-Town docks by the Confederation, the Canton of Basel-Town, and private enterprise amounts to 118 million francs.

The chief port authority is the Shipping Board of Basel, which has entrusted the current business of administration of the port to the subordinate Rhine Shipping Office. This office also superintends the legislation on the Swiss stretch of the Rhine. The railway facilities in the docks have been entrusted by the Canton to the Swiss Federal Railways under a special agreement. This agreement governs the apportionment of operational costs and proceeds. The Rhine docks of Basel are not free ports but do have extensive opportunities for the storage of goods in bond.

## DOCKS OF BASEL-COUNTRY

The docks of Basel-Country lie upstream from the St. Alhans Bridge and the railway bridge near the central part of the eastern border of the city. These bridges largely carry through-traffic between Switzerland and Germany. Above the railway bridge is the mouth of the Birs River which rises in the Swiss Jura hills. Slightly further upstream are the imposing buildings of the Birsfelden power house. To the right of the power house is the lock used by ships traveling to points above Basel. The dam has a head of 26 feet of water and the level of the upper pool lies 833 feet above sea level. The annual production of power runs to 550 million kilowatt hours. The lock itself is 590 feet long and 39 feet wide. A vessel takes between fifteen and twenty minutes to pass through the lock.[12]

The Basel-Country docks comprise port developments at Birsfelden and Auhafen. Together they have a usable wharfage of one and a half miles. The former is used primarily for storage of solid and liquid fuels. Beyond the dock an extensive industrial area has been prepared and opened for various kinds of enterprises. The area of the Auhafen is slightly upstream and, begun in 1951, already is covered with tanks, warehouses, and cargo-handling installations. Ownership and management of the Basel-Country docks are much the same as holds true of the Basel-Town docks.[13]

## SHIPS AND CREWS

The ships moored in June 1960 at the Basel docks represented several nationalities. The Swiss Rhine fleet at present numbers in the neighborhood of 400 vessels, but is not able to carry all the Rhine traffic destined for Basel. In this service also are German, Dutch, French, and Belgian vessels, much alike in size, appearance, and function. The arrival of foreign vessels is an everyday occurrence.

Some of the Rhine ships have propelling machinery; others have no power of their own. The latter have a capacity of between 1,000 and 3,000 metric tons. Powered barges always are smaller and have a capacity between 400 and 1800 metric tons. The ships on the Rhine carry a crew of from three to five men according to size. The deck hands or ship's boys have permanent quarters in the bows, whereas the captain and his family occupy the stern. Between these superstructures there commonly are from five to seven holds, only accessible via the hatches. The company's flag is flown from the masthead in the fore part of the ship, whereas other flags and light signals are hoisted in the rear.

*SHIPPING AND TRAFFIC*

In 1958, 8400 ships registered in the docks of Basel-Town and Basel-Country. Forty-four per cent of these belonged to the Swiss Rhine fleet and 56 per cent to foreign flags. They carried nearly 4.9 million metric tons or 38 per cent of the total Swiss foreign trade. Of the commodities passing through the Rhine docks, 94 per cent is inward trade and only 6 per cent outward bound from Switzerland.[14] This fact illustrates the continuing excess of imports over exports, and explains the further fact that a majority of ships arriving at Basel move down river in ballast.

The increase of unloaded tonnage shipped by the Rhine together with that by the Hüninger-Zweig canal, opened to navigation in 1923, is shown in Table 26. As Switzerland has little or no coal, the solid heating

26. THE UNLOADED TONNAGE SHIPPED BY THE RHINE TO-GETHER WITH THAT BY THE HÜNINGER-ZWEIG CANAL.

| Metric Tons | Years | | | | | |
|---|---|---|---|---|---|---|
| | 1910 | 1930 | 1937 | 1951 | 1957 | 1958 |
| | 64,700 | 1,099,887 | 2,966,265 | 4,592,413 | 5,396,360 | 4,868,013 |

Source: "The Docks of Basle-Town and Basle-Country," *Rheinschiffahrtsamt Basel,* mimeographed release, 1960, p. 2.

fuels are the leading import in terms of quantity. Next in order are petroleum and petroleum products, followed by grain and feeding stuffs. Both people and cattle depend on imported food and feedstuffs. The list of commodities shipped downriver includes ores, machines, apparatus, chemicals, and pharmaceutical finished products.[15]

Only about 7 per cent of the goods moved up stream to Basel is utilized in the cantons of Basel-Town and Basel-Country. The remainder is hauled by rail and/or highway to supply the urban and rural population of Switzerland. It is claimed that "the whole population benefits from the reduction in the cost of living made possible by the cheap freight rates on the Rhine." Moreover, the economic advantages accruing to the country are evident not only in the saving of freight costs but in the fact that before the development of Rhine navigation to Basel many goods had to be transloaded or stored at Swiss expense in foreign ports. Increases in local employment represent another advantage. As navigation only reaches the

Swiss border, there is little or no competition between water and rail transport. In fact shipping has brought much business to the Swiss Federal Railways.[16]

In our study of Rhine navigation, not much was learned about the costs of port development. Because of the recency of the growth of the ports at Basel, Table 27 represents the capital invested on Rhine shipping by the Swiss Confederation, the Cantons of Basel-Town and Basel-Country, and private enterprise. It is argued that the haulage over the Swiss

27. CAPITAL INVESTED IN RHINE SHIPPING BY THE SWISS CONFEDERATION, THE CANTONS OF BASEL-TOWN AND BASEL-COUNTRY, AND PRIVATE ENTERPRISE.

Source: "The Docks of Basle-Town and Basle-Country," *Rheinschiffahrtsamt Basel,* mimeographed release, 1960, p. 3.

| Area of Expenditure | Amount in Million Francs |
|---|---|
| Basel–Town docks | 118 |
| Basel–Country docks | 83 |
| Swiss contributions to Rhine River improvement between Strasbourg and Kehl/Istein | 50 |
| Expenditures on shipbuilding | 165 |
| Swiss capital expenditure on foreign shipping installations | 17 |
| Total | 433 |

highways also has benefited from Rhine shipping. Finally, it may be said that "collaboration between the Confederation and the Cantons of Basel-Town and Basel-Country, always in closest association with private enterprise, has proved of great value." Certainly the Rhine is so closely bound up with the interests of Switzerland that impediments and disturbances of any kind would have serious repercussions on the economic life of this mountainous country.[17]

## DOWN RIVER TO STRASBOURG

On the left bank of the Rhine and nearly opposite to the entrance of the Kleinhuningen basins I and II is the entrance to the Hüninger Canal. This canal leads to Mulhouse where it joines the Rhine-Rhone Canal that begins at Strasbourg, and runs via Mulhouse, Besançon, Dôle, and Lyons to the Rhone. Hence the Hüninger Canal gives a second route for shipping in addition to the Rhine itself. Although this canal has fifty-two locks and only allows the passage of vessels with a capacity of about 350 tons, it is of importance to Basel when the Rhine is either unusually high or low. Moreover the Hüninger Canal connects Basel to the whole inland waterway systems of France and Belgium.

Strasbourg, some 70 miles down river from Basel, is the natural head of navigation on the Rhine. Above Strasbourg the gradient of the river bed increases, especially in the last 15 or 20 miles below Basel. For example, the Istein bar near the village of Istein was a particularly dangerous section and could be negotiated only during periods of high water. Hence, from late autumn until snow melted in the spring, shipping to Basel usually was not attempted. To offset this difficulty a dam and locks (the "markt barrage") were constructed across the old bed of the river. This dam raised the level of the water to a height of 39 feet thereby flooded the dangerous rapids. At this point a canal on French territory, the Grand Canal d' Alsace, leads from the river and, bypassing the dangerous section, continues as a straight waterway for 24 miles to Fessenheim where the water diverted from the river to the canal joins the old course of the Rhine again. High locks at two points (Kembs and Ottmarsheim) are necessary to lift the vessels coming up stream to higher sections of the canal. The height of the lift at Kembs is 49 feet, and the associated power station has six generating sets with an annual production of about 900 million kilowatt hours. It is reported that the French inland waterway authorities plan on extention of the Grand Canal d' Alsace as far as Strasbourg.

The dam and locks at the Istein bar were damaged during an allied attack in 1944, and navigation on the open Rhine to Basel was no longer possible. After the war the importance of the dam to Switzerland was emphasized by the rapid reconstruction of the structure by Swiss engineering firms and labor. Hence, by the end of April 1946 the new dam was completed and navigation soon recommenced.[18]

The international quality of all these improvements to Rhine navigation is shown by financial contributions by Swiss authorities even though they are in French and German territory. Such action makes the bickerings over constructive action between or among our states over water problems look small indeed.

*AIRPORT*

Development of an airport for Basel represents another example of international cooperation in transport services. With the Jura range at its back, level land in sufficiently large amount for an airport is at a premium at Basel. The best opportunity for such a development is northwest of the city, but in that direction the boundary between France and Switzerland extends along a west-east line to the river. However, the problem was solved by building an international airport in French territory a few miles northwest of Basel. The port is known as the Basel Mulhouse airport as it also serves Mulhouse, the industrial capital of Alsace. A feature from the center of Basel to the airport is a specially constructed customs corridor that can be used without having to show a passport.

## II  *Strasbourg*

Strasbourg, in modern times, is a center of transportation with closely related administrative, commercial, industrial, and cultural interests. In addition to its Rhine port it is a hub of rail, highway, and canal services. It is situated in the southwestern section of the Rhine Rift Valley where the valley is bordered on the east by the steep face of the Black Forest and on the west by the equally steep slopes of the Vosges Mountains in Alsace. In its vicinity, Strasbourg commands the plain of Alsace between the lower slopes of the Vosges and the regulated channel of the Rhine. Since some portions of this plain are highly fertile, the city is a market center for agricultural products.

In considering Strasbourg's over-all situation it should be remembered that the upper or southern portion of the rift valley is boxed in by mountainous terrain that emphasizes the few inlets or outlets. In addition to the Rhine route for river, highway, and railway transport up and down the longitudinal axis of the valley, Strasbourg has  1] the Gate of Burgundy some 70 miles to the southwest  that furnishes a route for canal, rail, and highway transport to the Rhone Valley;  2] Saverne Gap, about 25 miles to the northwest between the high and low Vosges, that provides the lowest pass from the Rhine to Lorraine, and is utilized by the Rhine-Marne Canal, a major railroad, and a highway leading westward from Strasbourg; 3] a pass east from Karlsruhe, some 40 miles to the northeast and on the German side of the Rhine, that opens a rail and highway route between the Black Forest and the lower Odenwald. Although a few minor highways have been engineered through the bordering highlands, the routes named are the major present-day connections of Strasbourg and the upper rift valley with other sections of Western Europe.

The port of Strasbourg extends for about four miles along the Rhine. From the port, canals lead to the city which originally grew up on the Ill River some three miles from the Rhine. A traverse from east to west across this urban area first shows the Rhine crossed by rail and highway bridges, with the international boundary between West Germany and France at the middle of the bridges. Next comes the river port with its ten harbors and at the south a cluster of manufacturing establishments. The east-west traverse leads across the Marne-Rhine canal into the center of the city and the broad expanse of other portions of the built-up area. Further west is a railroad section with a display of "Marshalling Yards" and more factories. At the north are the industrial suburbs of Robertsau and Schiltigheim.

Strasbourg resembles Antwerpen in its historical vicissitudes in government and religion. Originally it was an important Roman military camp and city. After centuries of rule by bishops it became a free imperial city in the thirteenth century. The city accepted reformation, and in 1609 joined the Protestant Union. It was seized by Louis xiv in 1681, and that returned it to catholicism. More than a century later it participated in the French Revolution and embraced its views and actions. It passed to Germany in 1871 under the Treaty of Frankfurt, and was gained by France in 1919. Much of the city was destroyed in the Second World War, and it came again under German jurisdiction in 1940. The fact that Strasbourg has survived and prospered during these and other changes is a tribute to its people and its geographical situation.

The port of Strasbourg has grown in business until in 1959 it handled about 8 million tons of freight. Of this, half was carried on the Rhine, with the upstream traffic slightly more than the downstream. The port traffic of the two canals, the Rhine-Rhone and the Marne-Rhine, was nearly equal to the traffic on the Rhine itself.

Of the imports by water into Strasbourg, coal, petroleum products, and cereals are the leading items, but manufactured products, fertilizers, and foodstuffs are other items. Potash is shipped by water from the Alsatian mines via Strasbourg to the fertilizer industries and chemical works in Antwerpen. The heavy nature of the traffic illustrates the high value of cheap water transport. The further inland, the greater the value.

## STRASBOURG TO MANNHEIM

For about 100 miles down valley from Basel, the Rhine is the present boundary between Germany and France. At Lauterbourg, some 30 miles below Strasbourg, the boundary of France makes a sharp turn to the west. From this point both sides of the river are in Germany, and the Rhine becomes wholly German until it crosses the boundary of the Netherlands. Across the river from Lauterbourg, the German city of Karlsruhe commands a valley that leads eastward through the Black Forest providing an important route for railway and for the famous autobahn from Munich, which at Karlsruhe connects with the autobahn from Basel to Mannheim and Frankfurt.

From Strasbourg to Speyer the slope of the river's bed is very gentle, and before the regulating works of the present century the Rhine meandered in wide and ever-changing curves. In this long reach, cuts to aid navigation have been made across the necks of the meanders. According to Partsch the course of the Rhine in its Baden reach, even before 1903, had been shortened by 50 miles or 23 per cent of its former length, and the river has been strait-jacketed into a single channel walled in by dykes. As a result of an increase in the rate of flow, the river has cut deeper into its bed with a gain to navigation.[19] As developed, the channel is narrow and has a swift current. Hence, this channel from Strasbourg to Mannheim is one of the two reaches of the Rhine that requires the services of a pilot at all times.[20]

## III   *Mannheim-Ludwigshafen*

At Speyer the river enters the lower third of the Upper Rhine Valley. This third comes to vigorous commercial life at Mannheim where the Neckar, the first of the big eastern tributaries of the Rhine, joins the major stream. Here Mannheim, with its sister port, Ludwigshafen, forms the commercial center of an irregularly spaced group of residential and industrial suburbs and satellites (*Fig. 19*). The port is only 318 feet above the sea, a fact that shows how deeply entrenched the Rhine is in the high ground of central Europe.

Mannheim, as St. Louis on the Mississippi, is the farthest upriver port which can be reached by the larger barges and tow boats. According to Baskin, an average convoy on the Rhine between Duisburg and Mannheim will have a load of 5,000 tons.[21] It was severely bombed during World War II, but most of the buildings destroyed have been rebuilt. In the number of vessels arriving and clearing, and in the volume of traffic, the port of Mannheim-Ludwigshafen is second on the Rhine only to Duisburg-Ruhrort.[22]

Mannheim has the internal rectangularity of a Middle Western American city. The central section is encased by a boulevard within which are the financial and retail sections of the city. As the city lies in the triangular shaped area between the junction of the Rhine and the Neckar, the inlets, piers, and other port facilities are prominent features of the urban scene, and the sight, noise, and smell of shipping are ever present. The port area, however, is more extensive than the city as it includes the port of Ludwigshafen on the opposite or left bank of the Rhine, the industrial harbor north of the Neckar, and the Mannheim-Rheinau docks south of Mannheim on the right bank of the river (*Fig. 19*). Official reports state that Mannheim has 1,093 yards of quays, ten docks, and a dock railway.

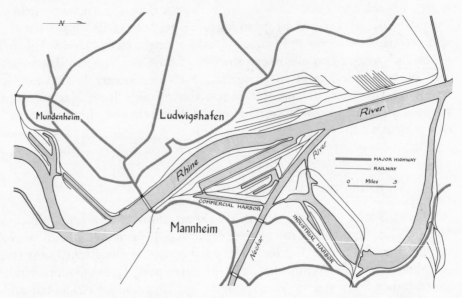

19.   *The port of Mannheim at the junction of the Neckar and Rhine rivers.*

A large movement of traffic at the port of Mannheim is of relatively recent origin. Its present importance involved two engineering achievements—one, the removal of obstructions to navigation at Bingen down-river, and the other, the development of a system of river transport under which powerful tugs draw barges with large carrying capacity. As has been stated, Mannheim is the farthest point up river that such large barges can reach. Today many smaller barges, propelled by their own engines, act as individual units; and because of their lesser draft, negotiate cargoes at ports above Mannheim and in connecting waterways.

Experience has shown that in competition for traffic with rail and highway services, river traffic largely is limited to heavy and bulky commodities. For example, at Mannheim the major river traffic is in chemicals, mineral fuels (coal and oil), building supplies such as iron and steel, cement, timbers, grain, and other basic foodstuffs.

Manufacturing in metropolitan Mannheim now employs more

people than the port and other commercial enterprises. As in many other places, the latter stimulated the growth of manufacturing activities. Present industry ranges from chemicals through cellulose, soap, and food processing to railway and electrical equipment. Manufacturing plants are widely distributed in the metropolitan area with several localized in industrial suburbs.

Both Mannheim and Ludwigshafen have a long record in the chemical industries. In fact before the First World War Ludwigshafen had the largest chemical enterprise in the world and stood at the head of the most powerful chemical trust in Europe. Mannheim also has been a major center in the growth of the German chemical industries. Chemical manufacturing in these two Rhine cities, however, is only a part of the development of the chemical industries in Germany. It should be understood that Germany's industrial and commercial fame in the chemical industries included the Ruhr District and the South German District along the Rhine, and three other districts—the Berlin District, the Saxony District, and the Bohemian District. Dyes, medicines, and potash fertilizers were allied products. The processes of manufacture of chemical and allied products are, in general, various combinations of grinding, mixing, roasting, distilling, compressing, crystallizing, and other processes employed by chemical science.[23]

Early German leadership in chemical manufacture was based on resources of potash, salt, sulphur, and coal. Because industrial chemicals are bulky and low priced commodities, freight charges form a big item in their cost. Hence, the manufacturers choose locations at which the raw materials can be assembled cheaply, and from which finished products can be shipped cheaply to market. Mannheim-Ludwigshafen on the Rhine waterway meet these requirements, as do Köln, Düsseldorf, Duisburg-Ruhrort, and certain other localities along the river. It should be understood, also, that the success of the chemical industries depended on the status of the chemical sciences, the organizing and administrative ability of the leaders, and on the skill and experience of available labor. In all these essentials, Germany, before the First World War, demonstrated leadership in each of its four industrial areas, but nowhere more definitely than along the Rhine.[24]

Mannheim's commercial and industrial activities are intimately related to the Neckar River. This eastern tributary is channelized with fourteen dams and locks to Stuttgart, a modern and growing industrial city. For many years the head of navigation was at Heilbronn, but in recent years the dams and locks have been extended to Stuttgart where a modern port is under construction. Stuttgart, with a population of more than 600,000, is the largest city in southwestern Germany. It is a center of rail, highway, and airway transportation and possesses a prosperous economy. The city is in a deep valley and climbs the surrounding wooded hills so that its vertical pattern ranges from 207 feet at the port to an altitude of 1,715 feet. One may question the utility of canalized rivers in such terrain, but it should be remembered that the Neckar is deeply incised in the upland, and its valley floor is only slightly above that of the Rhine. In its essentials, the site of Stuttgart is closely akin to Pittsburgh in the Allegheny Plateau.

As has been stated, the northern or lower end of the Upper Rhine Valley not only is of special interest in Rhine navigation but also as a focal area in the transportation pattern of Western Europe. This busy area is featured by the junction of two rivers and the coalescence of two valleys among deeply depressed surrounding uplands.

At its northern end the rift valley, occupied by the Rhine, is blocked by the Taunus Range much as the Swiss Jura blocks the southern end. This northern barrier turns the course of the Rhine westward to Bingen. Of this section of the river Bashkin states "This is the most difficult stretch to navigate. Its swift current, narrow channel, and shallowness requires the use of a pilot at all times."[25] At Bingen the river enters its 80-mile gorge by which it crosses the Taunus Range and other sections of the Rhenish Plateau. Although the Rhine turns westward, the floor of the rift valley opens to the east and northwest between the Taunus and the Odenwald to coalesce with the Hessen lowlands.

The Main River enters the southern border of the Hessen lowland at Aschaffenburg and in a great curve via Hanau, Offenbach, and Frankfurt reaches its junction with the Rhine at Mainz. Transportation routes and services focus on this urbanized lowland that has Frankfurt am Main and Mainz on the Rhine as centers for its diversified economy. As Mackinder pointed out, this sunken lowland is set in a broadly exposed and relatively infertile tableland into which deep valleys have been etched by the Rhine, the Neckar, the Main, and the Lahn.[26] In general, river, canal, railway, and highway routes follow the valleys. However, in modern times some sections of the arterial highways and autobahnen have been engineered across the upland surface.

IV   *Frankfurt am Main*

Frankfurt am Main, with a population of approximately 700,000, dominates the economy of the northern end of the Rhine-Main lowland. Its administrative leadership in its area became evident in the Middle Ages. The banking business owes much to the financial interests of Frankfurt, and the city has had centuries of experience in the publishing and printing industries.

With the growth of modern transportation Frankfurt has become Germany's leading traffic center. Three large dams and locks enable barges to reach the ports of the city, and resulting traffic makes Frankfurt the third largest inland port of the country. It was one of the first German cities to have railway services and has become one of the focal points in the railroad pattern of Western Europe. As the first German city to have an autobahn, it now is near the crossing of two of the major autobahnen and has ready access to others. Moreover, it claims to possess the largest airport in Europe.

With its transportation, commercial, and banking resources Frankfurt has attained a high rank in industry, especially in such manufacturing enterprises as paints, dyes, and inks that require highly skilled labor. To the east and on the Main River are Offenbach, an industrial town with leadership in leather goods, and Hanau producing automobile tires and articles made of gold and silver. At Rüsselsheim, on the river between Frankfurt and Mainz, automobile manufacturing adds to the industrial diversity to the Frankfurt-Mainz area. These and other activities give employment and produce a market for foods, coal, oil, and raw materials brought in by barge services on the Rhine and Main.

The harbors along the Main River at Frankfurt accomodate river craft up to 3000 tons. Each harbor has one or more distinctive functions. The West Harbor traffic consists largely of loading and unloading manufactured goods through its private, municipal, and bonded warehouses. The last named has an office for customs clearance. Its one basin has 47,732 square miles of water area with a depth of 3.70 meters, and its quays have a length of about 1,500 **meters**. The East Harbor is larger, with a river harbor and four basins **with a** depth of 3.70 meters. It has 7,780 meters of quays, a wharf for storing and loading commercial commodities, stores for staple goods, a petroleum section, and transshipment areas for such heavy materials as coal, sand and gravel, and building materials. Höchst Harbor handles staple goods and has eighteen special plants for transshipment purposes. The different sections are served by a belt railway that connects the harbors with the railways which serve this important commercial center on the Main River.

## v  Mainz

Mainz, the other commerce center of this metropolitan area, is located opposite the mouth of the Main where the Rhine impinges on the hilly terrain of the lower western flank of the rift valley. Moreover, Mainz has the further advantage of firm land above flood level on both sides of the river; hence providing not only good foundations for a bridge crossing, but for wharves and other construction.

Mainz has been a center of religious administration, a breaking point in transportation, and a strategic center since Roman times. It was the home of Johann Gutenberg (1398–1468), a German printer who reputedly was the first European to print with movable type. Near his statue a brass bar in the pavement marks the fiftieth parallel of latitude, a line further north than any point in continental United States. Since the Second World War a new university has come to life on the grounds and buildings of a German army camp.

Mainz handles a large part of the German wine trade as it is the port of the Rheingau. Here, between the south-facing slope of the Taunus and the Rhine, is a highly productive area where the vineyards and orchards represent a major basis of the local economy. The vineyards mantle the steep, terraced slopes of the Taunus where the sun warms the south facing slopes and afford protection from northern winds. In this general area, in the latitude of southern Canada, the Rhine, Main, Lahn, Moselle, and other rivers are deeply etched into the exposed and relatively infertile Rhenish upland. The sheltered slopes and valley bottoms are reputed to be the most productive agricultural areas in Germany. In this uplifted and maturely dissected section of the foreland, most of the people live in the valleys where, in large measure, agricultural land and transport facilities are localized. Under such conditions river and canal transportation witnessed an early development and thereby established river and canal transportation as an inherent part of the economy.

Perhaps the greatest claim of Mainz for renown is historic, as in

1254 Mainz and the nearby city of Worms founded the League of Rhenish Cities. This was a commercial enterprise that gave impetus to shipping and trade on the Rhine and a measure of protection to the seventy cities which obtained membership in the league.[27]

# 12

# Emphasis in Water Transportation

## STATED OR IMPLIED

I    *The Mediterranean*

The Mediterranean and Black seas, vast inland water bodies, together cover a space-area of more than a million square miles (1,145,-000). In size this area about equals the eastern United States; that is, the space area east of the 95th meridian, or in other words near the western boundary of the states that border the Mississippi River on the west. Both the Mediterranean and eastern United States thus designated are included in the North Atlantic Arena, recognized in this study as the most advanced segment of the world today.

In antiquity the Mediterranean and its bordering lands included most of the known world. At the time of the Roman Empire, Roman rule represented the world order and emphasized both the theory and practice of law, much as ancient Greece contributed the inherent qualities of philosophy and the arts. The Greeks also generated the curiosity in regard to space that became the basic inquiries of geography. Most of all, the Mediterranean was the arena where the Phoenicians practiced the beginnings of water transport, the techniques of navigation, and the organization of commerce. The effect on world development by these contributions of the Romans, the ancient Greeks, and the Phoenicians was so great that the Mediterranean has been called "the cradle of European civilization."

The climate of the Mediterranean has encouraged the progress of its economy and other segments of its culture. The climate is known as "the Mediterranean type," with hot, dry, storm-free summers and cool, rainy, stormy winters. The summers provide long periods with nearly perfect periods for sailing, whereas little or no navigation occurs in winter. Civilization advanced as water transport developed; and it rapidly advanced when, under Roman rule, the great system of Roman roads was integrated with the remarkable system of seaways.

The Mediterranean has an important service in modern transportation as a vital link in the Mediterranean-Asiatic ocean route. Ships from Western Europe and other areas enter the Mediterranean through the Strait of Gibraltar, sail nearly the entire length of the longitudinal axis of this great sea, and then at Suez escape through the man-made canal of the same name to the headwaters of the Red Sea. Here is the engineering structure that in terms of shipping connects the Occident with the Orient, the West with the East, and the Atlantic with the Indian Ocean.

In visualizing a permanent civilization that will generate an enduring world order, the generations of the future must discover the ways in which successful interaction of political and other forces may be expedited. New concepts of social, economic, religious, and political progress will be of the essence. Such concepts probably will come from years of effort in the many disciplines devoted to research. For example, may there be expected new principles and laws of time and space, i.e, of history and geography, as these two disciplines are cultivated in the years to come. The ideas of space-areas on the surface of the world have changed remarkably under the persistent geographic discovery, survey, and measurement that have followed the early efforts of the ancient Greeks. Moreover, the Roman Empire disappeared in the distant past, but history has shown that its influence in one way or another lasted for many centuries. Thus, history records the influences of the past on the affairs of the present; or in other words, of one world order on subsequent world orders.

In view of prevailing conditions in the current world order, there may be little or no hope for a world order that will endure. Chaos more nearly describes the present than progress. Yet harmony may be attained by combination of parts or ideas into a proportionate or orderly whole. As in world commerce, the whole may be unbalanced, but not the parts.

Attempts to harmonize the customs and attitudes of the whole world have been disastrous; but under the thesis of this study, if we begin with the North Atlantic Arena—the most enlightened part of the world—progress towards a stable civilization might be forthcoming. In this case, the eastern United States might generate the germ of leadership, as the Mediterranean did long ago. This will prove no easy task, as nearly every facet of the present world order is against the development of social, economic, and political leaderhip.

II    *The North Atlantic and the Commercial World*

The Commercial World, that is, the parts of the world equipped with the facilities and agencies of trade, cover much, but not all, of the land surface of the world. Large areas, such as the polar regions, have little or no trade and lie beyond the dimensions of the Commercial World as defined in this study. Within the Commercial World ten major divisions are of significance to shipping in that they furnish most of the cargoes, passengers, and mails carried by the seagoing vessels. These all-important areas are:    1] Western and Maritime Europe;    2] Eastern Europe, including the eastern Baltic, White, and Black sea outlets;    3] East Asia, comprising China, Manchuria, Japan, and the Philippines;    4] Malaya and the East Indies;    5] India;    6] Australasia;    7] South Africa;    8] Eastern South America;    9] Caribbean America;    10] the United States and southern Canada. These ten areas include at least 90 per cent of the world's population, about the same proportion of the world's natural resources, and do even a bigger percentage of the world's business. All of them have high strategic value in the operation of shipping on the world's trade routes. Of the ten, the first and last named are by far the most important.

Sea trade reaches practically all parts of the ten major divisions. Some sections of each division, however, are naturally so poor that they support few or no people. They are poverty belts within the productive regions and are handicapped by rugged surface, poor soil, arid climate, or some other condition imposed by nature. Furthermore, inland transportation reaches some areas adequately, whereas others lie beyond the end of steel or too far from roads or inland waterways. These conditions of nature or of transport facilities, as well as handicaps imposed by the absence of trading agencies or the existence of governmental or other social restrictions, notably affect the participation of a given area in world trade. Air services have brought some remote but rich mineralized areas into the Commercial World.

SEABOARD SECTIONS OF MAJOR DIVISIONS

Within each of the major productive divisions of the world, one or more sections of the seacoast stand out as focal areas to which lead both continental and oceanic transportation routes. These focal seaboard areas, with all their multiplicity of commercial, industrial, and financial institutions, climax the economy of the regions which they serve. As has been stated, the section of the Atlantic coast of the United States from Boston to Norfolk is the focal seaboard area for much of the United States just as the maritime area between the peninsulas of Brittany and Denmark plays a similar role for Western Europe.

In the focal points of international activity are concentrated the piers, the warehouses, the yards, the exchanges, the trading companies, the financial houses, and the other agencies and institutions which functionalize these critical points in the world's economy. Within the ports and at other points in the seaboard areas of Western Europe and the United States, and to some extent to the other focal seaboard areas, there has developed a large amount of manufacturing, much of which is directly related to port activities; sugar, petroleum, and metal refining are examples. Because sea transportation under most conditions is cheaper than land transportation, the raw sugar, the crude petroleum, or the partially reduced ores are brought as bulk cargoes to dockside refineries where they are further processed. Partially finished materials go to other manufacturing establishments, whereas the finished products may be used locally or are shipped to inland or overseas markets. The number and variety of commodities processed in some fashion at seaboard is surprisingly large, and thus manufacturing constitutes an important pursuit, actually or potentially, in the world's seaboard areas. Because of the high importance of transportation and trade in modern life, the seaboard sections have become highly influential in both national and international affairs. In many ways, moreover, the people of seaboard areas are cosmopolitan in outlook and internationally minded in world affairs. In some cases they suffer, however, in being physically and intellectually removed from the farming, mining, and other actualities of primary production. In many cases they tend to take other people's efforts as tributary to their own efforts and not infrequently display an intolerant attitude on national issues.

*PORTS AS FOCAL POINTS*

The big ports of the world such as London, Liverpool, Antwerpen, Rotterdam, and Hamburg in the major seaboard section of Western Europe and New York in our Eastern Seaboard not only are large and influential but they tend to become more so. Integrated shipping, rail, and other transport services breed trade. Conversely, expanding trade calls for additional rail and shipping services. This spiral gives momentum to the economic structure and is one of the major assets of great ports.

*OCEAN TRADE ROUTES*

Between the major commercial areas ships follow the routes which long experience has shown to be most practical. In many cases the routes represent agreements of governments or shipping agencies. In general, the routes conform to the shortest distance between the focal seaboard areas, to the configuration of the continent and offshore islands, to the presence of floating ice in certain seasons, to the position and volume of traffic of way ports, to the areas where export commodities are available, and to the distribution of coal and other fuels.

*DISTRIBUTION OF SHIPPING ON THE OCEAN ROUTES*

To serve the commercial regions of the world there are about 30,000 merchant ships, but not more than 8,000 are used in overseas business. On one summer's day in 1938, for example, Britain alone had 9,292 merchant ships, big and little, actually in service. Of the ships at sea at any one time, more than half are in the North Atlantic. Many are engaged in the coastwise trade of the United States and an even greater number in the North Baltic and Mediterranean seas and other coastal waters of Europe. Britain's trade with the Continent commonly is double that with America and employs a great number and variety of vessels. Of the ships in overseas trade, the largest number are employed in the North Atlantic, presumably between Europe and the United States. This amazing display of shipping in the Atlantic north of the Equator emphasizes the high importance in world affairs of the North Atlantic Arena, that is, of the lands bordering the North Atlantic Ocean.

*FLAGS OF IMPORTANCE IN SHIPPING*

Shipping is world-wide in its field of operation but highly localized in its ownership. All but two of the twelve flags of importance in the maritime world are flags of European countries. Hence, except for the shipping of the United States and Japan, most of the ships of the world are of European origin and are under European control.

## EUROPE'S DOMINANCE IN MARITIME AFFAIRS

The development of steam navigation in the nineteenth century brought great changes in the organization, facilities, and institutions of overseas trade and shipping. In large measure these developments were initiated in maritime Europe, especially in Great Britain. Gradually they were extended into the other major regions, and by the turn of the century a world pattern of sea lanes, fuel stations, ports, trading agencies, and credit institutions had come into existence. The vessels which activated the pattern, however, were built and owned in the maritime countries of Europe and were registered and operated under the flags of those nations. The pattern was world-wide in its dimensions, but the initiative which established and maintained it was localized in Western Europe.

## III   Western Europe

In terms of world order the rank of the nations in shipping is less important than the extraordinary dominance of Western Europe. This area, long the active heart of the Commercial World, has built and operated most of the world's ships. In these ships, goods from all parts of the world have moved to Western Europe, and from Western Europe other goods have moved to all parts of the world. Farmers, miners, lumbermen, and others in all regions have looked to Western Europe as a market area. For more than a century this has been part of the world order. The World Wars profoundly disrupted this order. They brought, for example, a sense of insecurity to nations dependent upon foreign flags for the movement of their overseas trade. Out of the disruptions occasioned by World War I the United States and Japan came forward as maritime nations. At the close of World War II the United States had an enormous fleet of vessels, most of which were built for wartime needs. Most of this shipping is not suited to peacetime competition. Fortunately, some of our fleet represents shipping built on a well-conceived long range plan.

The Rhine Valley has been continuously utilized as a route for some means of transportation; however, the means have varied conspicuously with changing conditions in the economy and with the impact of political rule. The greatest use has occurred in modern times with the appearance of railways, highways, waterways, and airways. Hence, with each new form of transportation the route has retained its significance. To a degree each means of transport plays a special role. Taken together they bring the areas served into effective commercial and social contact.

The present study is focused on the Rhine Waterway from the North Sea to Basel at the border of Switzerland. The Rhine Waterway follows the Rhine River, but at many points engineering achievements have modified its natural characteristics in order to facilitate its use by river craft and in handling commodities at its numerous ports. As the problems involved have been of notable variety—physical, commercial, financial, and political—the plans, designs, and means and methods of effectuation in developing this greatest of river waterways serve as models of what to do and in some cases of what not to do.

Historically, and now, in terms of highway and railway transportation, the Rhine Route is part of the routes from West Germany to North Italy. Up to the present time the shortest rail and highways traverse from north to south is from Zürich up the Reuss Valley to a tunnel under the St. Gotthard Pass and thence to the Ticino Valley and Milano in northern Italy. This railway revives the direct communication with Italy and makes Genova (Genoa) a Mediterranean port for West Germany. In ancient times when Roma (Rome) was the center of the Western world, the Roman roads followed several routes over or around the Alps, but much of the travel found its way into the Rhine Valley enroute to the North German Plain and the North Sea.

The number and variety of craft plying the Rhine greatly exceeds the number and variety working the Mississippi and Ohio waterways. The Rhine fleet, however, is made up of smaller craft with much smaller carrying capacity than the huge towboats and barges on the American waterways. In fact, some of the towboat-barges are so large they could not be used on the congested European rivers and canals.

In two respects the Rhine is much ahead of American operations: One is that the Rhine has well-planned river ports where vessels load and discharge in port basins rather than at quays along river side. These basin-ports are as well-built and maintained as the best ocean ports. The second is that in most cases along the Rhine the land is owned by the city, the county, or the nation or by a combination of the three jurisdictions. The right to build a warehouse or other facilities is leased to private interests but the control is maintained by legal authority. Along the Mississippi, railroads or other private owners commonly both own and operate the existing terminals. Under such conditions cooperative arrangements are difficult to achieve.

The Rhine River and its famous longitudinal valley always has been a proving ground in the affairs of Europe. Its significance grows out of many considerations including its unique position in Western Europe, its roll in the commercial and political structure of Europe and the world, its situation in regard to the North Sea arm of the Atlantic Ocean, its contributions to the manufacturing belt of Europe, its advantages of site and situation for the cities that have localized along its course, and finally in its relatively regular flow due to its large supply of melt water from the Alps.

# 13

# Amplification

There have been many brief periods when there seemed some hope of man's capturing the prize of a stable, permanent civilization. Arnold Toynbee, the celebrated English historian tells us that at least twenty-seven major nations have flourished, only to be lost in the limbo of forgotten peoples. Each in its day, doubtless hoped that its particular culture was permanent.—Lester O. Schriver

A PERMANENT CIVILIZATION would mean a continuing and improving world order. Achieving such an order will call for vision, leadership, and honest and determined effort on the part of many people. Vision not only must be defined, but it must be accepted and implemented by a kind of leadership unknown today. To a surprising degree, determined effort must march with the times and project the best of the past into the realities of the future. The world order is composed of a multiplicity of local orders, each occupying a space-area on the surface of the earth. Each order contributes to the total world order, but in varying amount and degree.

In this study "North Atlantic Arena" is used as a term of convenience to designate the order, civilization, or culture of an outstanding space-area on the surface of the earth. The designated area includes the North Atlantic Ocean with Western Europe on its eastern margin and the United States and Canada on its western margin.

The people who inhabit the earth present different stages of civilization, that is, distinctive divisions of the world order. Both economy and other aspects of civilization have reached their maximum development among the people in the North Atlantic Arena. These peoples possess distinctive characteristics that rate them at the top level of human accomplishment. This status should not generate a sense of superiority as compared with the people of the other world regions. Instead, they should develop an attitude of responsibility in harmony with the leadership attained. Whether it is realized or not, much of the hope for the future depends upon the leadership of the people of the North Atlantic Arena in developing their own areas and in upgrading or helping to upgrade the economy and way of life in other areas.

The status of transportation probably is the first measure of the economy of an area. Command of transportation and associated phenomena lead to progress, and without transportation advances in economy and culture are impossible under present-day conditions. Of the types of transport, water transport was selected for study because it has been in continuous evolution throughout recorded history. Advances in water transport have been associated with progress in civilization. Leadership in water transport has varied from time to time and from place to place, but always at some point on the periphery of Asia and Europe. More specifically, leadership of water transport on a commercial basis, with two exceptions, has localized on the periphery of Europe. Phoenicians, ancient Greeks, ancient Scandinavians, Venetians, Genoese, Germans, Portuguese, Spanish, Dutch, French, and English at different times have dominated both water transport and the world order. The only exceptions were 1] the period of leadership in water transport localized under the Carthaginians in northern Africa, and 2] in the United States in the first half of the nineteenth century. However, the contributions of the Japanese since the beginning of World War I should be recognized.

Experience from 1870 to 1914 demonstrated that ocean transport finds its minimum cost and reaches its maximum usefulness when it is world-wide in its operation. Moreover, since 1600 A.D. the Narrow Seas section of Western Europe has been the center of maritime activity. In fact, this small seaboard area has been the heart of the world's transportation services. For example, the invention and use of the steam engine in ship propulsion made it possible to introduce regularity of sailings and insure regular deliveries of mail, express, freight, and passengers. This helped to lower the cost of ocean shipping and many types of trade.

The high status of the utilization of natural and human resources attained in the North Atlantic Arena is based on experience gained from centuries of effort, advanced through the solution of inevitable social, religious, and educational conflicts in human development. For thirty centuries progress in water transportation was confined largely to the Mediterranean section of the Atlantic Arena. First the Phoenicians and then the ancient Greeks were the pacemakers. They organized chains of ports and learned the arts of trade and manufacture. The Phoenicians made Sidon and Tyre warehouse centers, thereby establishing the rudiments of commercial enterprise. The Romans built the world order of their time on command of sea routes on the Mediterranean and on their magnificent system of roads. They also became as famous in law as the Greeks had been in philosophy and art.

Control and operation of both sea and land transportation under Roman rule was an amazing achievement of antiquity. The Romans did not become a seafaring people, but utilized the skill and experience of the Greeks and Carthaginians in working the established routes from Roma (Rome) to other city-ports of the Mediterranean. The transportation and trade in grain and other essentials proceeded under Roman law. The whole structure became especially successful during the long period of peace inaugurated by Augustus Caesar.

The Romans found the development of naval power necessary in order to meet the depradations of pirates. To this end they built galleys propelled by oars so that swift action could be accomplished. For the most part, the oars were manned by slaves obtained from many areas. In patrolling the immense reaches of the Mediterranean, experience led to knowledge of sailing conditions, thereby leading to better understanding of the problems of navigation.

The construction and maintenance of their famous system of roads came to be a top accomplishment of the Romans. The system was so planned and built as to connect Roma (Rome), the central city, with other parts of the empire. Facilities of many types were constructed so that travelers could be well cared for and their travel expedited. The main roads needed police protection, and that became a function which employed many men. Overnight accommodations and fresh horses were available at the major centers. The central authority, moreover, was kept informed of operating conditions.

In part, integration of the water and land services was accomplished by a selective process. Where both services were available, as in the Lower Rhone Valley, the one most acceptable got the most business. In other cases the roads terminated at the docks, thereby expediting the ready exchange of goods. Probably it is possible to overstate the cooperation accomplished, but the whole organization stands as a milestone in the field of transportation.

The Decline and Fall of Rome was followed by the contributions of the city-states in the Mediterranean and the commercial leagues in the Danube and Rhine valleys, and in the North and Baltic seas. These commercially-minded organizations demonstrated the advantages of controlled trade. They were made up of merchants and established the power of money and methods of exchange. They laid the basis of the Discoveries Period which was to follow.

Bottled in the Mediterranean for fifteen centuries before Christ and fifteen centuries after Christ, civilization, in a single decade at the end of the fifteenth century, burst its bounds and escaped through Gibraltar to the high seas. Iberia changed from a frontier peninsula to the center of the Commercial World, and for the following century Portugal and Spain became centers of the world order. Tragic misuse of the inflowing wealth lost them the opportunity of maintaining their elevated position in maritime affairs.

Even before the end of the sixteenth century the European center of maritime affairs began its shift to the coast between the peninsulas of Brittany and Denmark. At this time the main continental routes reached the sea between these peninsulas, thereby making the Netherlands, France, and Great Britain the major Atlantic countries. They were the countries of destiny. Each, in the order named, took the center of the political stage. Britain, however, finally attained leadership, and eventually through its maritime policies the old concepts of commerce were replaced by ideas of free trade; that is, equal treatment of all flags in all areas.

The emergence of industrial and commercial enterprises led to the growth of many industrial districts—in England, the Netherlands, Belgium, France, and Germany. Taken together these districts created the European Manufacturing Belt that extended through Atlantic and Central Europe, that is, Western Europe. Population increased rapidly as did the methods and techniques of industry and trade. An ever-increasing demand for food for the population and raw materials for the manufacturing industries created a great volume of imports, balanced by an outflow of coal, steel, and such commodities as textiles, chemicals, drugs, hardware, and fertilizers. Profits resulted, and the countries became wealthy. This growth of highly localized industry, and widespread commerce became the world order as the nineteenth century turned into the twentieth century. This period marked a milestone in human development and, as will be presented later, gave promise of a stable and permanent peace.

In 1914 the unity of Western Europe was severed by the outbreak of World War I. Eventually, the war divided Central Europe from Atlantic Europe; that is, the Central Powers from the coastal countries known as the Allies. After the United States joined the Allies, the struggle on the Atlantic was intensified, and the maritime segment of the North Atlantic Arena was at war with the Eastern or continental segment. This represented a calamity of the first order, as the men, the money, and the efforts of the people most advanced in transport and civilization were directed to war instead of the advancement of a permanent and ennobling world order.

It will be remembered that at the end of World War I the German merchant fleet was distributed among the Allies. Britain, however, did not want the vessels allocated to them, as the Shipping Authorities preferred to build a new, modern fleet. In fact, the German vessels were sold back to Germany. In the years following the war the German government provided financial aid to the shipbuilding industry. Hence, by 1921–22 some 437 vessels were launched; and by 1928 Germany regained a merchant fleet equal to 80 per cent of its prewar fleet.

Political machinations in the postwar years so dominated German affairs that the remarkable revival of internal and external trade was almost completely overshadowed. The revival, however, reflected both the continental and maritime position of Germany; or in other words, the basic geographical qualities of the German space-area in the European scene and in the North Atlantic Arena. Germany, the largest segment of Central Europe, lies between the Balkan, Danubian, and Baltic countries and the Narrow Seas and other parts of Atlantic Europe, including the Lower Rhine Valley.

The varying eastern border of the North Atlantic Arena is illustrated by the postwar experiences of Austria, Hungary, and the Danubian countries. Under either the Soviet policies or the German programs of that time, there was no justification for the existence of these small countries on or near Germany's eastern frontier. After World War I the foreign trade of these small political units stagnated in a period of extreme depression for both the exports and the purchasing power declined. Into this dark period the imports of foods and raw materials needed in Germany's economic revival brought the needed relief. For example, the tragic separation of

Austria from Hungary lost the former its agricultural support and the later its industrial market. Trade with Germany helped remedy this situation. Furthermore, it is reported that Rumania found in Germany the best market in many years and that Germany imported 50 per cent of Bulgarian tobacco as well as 40 per cent of that from Greece. Moreover, Germany took 56 per cent of Hungary's lard exports and 80 per cent of that country's meat. Against the circumstances of the postwar years, these facts seem to have small stature; but they do suggest that if Germany had not allowed Hitler to plunge it into World War II the border countries might have been drawn permanently into the North Atlantic Arena. In this connection, it should be understood that Germany had the largest and best railway network in Europe. The German railways were of the essence in World War II, but they were not equal to the double task of supplying Italy with coal and supporting the German invasion of Soviet territory. In the latter, vast spaces, long distances, and severe weather were against them. In the post-war period, however, the German railroads for a time enabled German firms to supply continental Europe with the products of German industries and with overseas supplies.

The structure of Germany's import trade in 1913 shows the importance of the transportation pattern then and now. In that year about 50 per cent of Germany's imports came from neighboring countries. This statement is in harmony with the fact that on its land frontiers Germany was in direct contact with more countries than any other European nation. Trade across the national borders quite evidently was traditional and could be anticipated in times of peace. Some 34 per cent of Germany's imports came from other European countries, especially coal from Britain and ore from Spain and Sweden. This leaves 16 per cent to come from the ocean trades. Of this, nearly three-fourths originated in America and one-fourth to one-third originated largely in India and China. Percentages vary from time to time, but the assumption can be made that in general the pattern remains about the same as long as transportation, the demands for commodities, and the agencies of trade are maintained.

The foregoing amplification of Germany's transportation and trade illustrates the high importance exerted by the transport facilities in Germany in implementing its central position in Europe. Conversely, it also suggests that central position means little or nothing if the agencies of transport and trade are not present. But facilities and experience are needed in the operation of each of the major four types of transport.

If this amplification now directs attention to the thesis that the

North Atlantic Arena is the space-area of the world where future leadership may develop, emphasis should be given in time to the world order as the nineteenth century merged into the twentieth, and to the space-area on the face of the globe defined as the North Atlantic Arena. In the century of peace following the Congress of Vienna, the development of steam transport on the sea and steam-powered locomotives on the railways added a transport plant to the use of people and not only led to the recognition of Western Europe with its two divisions—Atlantic Europe and Central Europe—as the center of the Commercial World, but also as the leading domain of industry, science, education, finance, and politics. Here world leadership and authority localized to an amazing extent.

From this area of achievement and leadership, a great emigration occurred in the nineteenth century, especially from Europe to the United States and Canada. Throughout most of the century, emigration largely was from the British Isles, Scandinavia, and Germany; that is, from Western Europe. Hence, the fertile lands of North America were settled and developed by emigrants from Western Europe with similar educational status, social characteristics, religions, and attitudes to the people of the particular part of Western Europe from which they or their forebearers had come; namely, the English, Scottish, and Irish from the British Isles; the Scandinavians from Norway, Sweden, Denmark, and Iceland; the Germans from Germany; and the French from France. Hence, the basic settlements in each part of Anglo-America represented natural and desirable extension of some part of Western Europe, and thereby prepared for participation in the North Atlantic Arena.

Near the close of the nineteenth century the European emigration shifted. The mass of emigrants then came from Italy, the Balkan countries, and Russia, thereby changing immigration into the United States. Hence, great numbers of people with different languages, educational status, religious views, and social characteristics almost overwhelmed New York and other parts of the United States. This change of origin gave the German shipping lines an advantage over the British lines in carrying the highly profitable steerage business. For a time division of the emigrant traffic was made at annual conferences of representatives of the shipping lines of the two countries, but by the end of 1913 the conference had resulted in disagreement rather than agreement; and in terms of management of North Atlantic traffic, the two countries to all intents and purposes already were at war.[1] This matter became so controversial that eventually the United States in the Immigration and Nationality Act and its Amendments limited immigration, establishing quotas in favor of the Western European nations from which came the early settlers. This represented national legislation on a matter that affected international transportation.[2]

From the foregoing analysis, the conclusion may be reached that coordination of all the physical facilities and social experiences localized in Atlantic and Central Europe will be necessary before the Common Market, for example, attains its potentialities of leadership. Moreover, the ideas, methods, and techniques of leadership will be equally essential as the American component of the North Atlantic Arena prepares to take its part in the stable, permanent world order that Lester Schriver visualizes for the world culture of the future. The contribution of the American division of the North Atlantic Arena to a stablized world order remains to be stated.

## GREAT DOCUMENTS AS A SOURCE OF PROGRESSIVE THINKING

In looking toward a solution of the complex problems that now confront civilization, it appears wise to envisage the great documents that have marked progress in upgrading the human race. Every nation that has risen to eminence has produced documental milestones along the route. Christian nations look to the Bible as the foundation of their contribution. In the English-speaking world great documents—Magna Charta, Bill of Rights, Declaration of Independence, Constitution of the United States, and The Ordinance of 1787—sparked progress in the long struggle for civil and political rights and led to the recognition of fundamental laws and principles, written and unwritten, under which our governments are organized. These laws and principles are unchanging and continue as potently active today as in the past. Certainly they should provide a source of inspiration and guidance in the increasingly complex changes of the future.

## 2 The Rhine Route

General Reference for The Netherlands: *The Netherlands,* ed. Bartholomew Landheer (Berkeley: University of California Press, 1934). See specifically (a) Samuel van Valkenburg, "Land and People," pp. 3–14; (b) J. Anton de Haas, "Holland's Role in World Trade," pp. 164–75; (c) "Selected Bibliography," pp. 437–48.
[1] *Die Duisburg-Ruhrorter Häfen* (August, 1956), p. 20.
[2] Edward Gibbon, *The Decline and Fall of the Roman Empire* (New York: The Modern Library, 1932) III, 865.
[3] Margaret Reid Shackelton, *Europe, A Regional Geography* (London: Longmans, Green & Co., 1934), p. 4.
[4] Werner J. Cadman, "Frontiers Between East and West in Europe," *The Geographical Review,* XXXIX, No. 4

(1919), 605–24.
[5] Barbara Ward, *The Rich Nations and the Poor Nations* (New York: W. W. Norton, Inc., 1962), pp. 14–16.
[6] Emile Chaix, "Switzerland," in *The International Geography,* ed. Hugh Robert Mill (New York: D. Appleton & Co., 1900), p. 256.
[7] Joseph Partsch, *Central Europe* (New York: D. Appleton & Co., 1903), p. 320.
[8] H. J. Mackinder, *The Rhine* (New York: Dodd, Mead & Co., 1908), Chap. V, pp. 144–67.
[9] *Ibid.*
[10] F. J. Monkhouse, *A Regional Geography of Western Europe* (New York: John Wiley & Sons, Inc., 1960), pp. 89–94.
[11] *Ibid.,* pp. 48–55.

## 3 Mediterranean Beginnings

[1] For reliable coverage of water and land transport in the Mediterranean Sea consult: *Encyclopaedia Britannica,* Vols. for 1957 and 1964; *Encyclopedia Americana,* Vols. for 1957, 1959, 1962, and 1964; *Standard Encyclopedia of the World's Oceans and Islands,* ed. Anthony Huxley (New York: G. P. Putnam's Sons, 1962); Ellen Churchill Semple, *The Geography of the Mediterranean Region* (New York, 1931).
[2] Derwent Whittlesey, *Environmental Foundations of European History* (New

York, 1949), pp. 21–22. This book began with a request in 1939 from the group teaching Medieval and Modern history at Harvard University.
[3] *Standard Encyclopedia of the World's Oceans and Islands,* p. 75.
[4] *Encyclopaedia Britannica* (1962), XV, 209–10.
[5] See definition of "Fertile Crescent," insert Atlas Plate 52, *The National Geographic Magazine* (Dec., 1963). Scale 150 miles to the inch.
[6] "The History of the Phoenicians,"

An *Universal History* (London, 1779), II, 21–22.

[7] C. W. C. Oman, *Greece* (New York, 1907), II, 26–27. Oman questions the monopoly of the Phoenicians of seagoing trade, but shows that they controlled the main bulk of Aegean Commerce.

[8] Albert A. Trever, *History of Ancient Civilization*, I (New York: Harcourt, Brace & Co., 1936), 81.

[9] "The History of the Phoenicians," pp. 22–23.

[10] A. G. Keller, "Trade and the Advancement of Civilization," in H. E. Gregory, A. G. Keller and A. L. Bishop, *Physical and Commercial Geography* (Boston: Ginn & Co., 1910), pp. 223–31.

[11] Trever, p. 80.

[12] "The History of the Phoenicians," p. 22.

[13] *Encyclopedia Americana* (1962), XXI, 787; John Yeats, *The Natural History of Commerce* (London: Cassell, Petter, & Galpin, 1870), p. 327.

[14] *Encyclopaedia Britannica* (1962), XVII, 768.

[15] "The History of the Phoenicians," p. 2.

[16] *Ibid.*, p. 35; Trever, p. 88; I Kings 5:1–18.

[17] "The History of the Phoenicians," p. 36; Trever, pp. 88–89.

[18] "The History of the Phoenicians," p. 37.

[19] Oman, Chap. 1, pp. 3–19; Lionel W. Lyde, *The Continent of Europe* (London: Macmillan & Co., 1926), pp. 158–59.

[20] H. L. Jones, *The Geography of Strabo*, IV (London: Heinemann, Ltd., 1927), 7; Edward Cresy, *An Encyclopaedia of Civil Engineering* (London, 1847), Chap. IV, p. 40; Gustav Frederich Hertzberg and William Nickerson Bates, *Ancient Greece* (Philadelphia: Lea Brothers & Co., 1905), pp. 19–26.

[21] Oman, p. 4.

[22] Clive Day, *A History of Commerce* (New York: Longmans, Green & Co.,

1907), p. 18; Cresy, pp. 40–44.

[23] *Encyclopedia Americana* (1962), XIII, 379.

[24] "The History of the Phoenicians," p. 29; Cresy, p. 2; P. Vidal De La Blache, *Principles of Human Geography* (New York: Henry Holt & Co., 1926), pp. 471–78.

[25] *Encyclopedia Americana* (1962), XIII, 378–79.

[26] Trever, p. 166.

[27] H. DE B. Gibbins, *The History of Commerce in Europe* (London: Macmillan & Co., 1923), pp. 17–18.

[28] Trever, p. 490.

[29] Gibbins, pp. 18–19.

[30] M. P. Charlesworth, *Trade Routes and Commerce of the Roman Empire* (Cambridge, Eng., 1924), Chap. II, pp. 16–34.

[31] *Ibid.*, pp. 2–3.

[32] *Ibid.*, pp. 8–9.

[33] Anthony Trollope, *The Commentaries of Caesar* (New York: John B. Alden, 1885), p. 1

[34] Charlesworth, p. 13.

[35] Hutton Webster, *World History* (Boston: D. C. Health & Co., 1923), p. 142.

[36] Richard Carrington, *A Million Years of Man* (Cleveland and New York, 1963), pp. 244–45; *Encyclopedia Americana* (1964).

[37] Webster, p. 142.

[38] *Annual Report of the Board of Regents of the Smithsonian Institution, 1934* (Washington, D. C.: Government Printing Office, 1935), pp. 328–29; La Blache, pp. 374–75.

[39] *Annual Report of the Board of Regents of the Smithsonian Institute, 1934*, p. 348; La Blache, pp. 370–89.

[40] *Annual Report of the Board of Regents of the Smithsonian Institution, 1934*, pp. 357–62.

[41] *Ibid.*, pp. 349–50.

[42] *Ibid.*, p. 364.

[43] *Ibid.*, p. 363.

[44] Charlesworth, pp. 171–73.

[45] *Annual Report of the Board of Re-*

gents of the Smithsonian Institution, 1934.
[46] Charlesworth, pp. 170–75.

## 4 Penetration

[1] *Encyclopedia Americana* (1962), VIII, 477; *Encyclopaedia Britannica* (1962) VII, 61.
[2] H. DE B. Gibbins, *The History of Commerce in Europe* (London: Macmillan and Company, 1923), pp. 73–74; *Encyclopedia Americana* (1962), VII, 559.
[3] Gibbins, pp. 57–59.
[4] *Ibid.*, p. 32.
[5] Ernst Samhaber, *Merchants Make History* (New York: The John Day Co., 1964), pp. 116–18.
[6] *Ibid.*, p. 108.

[47] *Ibid.*, pp. 181–82.
[48] *Ibid.*, pp. 183–84.
[49] *Ibid.*, pp. 184–85.

[7] *Ibid.*, pp. 150–75.
[8] *Ibid.*, p. 135.
[9] Joseph Partsch, *Central Europe* (New York: D. Appleton & Co., 1903), pp. 131–32.
[10] Samhaber, pp. 116–18.
[11] Clive Day, *A History of Commerce* (New York: Longmans, Green & Co., 1907), pp. 90–113; L. Dudley Stamp and S. Carter Gilmour, *Chisholm's Handbook of Commercial Geography*, 16th ed. (London: Longmans, Green & Co., 1960), pp. 357–59.

## 5 Beyond Gibraltar—the Atlantic

[1] Lionel W. Lyde *The Continent of Europe* (London: Macmillan & Co., 1926), p. 166.
[2] Captain Ernesto de Vasconcellos, "Portugal," in *The International Geography*, ed. Hugh Robert Mill (New York: D. Appleton & Co., 1900), p. 382. Also for a good account of Prince Henry's accomplishments see: Elaine Sanceau, *Henry the Navigator* (New York: W. W. Norton & Co., Inc., 1947).
[3] Captain Alan Villiers, *Men, Ships and the Sea* (Washington, D. C.: National Geographic Society, 1962), p. 81; H. Morse Stephens, *Portugal* (London: G. P. Putnam's Sons, 1905), p. 141.
[4] Villiers, p. 84; J. H. Parey, *Europe and a Wider World* (London: Hutchinson's University Library, 1949), pp. 21–22.
[5] *The Columbia Lippincott Gazetteer of the World*, ed. Leon E. Seltzer (New York, 1961), p. 1509.
[6] Villiers, p. 89.
[7] M. M. Knight, H. E. Barnes, and

Felix Flügel, *Economic History of Europe* (Boston: Houghton Mifflin Co., 1928), pp. 267–68.
[8] Clive Day, *A History of Commerce* (New York: Longmans, Green & Co., 1907), p. 174.
[9] *Ibid.*, p. 176.
[10] Day, pp. 176–84; H. E. Gregory, A. G. Keller, and A. L. Bishop, *Physical and Commercial Geography* (Boston: Ginn & Co., 1910), pp. 236–40.
[11] Day, p. 123.
[12] *Ibid.*, p. 127.
[13] *Ibid.*, p. 176.
[14] James A. Williamson, *Maritime Enterprise, 1483–1558*, p. 30.
[15] *Philip's Historical Atlas*, p. 42.
[16] Williamson, p. 25.
[17] Gregory, Keller, Bishop, pp. 234–35.
[18] *Philip's Historical Atlas*, p. 42.
[19] Gregory, Keller, Bishop, pp. 239–40.
[20] C. C. Colby and A. Foster, *Economic Geography* (Boston: Ginn & Co., 1954), pp. 426–27.
[21] H. DE B. Gibbins, *The History of*

*Commerce in Europe* (London: Macmillan & Co., 1923), p. 61.

[22] *Ibid.*, pp. 67–68; Day, p. 420.

[28] "Report of the Committee to Advise as to the Measures Requisite to the British Mercantile Marine" (Chamber of Shipping of the United Kingdom and Liverpool Steamship Owners Association, July, 1917), I, iv.

[24] *Encyclopedia Americana* (1962), XX, 126; Gibbins, p. 85.

[25] George G. Chisholm, "The Continent of Europe," in *The International Geography*, ed. Hugh Robert Mill (New York: D. Appleton & Co., 1900), pp. 123–37.

[26] Gibbins, p. 159–60; Day, pp. 229–39.

[27] Chisholm, p. 135.

[28] Gibbins, pp. 138–40.

[29] *Encyclopedia Americana* (1962), p. 247.

[30] Alfred Kirchoff, "The German Empire," in *The International Geography*,

ed. Hugh Robert Mill (New York: D. Appleton & Co., 1900), p. 277.

[31] *Ibid.*, pp. 278–79.

[32] Gibbins, pp. 132–33, 159; Day, pp. 242, 246–47.

[33] Gibbins, pp. 138–39, 142–43.

[34] H. DE B. Gibbins, *Industry in England* (London: Methuen & Co. Ltd., 1896), pp. 358–59.

[35] *Encyclopedia Americana* (1962), XXVI, 659.

[36] Gibbins, *Industry in England*, pp. 285–86.

[37] *Ibid.*, pp. 285–86.

[38] *Encyclopedia Americana* (1962), IX, 504.

[39] *Encyclopaedia Britannica* (1962), XX, 526; Gibbins, *Industry in England*, p. 303.

[40] *Encyclopaedia Britannica* (1962), VIII, 526; Gibbins, *Industry in England*, pp. 303–4.

[41] *Encyclopedia Americana* (1962), I, 562–62h.

## 6 North Atlantic Developments

For statistical and other material in regard to the development of British shipping and trade the author is indebted to the *Reports of the Departmental Committee appointed by the Board of Trade to consider the Position of the Shipping and Shipbuilding Industries after the War* (London, 1918).

[1] Clive Day, *A History of Commerce* (New York: Longmans, Green & Co., 1907), p. 233.

[2] H. DE B. Gibbins, *The History of Commerce in Europe* (London: Macmillan & Co., 1923).

[3] Day, pp. 142–43; Gibbins, p. 144.

[4] Day, p. 191; *Encyclopaedia Britannica* (1962), VII, 869.

[5] Martin D. Stevens and Capt. James Pendelburg, *Sea Lanes, Man's Conquest of the Oceans* (New York: Minton, Balch & Co., 1935), pp. 212–14.

[6] Day, pp. 167–72; Townsend Warner, *Landmarks in English Industrial History* (London, 1930), pp. 128–29.

[7] Day, pp. 199–226; Thomas B. Macaulay, *The History of England*, I (Philadelphia: Porter & Coates, 1887), 48–50.

[8] Day, p. 225; *Reports of the Departmental Committee* (1918), pp. 70–71.

[9] *Encyclopaedia Britannica* (1958).

[10] S. A. Williams, *The Romance of English Trading* (London, 1928), pp. 112–18; Warner, pp. 128–29.

[11] *Reports of the Departmental Committee*, pp. 70–72. This basic source covers navigation policy and shipping in the seventeenth, eighteenth, and nineteenth centuries.

[12] W. Cunningham, *The Growth of English Industry and Commerce in Modern Times* (Cambridge, 1929), pp.

525–624; *Encyclopedia Americana* (1962), XII, 446.

[13] C. Earnest Fayle, *A Short History of the World's Shipping Industry* (London, 1928), pp. 214–25.

[14] Encyclopaedia Britannica (1962), II, 308.

[15] James A. Williamson, *The Age of Drake* (London, 1938), pp. 319–20; *Encyclopedia Americana* (1962), II, 247.

[16] R. H. Thornton, *British Shipping* (Cambridge, Eng., 1939), pp. 3–5; Stevens-Pendelburg, p. 215.

[17] Stevens-Pendelburg, pp. 217–19; Thornton, p. 5.

[18] Stevens-Pendelburg, pp. 210–12; Thornton, p. 33.

[19] Stevens-Pendelburg, p. 256; Thornton, p. 6.

[20] Stevens-Pendelburg, pp. 211–21.

[21] Stevens-Pendelburg, p. 256; Thornton, pp. 4–5.

[22] Stevens-Pendelburg, p. 238; Thornton, p. 7.

[23] Thornton, p. 8.

[24] *Ibid.*, p. 26.

[25] *Ibid.*, p. 33.

[26] Thornton, pp. 36–38; Stevens-Pendelburg, pp. 244–45.

[27] W. L. Marvin, "How Can American Ships Compete Successfully with Foreign Ships," Paper read at the twenty-ninth general meeting of the Society of Naval Architects and Marine Engineers, New York, Nov. 17–21, 1961.

[28] Edward Pulsford, *Commerce and the Empire* (London, 1903), pp. 27–29, 84–85; Thornton, p. 49.

[29] Stevens-Pendelburg, p. 213; Thornton, p. 55.

[30] Thornton, p. 7.

[31] Thornton, p. 8; Chap. IV, 59–74.

[32] Thornton, Chap. V, pp. 75–94.

[33] Joseph Russell Smith, *Influence of the Great War Upon Shipping*, Carnegie Endowment for International Peace (New York: Oxford University Press, 1919), pp. 3–350. This book constitutes a contribution of the first order of importance.

[34] Forrest Davis, *The Atlantic System* (New York, 1941), p. 127.

[35] Adapted from: Memorandum to H. Harrison Robson, Director of Emergency Shipping, U.S. Marine Commission, World War II, from Charles C. Colby who was Special Expert, Commodity Section, Division of Planning and Statistics, United States Shipping Board, World War I.

[36] *Ibid.*

[37] *Ibid.*

[38] *Ibid.*

[39] *Ibid.*

[40] S. S. Huebner, *Report on Steamship Agreements and Affiliations in the American Foreign and Domestic Trade, 1914* (U.S. House of Representatives, 63d Cong., Committee on Merchant Marine and Fisheries), Vol. 4, 29–30.

## 7 Lower Rhine in the Atlantic Arena

[1] Joseph Partsch, *Central Europe* (New York: D. Appleton & Co., 1903), pp. 313–14.

[2] *Rotterdam-Europoort* (Quarterly published by the Port of Rotterdam), No. 2 (1963), pp. 2–3.

[3] F. J. Monkhouse, *A Regional Geography of Western Europe* (New York: John Wiley & Sons, Inc., 1960), pp. 65–69.

[4] Jean Gottmann, *A Geography of Europe*, 3rd ed. (New York: Holt, Rinehart & Winston, 1962), p. 259.

[5] "Zuider Zee," in *Standard Encyclopedia of the World's Oceans and Islands*, ed. Anthony Huxley (New York: G. P. Putnam's Sons, 1962), pp. 323–24.

[6] Monkhouse, p. 49.

[7] Monkhouse, p. 52; Huxley, p. 323.

[8] Monkhouse, pp. 28–37; Monkhouse refers to John van Veene, *Dredge, Drain, Reclaim: The Art of a Nation,* 2nd ed. (1949), pp. 122–27.

[9] *Ibid.,* p. 36.

[10] Gottmann, pp. 255–89.

[11] Dr. C. G. van Leeweven, "Rotterdam, The Greatest Port in the World?" *Rotterdam-Europoort,* No. 1 (1963), pp. 1–5.

[12] Feliza Seyd, *The Rhine* (New York: Doubleday & Co., 1955), pp. 263–86.

[13] Arthur Veysey, "From Ruins to 2nd Place Port in 15 Years," *Chicago Sunday Tribune,* July 15, 1962, Sec. 2, p. 2. Also Helen Hill Miller, "Rotterdam—Reborn from Ruins," *National Geographic,* CXVIII, No. 4 (October, 1960), 527–35.

[14] *Encyclopaedia Britannica* (1962), XIX, 578.

[15] *Ibid.,* p. 578; Hendrik Riemens, *The Netherlands* (New York, 1944), Chap. I, pp. 3–28.

[16] I. F. Posthuma, "From Estuary to Island to Industrial Port," *Mermail* (1963), p. 6.

[17] *Ibid.;* *Encyclopaedia Britannica* (1962), XIX, 578.

[18] Posthuma, pp. 6, 13–15; Der Hafen Von Rotterdam (Rotterdam, 1960), p. 9 and Maps.

[19] Seyd, p. 278.

[20] Hendrik Kuipers, "The Changing Landscape of the Island of Rozenburg" (Rotterdam Port Area), *Geogr. Review,* LII, No. 3 (July, 1962), 369.

[21] Seyd, p. 278.

[22] "Rotterdam, Europe's Biggest, Busiest Port," *The Lamp,* Standard Oil Company (New Jersey) Vol. 44, No. 1 (Spring, 1962), 22.

[23] Seyd, pp. 280–81.

[24] *Encyclopaedia Britannica* (1962), I, 853.

[25] Monkhouse, p. 93.

[26] *Encyclopaedia Britannica* (1962), XIX, 578.

[27] Monkhouse, p. 93; *The Lamp,* p. 21.

[28] Kuipers, pp. 362–79.

[29] For more detailed account see Monkhouse, p. 68; *The Lamp,* pp. 18–25; Kuipers, pp. 362–78; Posthuma, pp. 3–41.

[30] Kuipers, pp. 373–75; Miller, Maps, pp. 534–35, 549–53; Posthuma, pp. 10–17.

[31] Kuipers, pp. 375–78; Miller, Maps, pp. 534–35, 549–53; Posthuma, pp. 10–17.

[32] H. J. Mackinder, *The Rhine* (New York: Dodd, Mead & Co., 1908), p. 290.

[33] *Encyclopaedia Britannica* (1962), II, 86.

[34] E. Havenith, "Antwerp, the United States and the Common Market," *Belgium Trade Review,* XVII, No. 11 (Dec., 1962), 11.

[35] Bank of Antwerp, *The Expansion of Antwerp,* January, 1960 (Antwerp, 1961), p. 17.

[36] *Ibid.,* p. 17.

[37] Lionel W. Lyde, *The Continent of Europe* (London: Macmillan & Co., 1926), pp. 261–62; *The Expansion of Antwerp,* p. 12.

[38] Riemens, pp. 18–19.

[39] *The Columbia Lippincott Gazatteer of the World,* ed. Leon E. Seltzer (New York, 1961), pp. 80–81.

[40] M. M. Knight, H. E. Barnes, and Felix Flügel, *Economic History of Europe* (Boston: Houghton Mifflin Co., 1928), pp. 270–71.

[41] Partsch, p. 299.

[42] *Encyclopaedia Britannica* (1962), II, 86.

[43] Bank of Antwerp, *The Expansion of Antwerp,* maps and entire brochure.

[44] Havenith, p. 10.

[45] *Ibid.,* p. 18; *Encyclopedia Americana* (1957), II, 48.

[46] Havenith, p. 22.

[47] *Ibid.*

[48] *Ibid.,* pp. 7, 10.

[49] *Ibid.*

## 8 Transport Structure of Atlantic Europe

[1] Dr. Erich Schwoerbel, "Duisburg in Rising Motorization in Inland Navigation," *Stadt und Hafen*, Vol. 9 (November 21, 1958), 961.

[2] *Annual Bulletin of Transport Statistics for Europe*, 1959 (Geneva: United Nations Economic Commission for Europe, 1960), pp. 7, 9.

[3] *Ibid.*, Table 12, p. 18. The percentages for France in 1958 were rail 19, inland water 6, and total road 75. Figures for Belgium and Switzerland were not given. On account of differences in methods of compiling basic statistics for the three modes of inland transport, and because statistics of road transport are based on estimates, the figures quoted must be regarded as orders of magnitude.

[4] *Ibid.*, pp. 17-21.

[5] *Ibid.*

[6] *Ibid.*, p. 22.

[7] *Ibid.*, Table 21, pp. 54-57.

[8] *Ibid.*, pp. 54-57.

[9] *Ibid.*

[10] *Ibid.*, pp. 90-93. Dumb barges and tankers refer to barges and tankers without power.

[11] Schwoerbel, pp. 961-81.

[12] *Ibid.*

[13] *Ibid.*

[14] *Ibid.*

[15] "The Docks of Basle-Town and Basel-Country," *Rheinschiffahrtsamt Basel*, Mimeographed release, 1960, p. 4.

[16] *Ibid.*, pp. 3-5.

[17] "Die Rheinschiffahrt im Kammerbezirk Duisburg," *Wirtschaftliche Mitteilungen*, Vol. 16, No. 14, (15 July 1960), 273-78.

[18] *Ibid.*, p. 274.

[19] *Ibid.*

[20] *Ibid.*

[21] Joseph Partsch, *Central Europe* (New York: D. Appleton & Co., 1903), p. 315.

[22] *Wirtschaftliche Mitteilungen*, p. 277.

## 9 The Ruhr Generates Commerce

[1] Chauncy D. Harris, "The Ruhr," *Scientific Monthly*, LX (1945), 25-29; "The Ruhr Coal-mining District," *Geogr. Review*, XXXVI, No. 2 (April, 1946), 194-221.

[2] Wilhelm Helmrich, *Wirtschaftskunde des Landes Nordrhein-Westfalen*, i.e., *The Economy of the State North Rhine-Westphalia* (Düsseldorf: August Bagel Verlag, 1960), pp. 62-88.

[3] In 1958 the Ruhr had 12 large cities of more than 100,000, six medium sized cities of from 68,000 to 95,000, and six rural districts and three sub-rural districts. From Gerhard Steinhauer, *Das Riviere: Profil einer Ungerwöhnlichen Landschaft* (Essen, 1959), p. 57.

[4] *Ibid.*, p. 58.

[5] Helmrich, p. 79.

[6] *Ibid.*

[7] *Ibid.*, p. 73.

[8] *Ibid.*, p. 76.

[9] Helmrich, p. 75.

[10] "How Clean Is My Valley," *Resources for the Future*, No. 8 (September, 1961).

[11] Steinhauer, p. 57.

[12] Helmrich, pp. 77-78.

[13] *Ibid.*, p. 77.

[14] *Ibid.*, pp. 77-78.

[15] *The Columbia Lippincott Gazetteer of the World*, ed. Leon E. Seltzer (New York, 1961), p. 669.

[16] Helmrich, pp. 78-80; Steinhauer, p. 60.

[17] *The Columbia Lippincott Gazetteer*, p. 669.

[18] Steinhauer, p. 59.

[19] Jean Gottmann, *A Geography of Europe*, 3rd ed. (New York: Holt, Rinehart & Winston, 1962), p. 425.

[20] Helmrich, p. 83.

[21] Steinhauer, pp. 17-22.

[22] *Ibid.*, p. 60.

[23] Helmrich, pp. 83-85.

[24] *Ibid.*

[25] T. H. Elkins, *Germany* (London, 1960), p. 111.

[26] Helmrich, p. 87.

[27] Steinhauer, p. 57.

[28] *Ibid.*

[29] *Ibid.*, p. 58.

[30] *Ibid.*, p. 60.

[31] Margaret Reid Shackelton, *Europe, A Regional Geography* (London: Longmans, Green & Co., 1934), p. 255.

[32] H. J. Mackinder, *The Rhine* (New York: Dodd, Mead & Co., 1908), p. 258.

[33] *The Columbia Lippincott Gazetteer*, p. 431; Mackinder, p. 290; Shackelton, p. 255.

[34] Joseph Partsch, *Central Europe* (New York: D. Appleton & Co., 1903), p. 258.

[35] *Ibid.*, pp. 258-59.

[36] Mackinder, pp. 290-91.

[37] *The Columbia Lippincott Gazetteer*, p. 431; Partsch, pp. 258-59.

[38] V. Neuburg, *Basle* (Switzerland: Basel Chamber of Commerce), p. 7.

## 10 Motivation of Petroleum Traffic

[1] *Report of the 80th Annual Meeting*, Standard Oil Company (New Jersey), May 23, 1962, at Chicago, Illinois, p. 6.

[2] "Der Rhein-Lippe-Hafen," *Stadt und Hafen*, Vol. 9 (November 5, 1958), 1000-1.

[3] *The Lamp*, Standard Oil Company (New Jersey), Vol. 44, No. 1 (Spring, 1962), 19.

[4] *The Lamp*, Standard Oil Company (New Jersey), Vol. 44, No. 2 (Summer, 1962), 23.

[5] *Ibid.*; *1961 Annual Report*, Standard Oil Company (New Jersey), pp. 17-19.

[6] *1961 Annual Report*, p. 19.

[7] *Ibid.*, p. 20; Bank of Antwerp, *The Expansion of Antwerp, January, 1960* (Antwerp, 1961), Map 1, "The Port of Antwerp," facing p. 4, and p. 18.

[8] "The Slochteren Field Discovery," *Oil and Gas Journal* (October 1964).

[9] *Oil and Gas Journal* (November 1964).

[10] *Ibid.*

## 11 Ports of the Upper Rhine Valley

[1] "The Rhine Docks of Basle-Town and Basle-Country," *Rheinschiffahrtsamt Basel*, mimeographed release, 1960, Part A, p. 1.

[2] V. Neuburg, *Basle* (Switzerland: Basel Chamber of Commerce), p. 3.

[3] *Rheinschiffahrtsamt Basel*, Part A, p. 1.

[4] *Ibid.*

[5] Neuburg, p. 6.

[6] "The Docks of Basle-Town and Basle-Country," *Rheinschiffahrtsamt Basel*, Part B, p. 1. The International Central Commission of the Rhine Navigation. Membership on the commission consists of all the countries through which the Rhine flows and Belgium, Great Britain, and the United States.

[7] *Ibid.*, p. 2.

[8] Les ports des deux Basel (Maps and text).

[9] *Rheinschiffahrtsamt Basel*, Part B, pp. 3-4.

[10] *Ibid.*, p. 5.

[11] *Ibid.*

[12] "The Docks of Basle-Town and

Basle-Country," *Rheinschiffahrtsamt Basel*, Part C, p. 6.

[13] *Rheinschiffahrtsamt Basel*, Part A, p. 2.

[14] *Ibid.*, p. 2.

[15] *Ibid.*

[16] *Ibid.*, p. 3.

[17] *Ibid.*, p. 4.

[18] *Rheinschiffahrtsamt Basel*, Part B, p. 7.

[19] Joseph Partsch, *Central Europe* (New York: D. Appleton & Co., 1903), p. 84.

[20] Henry S. Bashkin, "Trade and Navigation on the Rhine," *Foreign Commerce Weekly*, Vol. 38, No. 6 (1950), in *Outside Readings in Geography* (New York: Thomas T. Crowell Co., 1955), pp. 628–42.

[21] *Ibid.*, p. 634.

[22] Partsch, p. 84.

[23] C. C. Colby and A. Foster, *Economic Geography* (Boston: Ginn & Co., 1954), Fig. 257, p. 469.

[24] *Ibid.*, pp. 468–69.

[25] Bashkin, p. 630.

[26] H. J. Mackinder, *The Rhine* (New York: Dodd, Mead & Co., 1908), pp. 188–211.

[27] *Ibid.*, p. 199.

## 13 Amplification

[1] "The German Control Stations and the Atlantic Emigrant Traffic," *First Report of the Departmental Committee Appointed by the Board of Trade to Consider the Position of the Shipping and Shipbuilding Industries After The War* (London, 1918), pp. 5–13.

[2] *The World Almanac and Book of Facts*, ed., Harry Hansen (New York: New York Telegram and The Sun, 1961), p. 629.